Minorities

Other Books in the Current Controversies Series:

Minorities

David Bender, *Publisher*
Bruno Leone, *Executive Editor*

Brenda Stalcup, *Managing Editor*
Scott Barbour, *Senior Editor*

Mary E. Williams, *Book Editor*

CURRENT CONTROVERSIES

Cover Photo: © David Maung/Impact Visuals

Library of Congress Cataloging-in-Publication Data

Minorities / Mary E. Williams, book editor.
    p. cm. — (Current controversies)
    Includes bibliographical references and index.
    ISBN 1-56510-681-4 (lib. bdg. : alk. paper). — ISBN 1-56510-680-6 (pbk. : alk. paper)
    Minorities—Civil rights—United States. 2. United States—Race relations. 3. Race discrimination—United States. 4. Minorities—United States—Population. I. Williams, Mary E., 1960–   . II. Series.
    E184.A1M5433   1998
    305.8'00973—dc21   97-37077
                                               CIP

© 1998 by Greenhaven Press, Inc., PO Box 289009, San Diego, CA 92198-9009
Printed in the U.S.A.

Contents

No: Minorities No Longer Face Significant Discrimination

Chapter 2: Are Race Relations Improving?

Race Relations Are Not Improving

Race Relations May Be Improving

There is no evidence that white racism provoked the burning of southern black churches in the early and mid-1990s. The idea that the fires were part of a racist conspiracy has been promoted by several liberal commentators and the media. Moreover, advocacy organizations have raised alarm about the fires in order to solicit donations—many of which have been set aside not to rebuild churches but to support liberal causes.

Chapter 3: Which Policies Benefit Minorities?

ics, as a teaching tool to help inner-city black children learn standard English. However, there is no evidence that Ebonics improves language skills; in fact, reading and language test scores dropped at one California elementary school employing an Ebonics program.

Chapter 4: How Are Changing Racial Demographics Affecting America?

groups are unable to peacefully coexist, whites will most likely become a
despised minority. Euro-American culture and Western civilization are
therefore in danger of being eclipsed by less successful nonwhite cultures.

Contents

Chapter 1: Do Minorities Continue to Face Discrimination?

Yes: Minorities Continue to Face Discrimination

No: Minorities No Longer Face Significant Discrimination

Chapter 2: Are Race Relations Improving?

Race Relations Are Not Improving

Foreword

By definition, controversies are "discussions of questions in which opposing opinions clash" (Webster's Twentieth Century Dictionary Unabridged). Few would deny that controversies are a pervasive part of the human condition and exist on virtually every level of human enterprise. Controversies transpire between individuals and among groups, within nations and between nations. Controversies supply the grist necessary for progress by providing challenges and challengers to the status quo. They also create atmospheres where strife and warfare can flourish. A world without controversies would be a peaceful world; but it also would be, by and large, static and prosaic.

The Series' Purpose

The purpose of the Current Controversies series is to explore many of the social, political, and economic controversies dominating the national and international scenes today. Titles selected for inclusion in the series are highly focused and specific. For example, from the larger category of criminal justice, Current Controversies deals with specific topics such as police brutality, gun control, white collar crime, and others. The debates in Current Controversies also are presented in a useful, timeless fashion. Articles and book excerpts included in each title are selected if they contribute valuable, long-range ideas to the overall debate. And wherever possible, current information is enhanced with historical documents and other relevant materials. Thus, while individual titles are current in focus, every effort is made to ensure that they will not become quickly outdated. Books in the Current Controversies series will remain important resources for librarians, teachers, and students for many years.

In addition to keeping the titles focused and specific, great care is taken in the editorial format of each book in the series. Book introductions and chapter prefaces are offered to provide background material for readers. Chapters are organized around several key questions that are answered with diverse opinions representing all points on the political spectrum. Materials in each chapter include opinions in which authors clearly disagree as well as alternative opinions in which authors may agree on a broader issue but disagree on the possible solutions. In this way, the content of each volume in Current Controversies mirrors the mosaic of opinions encountered in society. Readers will quickly realize that there are many viable answers to these complex issues. By questioning each author's conclusions, students and casual readers can begin to develop the critical thinking skills so important to evaluating opinionated material.

Current Controversies is also ideal for controlled research. Each anthology in the series is composed of primary sources taken from a wide gamut of informational categories including periodicals, newspapers, books, United States and foreign government documents, and the publications of private and public organizations. Readers will find factual support for reports, debates, and research papers covering all areas of important issues. In addition, an annotated table of contents, an index, a book and periodical bibliography, and a list of organizations to contact are included in each book to expedite further research.

Perhaps more than ever before in history, people are confronted with diverse and contradictory information. During the Persian Gulf War, for example, the public was not only treated to minute-to-minute coverage of the war, it was also inundated with critiques of the coverage and countless analyses of the factors motivating U.S. involvement. Being able to sort through the plethora of opinions accompanying today's major issues, and to draw one's own conclusions, can be a complicated and frustrating struggle. It is the editors' hope that Current Controversies will help readers with this struggle.

Greenhaven Press anthologies primarily consist of previously published material taken from a variety of sources, including periodicals, books, scholarly journals, newspapers, government documents, and position papers from private and public organizations. These original sources are often edited for length and to ensure their accessibility for a young adult audience. The anthology editors also change the original titles of these works in order to clearly present the main thesis of each viewpoint and to explicitly indicate the opinion presented in the viewpoint. These alterations are made in consideration of both the reading and comprehension levels of a young adult audience. Every effort is made to ensure that Greenhaven Press accurately reflects the original intent of the authors included in this anthology.

> *"Whether integration has benefited minorities and American society continues to be a subject of debate among politicians, educators, and lawmakers."*

Introduction

For much of its history, American society separated whites from minorities. In the 1800s, for example, white settlers seeking land forced many Native Americans to move to reservations. Jim Crow laws required whites and blacks to use separate public facilities as recently as the 1960s. Social customs and local ordinances in the nineteenth and twentieth centuries often insisted that Hispanic Americans and people of Asian descent live in racially segregated neighborhoods. Even white ethnic minorities—Jews and immigrants from southern and eastern Europe—were excluded from many residential areas until the middle of the twentieth century.

Numerous historians argue, however, that segregation by law and by custom has had its most profound impact on African Americans. As proof, they point to the fact that the status of African Americans has been the subject of much of the controversy and legislation involving race. In the 1896 case of *Plessy v. Ferguson,* for example, the Supreme Court upheld the constitutionality of a state law calling for "separate but equal" facilities for whites and blacks in railroad cars. According to Joe R. Feagin, coauthor of *Living with Racism: The Black Middle-Class Experience,* "*De Jure* (by law) racial segregation in America was strengthened by this decision. For more than 50 years, many states used the 'separate but equal' rule to segregate the races in public schools, and in the use of transportation, recreation, sleeping, and eating facilities."

By 1940, deeply entrenched patterns of segregation separated whites and blacks in almost every area of life. However, public sentiment concerning race relations began to change in the years following World War II, and a movement involving civil rights organizations, labor unions, and churches started battling against the system of segregation. Arguing that segregation was discriminatory because facilities for blacks were inferior to facilities for whites, civil rights activists organized protests, demonstrations, and boycotts in support of desegregation. In the 1954 case of *Brown v. Board of Education,* the Supreme Court declared that racially segregated public education was "inherently unequal" and therefore unconstitutional. Several states and cities passed statutes that made racial discrimination in housing and in employment illegal, and in 1964, the federal Civil Rights Act outlawed segregation in most privately owned public facilities.

Racial integration remained the goal of most civil rights activism from the 1960s through the 1970s. In the 1980s and 1990s, though, many people began to question the outcome of efforts to bring the races together. Integrationist efforts, some commentators maintain, actually require blacks to assimilate into white society to become successful. These critics argue that when assimilation occurs, minorities abandon their own culture to adopt the customs and mores of the dominant society. This process, they insist, does not guarantee justice or equal treatment for the minority population. "Instead of equality," contends *Sojourners* editor Jim Wallis, "integration has meant selective assimilation for middle-class blacks while the urban underclass and rural poor are simply left behind. . . . [Integration] has always been and continues to be on white terms."

Others claim, furthermore, that integration has weakened the spirit of autonomy and community among African Americans. Before the advent of desegregation, these critics assert, blacks pooled resources and built strong communities and cultural institutions that allowed them to feel pride in their own achievements. Various commentators contend that the promise of success through integration has, ironically, lured many blacks away from the task of helping other blacks, resulting in the deterioration of formerly powerful African American institutions. According to Tony Brown, author of *Black Lies, White Lies,* integration has "diabolically . . . taught blacks not to want to go to school with one another, not to want to live with one another, and not to spend money with one another." For these reasons, some black leaders advocate abandoning integrationist efforts and returning to black self-reliance to benefit the African American community.

On the other hand, supporters of integration contend that its critics misunderstand the difference between assimilation and integration. While they agree that assimilation entails minorities' acculturating to the majority culture, they argue that this is not the true goal of integration. The real aim of integration, they maintain, is to transform American society into a multiracial democracy. According to John A. Powell, director of the Institute on Race and Poverty at the University of Minnesota Law School, ideally integration "allows the views and experiences of both the dominant group and minority groups to meet, informing and transforming each other." Joseph Lowery, head of the Southern Christian Leadership Conference, agrees with Powell, asserting that integration "is not the systematic movement of all things black into all things white. It is the emphatic movement of all things wrong into all things right." In the opinion of Powell, Lowery, and other proponents of integration, then, integration does not require the abandonment of black cultural values and allegiances; rather, black cultural values help inform the multiethnic conversation that aims to create a more egalitarian America.

Whether integration has benefited minorities and American society continues to be a subject of debate among politicians, educators, and lawmakers. *Minorities: Current Controversies* explores this issue as well as arguments concerning discrimination against minorities, the state of race relations, public policies designed to aid minorities, and the effects of changing racial demographics on American society. Examining these topics will illuminate today's dialogue between America's minority and majority cultures.

Chapter 1

Do Minorities Continue to Face Discrimination?

Chapter Preface

Hazel Johnson, a resident of a predominantly black housing project in Chicago, calls her neighborhood the "Toxic Doughnut" because it is surrounded by waste dumps and factories that discharge noxious pollution. Alarmed by the illnesses of several family members and neighbors, she canvassed her neighborhood to see if the area's health problems could be linked to its polluted environment. After discovering an unusually high number of cancers, respiratory diseases, birth defects, and early deaths, Johnson founded the People for Community Recovery (PCR) and began lobbying for improved environmental standards in Chicago's South Side.

The PCR is one of many organizations charging that sources of toxic waste are disproportionately found in minority neighborhoods. These groups contend that government agencies do not adequately respond to the impact of numerous hazardous facilities in minority communities, thereby contributing to a form of discrimination termed "environmental racism." In 1992, for example, a *National Law Journal* study found that companies were, on average, fined more than three hundred thousand dollars for toxic waste violations in white neighborhoods and only fifty-five thousand for similar violations in minority neighborhoods. The study also revealed that the Environmental Protection Agency (EPA) waited longer to decide if hazards in minority communities warranted being placed on "Superfund," the government's list of high priority cleanup sites. Furthermore, the study showed, Superfund sites in white neighborhoods were cleaned up in less than ten years while it took between twelve and fourteen years for the EPA to clean up such sites in minority areas. Many activists claim that such unequal treatment on the part of the EPA encourages hazardous facilities to locate in minority areas where they face less governmental scrutiny. This siting pattern, they argue, increases the chances that people of color will be exposed to high levels of toxins.

Several commentators dispute the claim that minority communities are disproportionately affected by environmental hazards. They often cite a University of Massachusetts study that concluded that hazardous waste facilities are more likely to be found in neighborhoods with a higher percentage of white working-class inhabitants than minority inhabitants. Such findings suggest that the placement of these facilities may have more to do with the lower economic status of the community than with the race of its residents, analysts contend. Moreover, some argue, the information used to support claims of environmental discrimination is mostly anecdotal. None of the studies contain evidence that actually proves that living near waste dumps or chemical plants causes health problems, these experts maintain.

The authors in the following chapter debate claims of environmental racism as well as several other forms of discrimination.

Racial Discrimination Is a Serious Problem

by Leith Mullings

About the author: *Leith Mullings is a professor of anthropology at the City University of New York Graduate School.*

Racism continues to be a real force in American life with severe consequences for millions of people. What is more, aspects of it can be scientifically measured. Hopefully, this is old hat for those who have been supportive of civil rights struggles but, unfortunately, we must continue to assert and demonstrate it. Because the right, as well as segments of the liberal camp, argue that affirmative action is based on past discrimination that no longer exists, it continues to be necessary to point out that discrimination is demonstrable and real today.

Examples of Racial Discrimination

Studies document hundreds of examples of racial discrimination every year. For example, the Federal Office of Personnel Management report that when education, performance rating, and other factors are held constant, African Americans are twice as likely as whites to be dismissed from government jobs, and no one can explain why. Federal Reserve Board studies find that in several cities, African Americans are turned down for loans at two-and-a-half-times the rate of whites. In a study by the Urban Institute in 1991, teams of equally qualified, equally articulate, conventionally dressed black and white men applying for jobs, found pervasive and widespread discrimination against young black men. In the same year, *Harvard Law Review* published a study that examined 90 car dealerships in Chicago. Black and white, male and female researchers were sent out to bargain for the same automobile with a list price of $11,000. All relevant factors were controlled—they had identical strategies, used the same language, had the same amount of money for a down payment, wore the same style of clothing. The only differences were gender and race. Euro-American men were able to buy the car for an average of $11,305; Euro-American women for $11,504; African American men had to pay $11,783 for the same car; and

Reprinted from Leith Mullings, "Racism Remains Pervasive," *New Politics*, Summer 1995, by permission of the author and *New Politics*.

African American women were charged \$12,300. If that happens to African Americans when they buy a car, think about what happens to them when they buy a house.

Some argue that African Americans born into middle-class families no longer suffer the effects of racism. But one need only examine the numerous studies of employment, income, housing discrimination, and patterns of awarding mortgages and contracts, to note the pervasive nature of racism. Black middle class people encounter forms of personal and institutional discrimination every day, from the infamous examples of trying to take taxis to violent—and sometimes deadly—encounters with police officers. African Americans, regardless of income, experience racism.

Shifting our focus to look at the positions in society held by white men, we find that white men constitute 95 percent of senior corporate executives, 92 percent of the Senate, 97 percent of school superintendentships, and one could go on and on.

The point is that racism is not a legacy of the past. It is an active, destructive aspect of the present and at the heart of it is economic exploitation. It is this *exploitation* that distinguishes racism from some of the other forms of intolerance.

A Warfare of Ideas

Why are affirmative action policies—which were developed to help to dismantle segregation and to force institutions to grant equal opportunity—being debated now? It is critical for us to understand the social context in which this discussion arises and its importance for the right-wing agenda. On the international level, the context is one of ascendent globalized capitalism. This is a time when few institutions can stand against multinational corporations; a time in which inequality among regions of the world, among countries, and between classes is increasing at historic rates.

In the United States between 1973 and the present, real incomes have fallen significantly for 80 percent of American workers. Simultaneously, the U.S. has experienced the most massive redistribution of wealth and income upward to the rich, producing conditions of severe insecurity for the majority of Americans.

The agenda of the right is to consolidate the process begun during the Reagan regime and, as Frances Fox Piven has pointed out, to destroy the admittedly minor redistributive functions of the state. In carrying out this agenda, the right devised a comprehensive strategy. They developed: 1) a mass movement through the Christian Coalition; 2) political institutions through the Republican Party and the "Contract with America" and 3) most significantly, for our purposes, an extensive ideological apparatus that includes think tanks; books, publications, publishers and

> *"Racism continues to be a real force in American life with severe consequences for millions of people."*

publicists; and the popular media, most notably the radio talk shows. They recognized, long before elements of the left, the importance of ideological warfare.

Race is central to this strategy: the attack on affirmative action, on immigration, on welfare all masterfully manipulate racial symbolism to distort real issues of inequality. Symbols evoke feelings and motivations, not necessarily rational thought. Whereas affirmative action, problematic as it is, speaks to the fact that inequality is structured into the social system, the attack on affirmative action presumes that systemic, institutionalized discrimination no longer exists. Racial inequality must then be attributable to inequalities inherent in the population. This is not a new argument: through U.S. history, the parallel paradigms of biological and cultural inequality have rationalized the exploitation of African Americans. Today, assertions of biological inferiority are formulated through "the bell curve," and cultural inferiority through concepts of "the underclass" and "the culture of poverty." Make no mistake, the bottom line of the anti-affirmative action argument is that white men continue to hold the vast majority of positions of power because women and minorities are inferior. The "bell curve" along with the campaign around family values tell us that the reason for underrepresentation is not white privilege, but biological and cultural inferiority.

> *"Studies document hundreds of examples of racial discrimination every year."*

Creating Divisions Among People

Thus, notions of racial difference once again create divisions among people who should have interests in common, and facilitate the management of dissent. Despite the fact that the major beneficiaries of affirmative action have been white women, it is affirmative action's possible benefits for African Americans that seems to be most effective in stimulating anger. The right's contemptible and contemptuous use of race is not the creation of conspiracy theorists; it is a strategy carried out with knowledgeable cynicism. Discussing the affirmative action debate, William Kristol, chief strategist for the Republican Party, remarked, "It's a winner for us any way you look at it."

In this controversy, we have a graphic demonstration of what many social theorists have discussed: the ability of the dominant class to define the terms of the debate and thereby control dissent. We are imprisoned in a discussion of affirmative action, a policy which has had some successes but has hardly touched the real structure of power.

At a time when the U.S. has become the world's most stratified industrial country, David Roediger's work, *The Wages of Whiteness*, is instructive. He points to the manner in which recruiting workers to whiteness has historically served to persuade white workers to support policies that are not in their interest. The majority of white men who are not in the top one percent of the population owning 48 percent of society's net wealth, have reason to be angry—but not at black people. Their grievance is deliberately steered toward those who are not responsible for their problem.

We, on the left, need to have the courage and the imagination to move beyond the boundaries constructed by the right. For too many of us, identity politics leads us to deconstruct race, but to downplay racism. Much of identity politics has been about "deconstructing" cultural symbolism and discourse, not about challenging the hierarchy of power that undergirds the structure of race relations.

Affirmative Action Is Not Enough

We need to state clearly that affirmative action does not go far enough. In the absence of structural transformations that definitively deal with all forms of unequal power and discrimination, measures at any limited level, such as affirmative action, have a stopgap quality. Affirmative action is a liberal rather than a radical reform, fraught with the contradictions of liberalism. It addresses problems, but in a partial manner that does not adequately speak to poverty, unemployment, and the "savage inequality" of capitalism. For those of us who have a vision of a humane society of equal opportunity, this does not mean that we reject affirmative action, but that we take creative approaches to constructing programs that seek to abolish all forms of privilege. As Gertrude Ezorsky has pointed out in *Racism and Justice: The Case for Affirmative Action,* since women comprise more than 50 per cent of the population, to the extent that affirmative action benefits women and underrepresented minorities, it is a policy that benefits the majority of Americans.

> *"It is necessary to support programs that expand opportunity and equality among all people, and . . . to break down the continuing racial boundaries to equal opportunity."*

Given our theoretical knowledge about the ways in which race and class are not exclusive but intertwined concepts, there is no contradiction between advocating universalist policies, such as health care and full employment and, at the same time, fighting for desegregation of the workplace and racial justice through affirmative action measures. It is necessary to support programs that expand opportunity and equality among all people, and simultaneously to struggle to break down the continuing racial boundaries to equal opportunity. This is critical because the struggle against mobile, globalized capital requires integration of the workplace at the national and international level. . . .

As the demagogues once again try to shift attention away from the declining life chances of the American worker, it is critical that the left maintain an anti-racist perspective. We must use our skills with greater creativity and tenacity than our opponents of the right, forging links to social movements that truly attempt to abolish all forms of race, gender and class privilege.

Minorities Face Lending Discrimination

by Jim Campen

About the author: *Jim Campen, an associate for the bimonthly progressive journal* Dollars & Sense, *teaches economics at the University of Massachusetts in Boston.*

As appalling as it was, an annual report on mortgage lending shocked few observers when the Clinton Administration's top regulators unveiled it before the Senate Banking Committee in early November 1993. In keeping with past patterns, black mortgage applicants were turned down more than twice as often as whites in 1992. Indeed, the most closely watched single number indicated that things were getting worse rather than better: The ratio of the black denial rate to the white denial rate rose from 2.16 to 1 in 1991 to 2.26 to 1 in 1992.

Acknowledging Discrimination

What was different in 1993 was the response to the statistics. Instead of denying the obvious as they have in the past, government officials acknowledged that discrimination is "alive and well in America," as Housing Secretary Henry Cisneros put it. Bank regulators, along with Attorney General Janet Reno, testified that they are intensifying efforts to identify and punish lenders who discriminate.

And bankers, rather than disputing charges that they had discriminated, emphasized their efforts to do better. Since researchers found what one Massachusetts banker referred to as a "smoking gun" in October 1992, bankers have recognized that they can no longer offer credible denials. The crucial evidence, from a study by the Federal Reserve Bank of Boston, finally established beyond a reasonable doubt that banks discriminate along racial lines when making mortgage loans.

The banks' quandary is the triumph of a nationwide grassroots "community reinvestment" movement that for over twenty years has been employing innovative strategies to challenge banks' failure to meet the credit needs of low-income and minority neighborhoods and individuals. That banks discriminate

Reprinted from Jim Campen, "Lending Insights," *Dollars & Sense*, January/February 1994, by permission. *Dollars & Sense* is a progressive economics magazine published ten times a year. First-year subscriptions cost $16.95 and may be ordered by writing *Dollars & Sense*, One Summer St., Somerville, MA 02143, or by calling 617-628-2025.

has, of course, long been obvious to those receiving the short end of the stick. But community advocates recognized that obtaining proof of discrimination would be the key to combatting it. So, they fought not only for laws that regulate banks, but also for requirements that banks furnish relevant information on their lending practices. They then used this data to publicize banks' abysmal performances, sparking the public outrage necessary to make banks more responsive to the needs of low-income and minority communities.

> *"Black mortgage applicants were turned down more than twice as often as whites in 1992."*

Their first major legislative victory was the 1975 enactment of the Home Mortgage Disclosure Act (HMDA—pronounced *HUMdah),* which required each bank to report the number and dollar amount of the mortgage and home improvement loans by census tract (census tracts are areas a few blocks square, containing a few thousand people, for which detailed demographic and socio-economic data are available). Two years after HMDA took effect, Congress adopted the Community Reinvestment Act (CRA). The CRA declares that banks have an "affirmative obligation" to serve the credit needs of local communities, including low and moderate income areas—which are often communities of color. A lesser-known set of *fair lending laws,* including the Fair Housing Act of 1968 and the Equal Credit Opportunity Act of 1974, explicitly prohibit racial discrimination. Only very recently, however, have bankers and regulators begun to take the CRA and the fair lending laws at all seriously.

The Information Game

In the absence of earnest enforcement efforts by bank regulators, it fell primarily to independent community-oriented researchers to document discriminatory lending practices. Their efforts to build this case, beginning with the struggle to enact HMDA, have followed a recurring pattern.

Typically, community groups made charges only to see them dismissed by the banks as unsupported by solid evidence. The groups then struggled to make more data available, so researchers would be able to produce more definitive results. Consistently, though, the banks and their defenders (including, in many cases, the regulatory agencies) criticized the resulting studies as inconclusive. The limited nature of the data available, they argued, made it impossible to rule out other possible explanations of racial disparities in lending patterns. But with this maneuver, the banks backed themselves into a corner: They were now in no position to deny demands from community advocates for additional data to fill out the picture. So another round would begin, as researchers used the more extensive data supplied by the banks to produce results even more suggestive of racial discrimination.

By the end of the 1980s, this cycle had yielded an impressive array of studies that combined HMDA data with Census Bureau information on the racial composition and income level of census tracts in order to document mortgage lending discrimination. The *Atlanta Journal-Constitution*'s Pulitzer Prize–winning series "The Color of Money" (May 1988) compared stable, middle-income neighborhoods that were at least 80% white to those that were at least 80% nonwhite. It found that between 1984 and 1986, Atlanta banks and savings & loans (S&Ls) made 4.5 times as many loans per 1,000 single-family structures in white neighborhoods as in comparable black neighborhoods.

In city after city, studies documented similarly dramatic racial disparities in mortgage lending. Between 1981 and 1987 in Boston, for instance, banks made 2.9 times as many mortgage loans per 1,000 housing units in low-income white neighborhoods as in minority neighborhoods with similar incomes. In Detroit, the ratio of the mortgage lending rate (loans per 1,000 homes) in middle-income white neighborhoods to that in middle-income black neighborhoods rose every year between 1981 and 1986, reaching 3.14 to 1 in 1986. Similar patterns appeared in Chicago, Los Angeles, Milwaukee, and New York as well as in 14 cities observed by the Center for Community Change. A survey of 23 studies by Professor Anne Shlay of Temple University showed that all 23 found a negative impact of race on conventional mortgage lending.

Reactions to the Studies

Bankers acknowledged that these results were troubling, but argued that they didn't prove that banks were discriminating. First, the bankers suggested that the low level of lending in minority neighborhoods might reflect a low level of applications rather than a high level of bank denials. They also pointed out that the data referred only to the location of the homes being purchased. Since it provided no direct information about the race or income level of the applicants, they argued that the data failed to prove discrimination against minority individuals.

These defensive arguments by bankers helped make it possible for the community reinvestment movement to finally succeed in broadening the scope of HMDA. As part of the S&L bailout bill adopted in August 1989, HMDA was amended to require banks to report on all mortgage applications received, rather than just on loans made. Beginning January 1, 1990, banks had to record the race, income, and sex of each applicant, the result of the application, and the previously required information on the census tract in which the home was located.

> *"Crucial evidence ... established beyond a reasonable doubt that banks discriminate along racial lines when making mortgage loans."*

In October 1991, the Federal Reserve reported the results of its analysis of the expanded HMDA data for 1990. It was the most extensive set of mortgage lending data ever assembled—more than six million loan applications reported by over 9,000 mortgage lenders. The most striking single result of their analysis was the difference in denial rates for black and white applicants. Overall, 34% of black applications for conventional home mortgages were rejected, compared to a 14% rejection rate for whites. (Hispanics were rejected at a 21% rate; rejection rates for Asians were slightly lower than for whites.) Large differentials persisted even when comparisons were limited to applicants in the same income categories. In many cities, high-income blacks experienced higher denial rates than low-income whites.

> *"In many cities, high-income blacks experienced higher denial rates than low-income whites."*

Lenders could no longer claim that low levels of lending resulted solely from a lack of demand for loans by minority applicants rather than from their own decisions on which applications to accept. They were, however, quick to adopt a fallback position. In its response to the grossly unequal denial rates revealed by the expanded HMDA data, the American Bankers Association (ABA) emphasized that the data didn't include "information critical to judging the creditworthiness of loan applicants." It was entirely possible, the bankers suggested, that differences in applicants' credit histories, wealth, job instability, or other economic characteristics accounted for the more frequent rejection of minority loan applicants. ABA chief lobbyist Ed Yingling maintained that "the HMDA numbers don't show a whole lot; they don't mean a whole lot."

These denials persisted in the face of both statistical and tangible evidence of racial discrimination by banks. Court cases and case studies compiled by community-based organizations supplemented the faceless statistical studies with the stories of real human beings. Banks were closing offices in minority neighborhoods while opening them elsewhere, and new surveys revealed that banks had disproportionately few black executives. It would have been perverse, in light of all this evidence, for anybody to doubt that banks were in fact discriminating.

But that did not deter the banking industry from commissioning social scientists to argue that the case for discrimination was based entirely on "circumstantial evidence." They took the position that, according to the standards of statistical research in the social sciences, the conclusion had not been proven beyond a reasonable doubt.

The "Smoking Gun"

Meanwhile, researchers at the Federal Reserve Bank of Boston—which has been a somewhat liberal outpost in the overwhelmingly conservative Federal Reserve System—were pursuing another path. If conclusions had been limited by missing data, they reasoned, why not collect and analyze all of the data necessary to resolve the issue? Taking advantage of the Fed's status as a banking regulator, they were able to conduct the first study to take into account virtually all of the factors used in mortgage lending decisions. They asked the 131 banks in the Boston area that had received 25 or more mortgage applications in 1990 to review their loan files and gather 38 additional pieces of information for each application from a black or Hispanic (about 1,200 applications) and for a randomly selected set of 3,300 applications by whites. Once again, the banks' attacks on the alleged insufficiency of existing data had led to the gathering of more and better information.

Using a special variant of the standard statistical technique known as multiple regression analysis, the Boston Fed's analysts then sought to explain why minorities in the Boston area were denied mortgages 2.7 times as often as whites. To what extent, the researchers asked, did legitimate factors account for the disparity?

Banks, hoping to be exonerated by the Boston Fed's study, were dismayed at the results. The additional information showed that, as the banks claimed, blacks and Hispanics were on average poorer, had worse credit histories, and requested mortgage loans that were larger relative to their incomes. But it also showed that these and similar factors only told part of the story. Even if black and Hispanic borrowers had been just as creditworthy as the average white applicant with respect to all 38 of the factors considered, they still would have been 56% more likely to be denied a mortgage. Only the applicants' minority status could account for the difference. As Alicia Munnell, who was then the Boston Fed's Research Director, put it, "The study eliminates all the other possible factors that could be influencing decisions." The long-sought "smoking gun" had been found.

> *"Banks were closing offices in minority neighborhoods while opening them elsewhere."*

The Boston Fed offered a plausible account of the way that discrimination took place. As most of those who have sought home mortgages know from personal experience, the application process can be complex and intimidating. The Boston Fed's data showed that only 20% of all applicants had flawless credit records. Within that group virtually all applicants were approved, regardless of race. But the great majority of applicants—including most of those ultimately receiving loans—had one or more imperfections in their loan files. These problems could have legitimately justified denying them mortgage loans.

To be successful, applicants generally need help and counseling, and often benefit from a willingness on the part of bank personnel to "stretch" or overlook one or two of the requirements. Whites appeared to have received this assistance more frequently than blacks or Hispanics—perhaps because the loan officers, who were overwhelmingly white, were simply more comfortable with other whites. Even though there may have been a valid technical reason for every denial of a minority application, banks were still guilty of treating white and minority applicants unequally. As activist Bruce Marks of the Boston-based Union Neighborhood Assistance Corporation explained, "it's a mortgage minefield," and banks are much more likely to guide white applicants through it.

After the Smokescreen Clears

Pushed beyond the stage of denial—in spite of the inevitable, and quickly discredited, objections published by *Forbes, Business Week,* and the *Wall Street Journal*—bankers and federal regulators have begun to recognize the value of measures that had been urged on them for years by community advocates. Bank responses have included taking a systematic "second look" at minority loan applications recommended for denial; training bank employees to increase understanding of fair lending issues and sensitivity to cultural differences; hiring more minority loan officers; revising certain traditional credit standards that are biased toward white cultural practices; forging working relationships with realtors and appraisal firms that have positive records in minority communities; developing new mortgage lending products adapted to the special circumstances and needs of minority borrowers; and using internal "testing" programs to identify whether or not bank employees are in fact offering equal treatment to minority applicants.

> *"Even though there may have been a valid technical reason for every denial of a minority application, banks were still guilty of treating white and minority applicants unequally."*

At the same time, the four federal bank regulatory agencies have begun taking steps to ensure that banks are complying with fair lending laws. One agency, the Office of the Comptroller of the Currency (OCC), estimated in November 1993 that it would complete 20 in-depth fair-lending examinations by the end of 1993. The OCC also announced that it would begin the use of undercover testers to detect racial discrimination at the pre-application stage of the mortgage lending process. For the first time, regulators are actually referring cases to the Justice Department when their own investigations suggest that discrimination is occurring. And, most dramatically, the Federal Reserve Board denied a routine application by Connecticut-based Shawmut Bank to acquire a smaller bank in New Hampshire, citing the ongoing Justice Department investigation of Shawmut's alleged lending discrimination.

These things happened only after Congressional hearings had brought to light what Deepak Bhargava of the Association of Community Organizations for Reform Now (ACORN) characterized as "a long and sorry record" of regulatory failure. Even New York's Republican Senator Alphonse D'Amato was moved to ask whether the "regulatory agencies [were] asleep at the switch, or worse, turning a blind eye?"

In fact, between 1978 and 1990 three successive directors of the OCC's fair lending office resigned in frustration at the attitude of the agency's leadership, which not only refused to allow them to take the steps they regarded as necessary to enforce the law, but even refused to release reports documenting possible discrimination. A single community organization in one medium-sized Ohio city, the Toledo Fair Housing Center, was able to identify and successfully pursue numerous cases of lending discrimination annually, while all four of the federal bank regulators—taken together—only referred one case of racial discrimination in lending to the Department of Justice in 18 years. And until its September 1992 settlement requiring Georgia's Decatur Federal Savings & Loan to pay $1 million to 48 black applicants denied mortgage loans, the Justice Department had never charged a single bank with racial discrimination in mortgage lending.

The Power of Disclosure

It remains to be seen whether, and to what extent, this story will have a happy ending. It will be years before we know whether the hard-won gains by community-based groups and their advocates will bring about an actual reduction in lending discrimination.

The Boston Fed study established the *fact* of discrimination in mortgage lending. But with its narrow focus on data from completed loan applications, the study did not attempt to measure the full *extent* of discrimination. For example, many potential minority borrowers encounter responses to their initial contacts with banks that discourage them from ever applying, and the property values recorded in loan files may have been furnished by appraisers who systematically undervalue homes in minority neighborhoods.

The community reinvestment movement is right to insist that banks are obliged by the CRA to do more than simply deal fairly with the loan applicants who come through their doors. A whole range of aggressive, affirmative initiatives will be necessary to extend credit and financial services to currently underserved communities. Moreover, without constant pressure from community groups, regulators will likely bow to pressure from banks and fail to enforce community-oriented laws and regulations.

If properly enforced, disclosure laws should continue to be useful. Many aspects of the normal operation of our economic system cannot stand the light of day. With that in mind, the community reinvestment movement has recently been emphasizing its long-standing call for the extension of disclosure requirements to the realm of business lending.

Activists believe that businesses based in low-income communities and those owned by minorities have had an even harder time obtaining credit than minority home-buyers. But until there is something comparable to HMDA for small business lending, it will be impossible to persuasively document the existence and extent of the problem. And as the ongoing struggle for fair mortgage lending has demonstrated, exposing the nature of a problem can go a long way toward forcing its solution.

Environmental Racism
Is a Serious Problem

by Salim Muwakkil

About the author: *Salim Muwakkil is a senior editor of* In These Times, *a bi-weekly progressive journal.*

A government sting operation that allowed illegal dumpsites to operate for years in several of Chicago's predominantly black neighborhoods has triggered outrage from city residents and sparked renewed interest in the fledgling environmental justice movement.

Operation Silver Shovel, the FBI's colorfully named but tawdry caper, featured a government informant, or "mole," who reportedly bribed aldermen and other city officials to look the other way as he illegally dumped thousands of tons of waste material—some of it hazardous—into their jurisdictions. According to officials at Chicago's Department of the Environment, more than 3 million cubic yards of debris have been dumped illegally on eight sites, and the cost of the cleanup has been estimated at $15 million.

"We just weren't respected at all," says Judge C. Watkins, who lives at the foot of a four-block-long, 70-foot-high mountain of debris created by the government mole, on the city's West Side. Watkins has been deeply involved in his community's furious but fruitless efforts to force a cleanup of the dumpsite. Oddly enough, the existence of what has come to be called "the mountain" was the major issue in the ward's previous aldermanic campaign. "A reasonable person knew there was no way that much debris could be dumped without a person in authority knowing what was really happening and allowing it to continue."

The Campaign Against Environmental Racism

The huge scale of the dumping operation and the lack of official response attracted many environmental activists to the cause and refocused attention on environmental racism, an issue with which Chicagoans are quite familiar. The city's predominantly African-American and Latino southeast side has long been notorious for containing the greatest single concentration of hazardous waste sites in the nation.

Reprinted from Salim Muwakkil, "Moving Mountains," *In These Times*, February 19, 1996, by permission of the author.

But the city is also noted for Hazel Johnson, the feisty grandmother who since 1982 has mounted a spirited struggle against waste dumps, landfills and other industrial polluters—and has won a few battles along the way. Her grass-roots group, People for Community Recovery, has inspired similar anti-pollution efforts across the country in neighborhoods ravaged by the by-products of environmental racism.

> *"Three out of five African-Americans and Latinos live in communities with one or more hazardous waste sites."*

The concept of environmental racism was pioneered by the Rev. Benjamin C. Chavis, who, as executive director of the Commission for Racial Justice of the United Church of Christ, co-authored with Charles Lee a 1987 study revealing that although the poor of all races are more likely than middle- or upper-income groups to live near hazardous waste sites, "race [is] consistently a more prominent factor in the location of commercial hazardous waste facilities than any other factor examined." The report, titled *Toxic Waste and Race in the United States,* found that three out of five African-Americans and Latinos live in communities with one or more hazardous waste sites.

The study cited a battery of other chilling statistics to support its claims. Childhood cancer rates are several times the national average in Latino farm communities where pesticides are used. Because of the bad quality of air in urban black communities, young black men die of asthma at three times the rate of young white men. African-Americans' high rates of cancer, respiratory disorders, renal malfunctions and heart disease have also been linked to the high concentrations of industrial pollutants disproportionately found in minority communities.

"For black people, this is the worst attack we've had since the Middle Passage, because the chemicals that we're getting exposed to are causing long-term, multi-generational damage," says Connie Tucker, executive director of the Atlanta-based Southern Committee for Economic and Social Justice, a network of groups seeking environmental justice. Tucker's group is one of many that have mushroomed since the United Church of Christ study appeared in 1987.

A Worsening Situation

But despite greater awareness of environmental racism, the situation has worsened. According to a 1994 update of the Chavis-Lee report, conducted by the United Church of Christ along with the National Association for the Advancement of Colored People and the Washington-based Center for Policy Alternatives, the concentration of people of color living in zip code areas with commercial hazardous waste facilities increased from 25 percent of the local population in 1980 to nearly 31 percent in 1993.

A host of additional studies have reinforced Chavis and Lee's initial conclusions about the primacy of race in placing a community at risk. One 1992 analysis by the *National Law Journal* found that minority communities get less environmental protection from government agencies. The *Law Journal*'s analysis found that the Environmental Protection Agency (EPA) required less comprehensive cleanup of polluted black communities and penalized polluters of black areas less severely than those in white areas.

Robert Bullard, director of Clark Atlanta University's Environmental Justice Resource Center, organized the First National People of Color Environmental Leadership Summit in Washington, D.C., in 1991. The conference, designed to connect the varied organizations concerned with these crucial issues, attracted representatives from more than 300 groups. Bullard also intended for the conference to give public notice that traditional notions of environmentalism no longer were relevant. "Environmentalists are not just white people who are interested in birds and whales," Bullard said at the time. "[African-Americans] are also environmentalists, because we drink the water, we breathe the air and we live on the land."

Though it's comparatively young, the environmental justice movement has been surprisingly effective in attracting mainstream attention. A national lobbying effort convinced President Clinton to sign an executive order in February 1994, directing 17 federal agencies to address environmental racism. The order requires the affected agencies to "make environmental justice a part of all they do." In an attempt to help provide some context for the new initiative, the EPA has established the National Environmental Justice Advisory Council, which includes researchers familiar with the issue.

Environmental Equity

The EPA and the Justice Department are currently investigating charges of environmental racism in Louisiana and Mississippi. The decision by the agencies to get involved marks the first time the federal government has encouraged the use of the 1964 Civil Rights Act in community environmental battles.

"The administration sent an important message with Clinton's order," says Chavis, who now is executive director of the National African-American Leadership Summit. "We have to set a long-term goal of a sustainable society that is economically viable and environmentally safe. And it's very important that we ensure environmental equity."

"The chemicals that [blacks are] getting exposed to are causing long-term, multi-generational damage."

For people like Watkins, whose house abuts the "mountain" on Chicago's West Side, environmental equity is not just a clever slogan or the current cause célèbre. And that sense of urgency can help forge important interracial alliances.

In Homer, La., a small town 65 miles northeast of Shreveport, an interracial coalition called Citizens Against Nuclear Trash (CANT) formed to fight

Louisiana Energy Services' (LES) plan to locate a uranium enrichment plant in their town. Although Confederate flags still fly high in this isolated part of the Old South, the threat of the LES plant helped bridge ancient racial divides. CANT is thoroughly integrated; Roy Mardis, a 39-year-old black man, is a member of the group's executive board and its unofficial spokesman. He has traveled across the state soliciting support for the anti-nuclear fight and has been startled by the grass-roots support he's received.

"Minority communities get less environmental protection from government agencies."

In this and other ways, the environmental justice movement provides the nexus between theory and action that progressives have long sought. Beverly Wright, director of Xavier University's Deep South Center for Environmental Justice in New Orleans, understands that grass-roots activists for the most part are women concerned about their families. "If you get information to a mother that her children may be harmed by toxic chemicals, then you have organization," Wright told *Emerge* magazine.

In the "Call To Action," which followed the 1991 Washington environmental summit, organizers wrote that "a new international movement of indigenous and grass-roots peoples was born." The authors of the document distinguished the summit's participants from traditional mainstream environmental and social justice organizations, noting that they seek "a global vision based on grass-roots realities" and are evolving from the bottom up. "We have come together around many issues in many lands to unleash the power of our united will in a common struggle for a new environmental movement," the document reads: "A movement to eradicate environmental racism and bring into being true social justice and self-determination."

It's an ambitious agenda, but somebody's got to do it.

The Criminal Justice System Discriminates Against Hispanics

by Ron Nixon

About the author: *Ron Nixon is a general assignment reporter for the political journal* Southern Exposure.

Shortly after the Million Man March of 1995, findings of the Sentencing Project (a research and advocacy organization on criminal justice policy in Washington, D.C.) showed that the number of African American men incarcerated in U.S. prisons had increased 31 percent, to one in three, during the five-year period from 1989 to 1994. The report was immediately greeted with great public outcry and national comment from politicians, media pundits, and civil rights groups. Lost in the dialogue was that the number of Hispanic inmates had also increased during the same period.

When there is a discussion of race and the legal system, the terms are almost entirely framed in black and white. Part of the problem, says Marc Mauer, author of the Sentencing Project's report, is that due to different methods of information gathering, data on Hispanics is unreliable, and not all states bother to keep the information.

"Obviously people have not felt it appropriate to try to gather the information," says José Gaitan of the Hispanic National Bar Association (HNBA). The absence of reliable data makes statistical calculation difficult, but data that is available clearly shows the disproportionate impact of the criminal justice system on the Hispanic population.

The Image of Crime

Driven by measures like "three strikes and you're out," tougher sentencing laws, and anti-immigration furor, Hispanics and other people of color have become, for many, the very image of crime. In communities across the country,

Hispanic parents, politicians, and community leaders feel that the war on crime has escalated into a war on the Hispanic population. According to the Sentencing Project's review of Department of Justice data, Hispanics constitute the fastest growing segment of the minority population in state and federal prison. From 1980 to 1993, . . . the percentage of [prison inmates who are Hispanic] rose from 7.7 to 14.3 percent (this does not include Hispanic inmates incarcerated in INS prisons). During this same period, the number of inmates has tripled from 163 to 529 per 100,000 Hispanic residents. In contrast, Hispanics make up 10 percent of the U.S. population. The U.S. Census also predicts that by the year 2020, the Hispanic prison population, ages 18–34, will grow to 25.6 percent.

> *"Data . . . clearly shows the disproportionate impact of the criminal justice system on the Hispanic population."*

Adding to the alarming significance of these figures, the authors of the report say the numbers probably reflect undercounting and are attributed to bias in the nation's sentencing laws. They concluded, "While we have no available data regarding other factors which correlate with a higher likelihood of incarceration . . . the findings here are of such magnitude that they raise serious questions about the racial implications of current drug policies."

The U.S. Sentencing Commission came to the same conclusion in a 1995 report. In its 242-page report issued to Congress, the Commission found that sentencing laws had a disproportionate impact on Latinos and blacks. Hispanics compose 16 percent of those sentenced on drug charges to state prisons, though whites make up the vast majority of the nation's drug users. The Commission recommended that Congress change the law to address the disparity. A Republican Congress, with the support of President Clinton in a rare bipartisan move to appear tough on crime, refused to follow the recommendations for one of the few times in the Commission's history. "These politicians have bought into the idea that the solution to crime is building more prisons and locking people up," says Juan Figueroa of the Puerto Rican Legal Defense Fund (PRLDF) in New York City. "The Latino prison population has exploded because of continued discrimination and institutional racism."

Hispanics Are Underrepresented in Law Enforcement

But if Hispanics are overrepresented in the prison population, they are vastly underrepresented in all other aspects of the criminal justice system, says Gaitan. Data from the Department of Justice (DOJ) Bureau of Justice Statistics in 1995 support his observations. According to the DOJ, Hispanics make up 1 percent of all judges, 3 percent of all lawyers, 9 percent of all police detectives, and 5 percent of all correctional officers. In addition, there is only one Hispanic federal U.S. Attorney and there has never been a Hispanic U.S. Supreme Court Justice. Nationally, there are only 651 Hispanic judicially elected officials (e.g., judges, police chiefs, justices of the peace) says Rosalind Gold of the National Association of Latino Elected Officials (NALEO). That is actually a small number when you consider that the majority of U.S. Hispanics are concentrated in eight states. "What this means is that at all levels of government and in the private sector you have people making decisions who are not sensitive to a large segment of the population," says Carlos Ortiz of the Hispanic National Bar Association.

The lack of Hispanics at the local law enforcement level appears to have the most impact on how Hispanics are treated in the criminal justice system. After the Rodney King incident in California, two reports documented the rampant use of excessive force and racial harassment by local law enforcement agents against Hispanics and African Americans (the 1996 filmed beating of two illegal Mexican immigrants at the hands of California law enforcement officials was another painful reminder). The reports concluded that racially intolerant attitudes and conduct reflect management failures, not just problems with individual law enforcement agents. Another California report found that police make unfounded arrests (where the suspect is innocent, there was inadequate evidence, or there was an illegal search and seizure) at higher rates for people of color than for whites. For Hispanics the rate was more than double that of whites.

> *"[Many] feel that the war on crime has escalated into a war on the Hispanic population."*

Perhaps more revealing is a survey conducted by the City of Los Angeles in January 1996 which shows that even some Latinos in law enforcement are harassed. The survey, conducted by the L.A. City Council Personnel Department, found that 57 percent of Latino officers in the bilingual police service found themselves resented and the target of negative jokes or comments. In the nation's capital, the Justice Department's Office of Civil Rights, acting on a 1993 complaint filed by a dozen Hispanic officers, ruled in 1996 that the D.C. police department routinely treats Hispanics unfairly. In one reported incident, a Latino officer was suspended for 25 days when he intervened to stop a white officer from using an illegal choke hold on a Latino resident.

The "War" on Gangs

Nowhere is the impact of having few Hispanics in law enforcement felt more than in the current "war" on gangs. In many areas, local law enforcement officials have begun what they called gang profiling: stopping suspected gang members for photos or denying them access to certain areas because of the way they are dressed. "Stereotyping and institutional racism make it hard for cops to separate the hard core gang members from other people who hang out in certain areas or dress a certain way," says Northern California American Civil Liberties Union (ACLU) attorney Edward Chen. "In some areas, this profiling has turned into outright harassment," says Chen. "The definition of 'gang' is so broad that you could label the Los Angeles Police Department a gang." Chen, who has handled cases against gang profiling, says the practice is escalating. In some cities, police simply walk up to young Hispanic men and women and take their pictures for a "gang mug book," oftentimes without the permission of the youths and even if they have no criminal record, says Chen.

"The Latino prison population has exploded because of continued discrimination and institutional racism."

These profiles are ultimately fed into local gang databases which, according to proponents, are supposed to keep an accurate account of gang members and track their future movement. In cities like Denver and Los Angeles, whose gang databases were investigated by local media, Hispanics and African Americans were found to make up the majority of names listed in the databases. In Denver the gang list contained 6,567 names, almost all Latino and black. In Los Angeles a Government Accounting Office study found that 44 percent of those on the database, again mostly black and Latino, had no criminal record. In San Jose, California, 97 percent of the young men on the gang database were people of color. In 1993 the Federal Bureau of Investigation (FBI) even considered its own database, but shelved the measure after public outcry lead by the ACLU asserted that a database of gang members would perpetuate racist stereotypes about young men of color.

Evelyn Ramirez-Claire of Redwood City, California, knows the problem of gang profiling firsthand. The mother of two boys sued an amusement park and a shopping mall after park security personnel, acting on local law enforcement protocol, stopped and detained her sons and their friends because they were dressed in "gang attire." Although both establishments settled out of court and agreed to end the profiling practice, the incidents leave a bitter taste for Ramirez-Claire. There is little doubt in her mind why her sons were stopped and accused of being gang members—their ethnicity. The suits, Ramirez-Claire hopes, will call "law enforcement [officials'] attention to what they are doing and the long-term effects."

Despite complaints about gang profiling from parents such as Ramirez-Claire, some consider the measure an effective way to curb gang activity and crime and don't see it as singling out Hispanics or blacks. "My response is, yes, those who claim to be in a gang happen to be black or Latino," says Dennis Cribari, who is co-director of the Denver Latino Peace Officers Association. "But it's not my fault. I didn't label them. It's what they claim." He says, "I don't see these profiles as unfair except in that our emphasis is targeting gang members no matter what their color. I leave it to other people to draw their own conclusions."

Bias Pervades the Criminal Justice System

Unfortunately, reports from around the country suggest that the racial stereotyping and discrimination against Hispanics on the streets have filtered up through other parts of the criminal justice system, and issues such as poor representation, language barriers, and a lack of cultural competency on the part of officials only make things worse. A report on arrests of women for felony drug charges in Queens County, New York, by criminal justice analyst Tracy Huling found that local drug laws disproportionately affect Hispanic women. According to Huling, 83 percent of Hispanic women arrested received prison sentences, while only 50 percent of white women and 52 percent of black women were sentenced for the same crimes even though all of the women had similar backgrounds and no prior criminal record.

A review of 150,000 criminal cases in Connecticut by the *Hartford Courant,* one of the state's largest daily newspapers, found that a Hispanic or African American man paid twice as much bail as his non-Hispanic white counterpart. In drug cases, the amount of bail was four times higher. For Hispanic women with no prior record, the amount of bail was 197 times higher than the amount paid by non-Hispanic white women. A comprehensive study of plea bargaining (where the defendant makes a "deal" with law enforcement officials for a lighter sentence) by the *San Jose Mercury News* found that non-Hispanic whites, on average, get better deals than African Americans or Hispanics, even when the crime is the same. Of the 71,668 adults without a prior record and charged with a felony reviewed by the *News,* one third of whites had their charges reduced to a misdemeanor or less, while only one quarter of Hispanics and blacks did so. As a result of these tougher plea bargaining deals, Hispanics were sent to state prison for drugs at twice the rate of whites. White offenders got community-based rehabilitation more than twice as often as did Hispanics or blacks.

In addition to bias in the criminal courts, Hispanic youth face problems from a measure pioneered by California cities using civil injunctions against alleged gang members. Instead of filing criminal charges against gang activities, cities are now taking alleged members of gangs to civil court and suing them to restrict them from entering certain areas, engaging in particular activities, or even being seen in public together. According to legal experts

> *"Police make unfounded arrests . . . at higher rates for people of color than for whites."*

like Chen of the ACLU, by pursuing civil cases instead of criminal charges, cities can get quicker action against alleged gang members. The burden of proof is not as high nor does the accused have a right to a lawyer or trial by jury. In the city of San Jose, at least 38 Hispanics received an injunction against them that, according to Chen, "prohibits them from engaging in a variety of constitutionally protected and innocent activities in the neighborhoods, including associating with other defendants, communicating with persons in vehicles, or making loud noises of any kind."

"At all levels in the criminal justice system, Hispanics feel that the system is stacked against them," says Ortiz of the HNBA. To address the disparities and discrimination in the legal system, organizations like the HNBA, the Latino Peace Officers Association, the PRLDF, and the Mexican American Legal Defense and Educational Fund (MALDEF) are pushing for the inclusion of more Hispanics in all levels of the criminal justice system.

Both MALDEF and the HNBA are pressing for the appointment of more Hispanic judges to the federal and state bench and are working with the Clinton Administration to get a Hispanic justice appointed to the Supreme Court. The Latino Peace Officers Association is recruiting more Hispanics to the police force. Professor Michael Olivas of the HNBA is working to increase the number of Hispanic students who attend law school and the number of tenured professors at these schools. A report published by Olivas in the *Chicano-Latino Law Review*, found that law schools have an abysmal record of attracting Hispanic law students and professors. Consequently, Latinos make up a tiny proportion of students in the nation's law schools.

At the same time that Olivas and other advocates are struggling to get more Hispanics into the nation's law schools, many schools, following the example of the University of Texas, are seeking to eliminate programs that make special efforts to recruit people of color. Certain politicians, such as Texas U.S. Senator Phil Gramm, have attacked these programs as racial quotas. "We're not asking for quotas," counters Gaitan. "We're talking about qualified people. Having police and court officers who are sensitive to issues of ethnic and racial bias that are manifest in our court system will help to eliminate a lot of the bias." Ultimately, says Figueroa, having more police officers, lawyers, and others who are Hispanic can make a difference. "But I would say it wouldn't make a big difference," he says. "It doesn't change the basic lack of support for our communities. As a community's economic base deteriorates, people scapegoat. Economic issues have to be addressed in a fundamental way if we are to get justice."

> *"Stereotyping and institutional racism make it hard for cops to separate the hard core gang members from other people who hang out in certain areas or dress a certain way."*

Blacks Encounter Constant Discrimination from Police

by Charles Bates

About the author: *Charles Bates is a diversity counselor in St. Paul, Minnesota.*

By most American standards, I am a successful man. I am moderately prosperous, a professional in my field, have good health, and my adult children love me. I have my problems, but who doesn't? There may be one difference between you and me: I am a black male.

Many would say, "So, what's the difference?" Let me answer you with what happened to me on Tuesday, November 23, 1994, my 52nd birthday.

A Criminal Suspect

I had just left a planning meeting with a corporate client, and was on my way to meet my partner at the Merriam Park library in St. Paul. When I entered the library to search for her, a law enforcement officer, who was on the phone, locked my gaze. I looked back at him accepting his study as curiosity. As I searched the stacks for my partner, the officer continued to follow my movements, changing his posture to keep me in view. Not finding her in a cursory search, I crossed the room to look again. The policeman was still watching me intently. Curious, I walked toward him to ask if I might be of help. He placed his hand on his gun and said, "Stop right there. Show me your hands."

Stunned, I complied. He asked why I was looking at him. (I was wondering the same about him.) He demanded my name. I gave it to him. Confused by his threatening tone, I asked why. He said that he was looking for a black man.

I was dressed in a tailored, conservative suit and tie. I had all the appearances of conventional respectability and I thought I should not automatically be considered a criminal. I asked if his tracking me meant that all black men looked alike. With his hand still on his weapon, he answered, "Yes." This was not the answer I expected. A response like that did little to instill a sense of well-being in me as a citizen. With a mixture of confusion and exasperation, I spread my

Reprinted from Charles Bates, "How Many Roads Must a Man Walk Down Before They Call Him a Man?" *Prison Mirror*, January 1, 1995. Reprinted with permission.

arms in despair and announced that I was walking away.

I crossed the foyer, but could not ignore the sadness I experienced in my stomach. So I turned to him, held my hands in plain view, and said, "Sir, I find it upsetting that I am denied the experience of protection from law enforcement. For you to say all blacks look alike and confront me the way you did causes me to feel sad and unsafe."

He put his hand on his gun again, approached me, and announced that he was looking for a 6-foot, 175-pound black man. (I am a 6-foot 2-inch and 220-pound black man.) I replied that I understood the difficulty of his position (I have taught diversity training for Twin Cities law enforcement officers) but that his contention that all black men looked alike caused me to feel unsafe and un-represented by him. He replied, "That's too bad," and left.

Everyday Racism

I found my partner and we prepared to leave. But by this time we had at-tracted an audience in the quiet of the library. The librarian and two patrons wit-nessed the interaction and came over to offer their concern about the officer's behavior. A young white male volunteered that the police were looking for a black man with a goatee. (I wear only a mustache.) He told us he had been in the library preparing an article on racism for his school newspaper. "I've never seen everyday racism be-fore," he said excitedly, "and here it is, right in front of my eyes!"

> *"[The officer's] contention that all black men looked alike caused me to feel unsafe and unrepresented by him."*

While we were all talking, the police officer came back inside. He walked up to our group and demanded to know if the librarian knew me. "Yes," she said, "he's a customer."

"What's his name?" asked the officer.

"I don't know," replied the flustered librarian. "We have so many . . ."

My partner was upset and restated my name. The officer said, "There's a black man out there who wants to kill a cop." He added that I was "eyeballin' him."

I reiterated something to the effect that his continued pursuit of me even though I did not fit the suspect's description left me upset and unsettled. I told him I was a law-abiding citizen who now felt unsafe.

"Have a nice day," he said sarcastically as he turned his back.

My partner later told me that she thought the reverse was true: "There was a cop who wanted to kill a black man."

Unchanging Stereotypes

As I think about what happened, I realize my pain is in the law enforcement officer's inability to see me. He looks, but I am invisible to him. He sees instead a stereotype of his own making. He does not allow me to liberate myself from his damaged, frozen, and negative image. No matter what I do, I remain a perpetual suspect of crime. I fear that underneath the stereotype may be what my partner deduced, the fear I share with almost all black men, his desire to shoot a black man. I fear that beneath that desire may be the "black man" who is his own self. The self that he fears, loathes, and places outside himself onto the embattled group of black men who carry the image and blame for this fear he has of himself. A line from *Blowin' In The Wind* comes to mind, "How many roads must a man walk down before they call him a man?" What do I have to do to be able to relax and enjoy the privilege of unencumbered citizenship? The song's refrain answers me, "The answer my friend is blowin' in the wind."

> *"No matter what I do, I remain a perpetual suspect of crime."*

With his hand still on his weapon, the officer left. I stood there stunned. Those who had joined me, and the on-lookers who had kept their distance, were wide-eyed and disturbed. I drove home carefully, on side streets and well under the speed limit to my home on Summit Avenue. The officer rejoined the search justified that he was doing a good job. The young white male went home to finish writing a story on racism for his school paper.

Racial Discrimination Has Abated

by Dinesh D'Souza

About the author: *Dinesh D'Souza is the John M. Olin Scholar at the American Enterprise Institute and author of* The End of Racism: Principles for a Multiracial Society.

As America becomes an increasingly diverse society, advocates of multiculturalism argue that blacks and nonwhite immigrants are jointly vulnerable to racism and racial discrimination at the hands of whites, especially white males. In the multicultural paradigm, white bigotry is not merely overt but is also expressed through a "melting pot" ideology that promotes white supremacy and compels people of color to assimilate to Western norms that are alien to them. "It's because of Eurocentric control of the public school curriculum," writes African American novelist Ishmael Reed, "that the United States produces generation after generation of white bigots."

Consequently, activist scholars such as Andrew Hacker, Derrick Bell, and Ronald Takaki call for laws and educational policies that would ensure an equal distribution of power and influence to all cultural groups. Takaki calls for "the creation of a new society . . . where there's no center and there's no margin," in which all cultures participate fully and receive equal recognition. As the term suggests, multiculturalism is based on a doctrine of many cultures, which are all presumed to be on the same plane. Its guiding principle is cultural relativism: the doctrine that all cultures are basically equal. Multiculturalists are united in their denial of Western cultural superiority.

Yet the multicultural assumption that African Americans, Mexicans, Cubans, Koreans, and Lebanese—not to mention women, homosexuals, and the handicapped—all experience a shared victimization is unhistorical and simpleminded. Women, for example, were not systematically enslaved in America, and only a few women over the centuries have even vicariously portrayed their plight as one of enforced servitude. Similarly, although immigrant groups (in-

Excerpted from Dinesh D'Souza, "Solving America's Multicultural Dilemma." This article appeared in the January 1996 issue and is reprinted with permission from the *World & I*, a publication of The Washington Times Corporation, ©1996.

cluding white immigrants from southern and eastern Europe) experienced nativism and exclusion, discrimination against them was far less comprehensive than that against blacks. Even today, many Americans may not like Asians, regarding them as clannish, or Hispanics, charging them with laziness, but few people consider these groups inferior. Racism is what it always was: a doctrine of biological superiority and inferiority. To this degree, racism in America remains primarily a black-and-white problem because it is only concerning African Americans that rumors of inferiority persist. . . .

A Historic Junction

Blacks as a group stand at a historic junction. Very few people in the civil rights leadership recognize this: Convinced that racism of a hundred varieties stands between African Americans and success, most of the activists are ready to do battle once again with this seemingly elusive and invincible foe. Yet blacks have seen incredible gains over the past generation and there is now a thriving African American middle class, the first such group in American history. Sadly, the success of the black middle class has partially contributed to the deepening miseries of the inner city: Millions of African Americans have seized their opportunities and moved out, taking with them valuable skills and resources and leaving the ghetto to its worst and most vulnerable elements.

What black activists like Jesse Jackson seem to miss is that the agenda of securing legal rights for blacks has now been accomplished, and there is no point for African Americans to increase the temperature of accusations of racism. Historically, whites have used racism to serve powerful entrenched interests, but what interests does racism serve now? Most whites have no economic stake in the ghetto. They have absolutely nothing to gain from oppressing poor blacks. Indeed, the only concern that whites seem to have about the underclass is its potential for crime and its reliance on the public purse. By contrast, it is the civil rights industry that now has a vested interest in the persistence of the ghetto, because the miseries of poor blacks are the best advertisement for continuing programs of racial preferences and set-asides. Publicly inconsolable about the fact that racism continues, many professional minority activists seem privately terrified that it has abated.

> *"Blacks have seen incredible gains over the past generation and there is now a thriving African American middle class."*

Formerly a beacon of moral argument and social responsibility, the civil rights leadership has lost much of its moral credibility and has a fair representation of charlatans who exploit the sufferings of the underclass to collect research grants, minority scholarships, racial preferences, and other subsidies for themselves. Progressive blacks who wish to keep the spirit of the civil rights movement alive might consider a sit-in at the offices of the NAACP [National Association for the Advancement of Colored People] at which they demand that the organization commit itself to measures to address the plight of the poorest blacks.

Discrimination Has Subsided

The real issue in America today is not whether taxi drivers pass up young black males, or whether shopkeepers follow them around in stores. Racial discrimination does exist and cause harm, but it has vastly abated over the past few decades. Racism is no longer the main reason that African Americans are uncompetitive with other groups in academic achievement or economic performance. Indeed, if racism could somehow be abolished overnight, black failure—especially the failure of the black underclass—would continue to hold back the African American community. And it is the persistence of black failure that gives empirical support to suspicions of intrinsic black inferiority.

The most serious challenge faced by African Americans today is not white racism, contrary to what liberal pundits assert. And it is certainly not genetic deficiency, contrary to the insinuations of *The Bell Curve* by Richard J. Herrnstein and Charles Murray. Rather, the greatest problem for blacks is that they have developed a culture that was adaptive to past circumstances but is in many respects dysfunctional

> *"There is no point for African Americans to increase the temperature of accusations of racism."*

today. Thus, the task ahead is the one that Booker T. Washington outlined almost a century ago: the mission of building the civilizational resources of a people whose culture is frequently unsuited to the requirements of the modern world. Much of the black underclass is so unskilled and unproductive, African American pastor Eugene Rivers writes, that even the old slaveowners would have no use for them.

Sadly, the habits that were needed to resist racist oppression or secure legal rights are not the ones needed to exercise personal freedom or achieve success today. As urged by black reformers, both conservative and liberal, the task ahead is one of rebuilding broken families, developing educational and job skills, fostering black entrepreneurship, and curbing the epidemic of violence in the inner cities. Because the government is not in a good position to improve socialization practices among African Americans, the primary responsibility for cultural restoration undoubtedly lies with the black community itself. "When we finally achieve the right of full participation in American life," Ralph Ellison wrote, "what we make of it will depend upon our sense of cultural values, and our creative use of freedom, not upon our racial identification."

Proposals for Black Self-Improvement

Reformers like Stanley Krouch, Thomas Sowell, and John Sibley Butler have offered specific recommendations for black self-improvement. One proposal is for middle-class African Americans to voluntarily establish Big Brother programs in which they "adopt" poor black children and expose them to more productive habits of behavior. The National Urban League has a pilot program to convince successful blacks who have benefited from affirmative action to invest in the economic revitalization of inner cities. Another proposal is for black groups to conduct summer camps in which students are taught entrepreneurial skills. John Sibley

> *"Racial discrimination does exist and cause harm, but it has vastly abated over the past few decades."*

Butler argues that blacks should emulate Koreans and set up rotating credit associations that establish pools of capital for members to set up new businesses. Reformers such as Eugene Rivers, Charles Ballard, Kimi Gray, Jesse Peterson, Johnny Ray Youngblood, and Reginald Dickson are going beyond advocacy, setting up teen pregnancy programs, family support initiatives, community job training, instruction in language and social demeanor, resident supervision of housing projects, and privately run neighborhood schools.

Even some of the old civil rights veterans are starting to realize that timeworn panaceas won't work. As Harlem's Rev. Calvin Butts puts it, "Our community has now become the dumping ground for every social service in the world. Harlem's salvation is not more AIDS hostels, drug rehab centers, homeless shelters, or low-income housing, but more businesses and middle-class people who buy condos or co-ops."

To Be a Truly Modern People

We can sympathize with the magnitude of the project facing African Americans. To succeed, they must rid themselves of aspects of their past that are, even now, aspects of themselves. The most telling refutation of racism, as Frederick Douglass once said about slavery, "is the presence of an industrious, enterprising, thrifty and intelligent free black population." For many black scholars and activists, such proposals are anathema because they seem to involve ideological sellout to the white man and thus are viewed as not authentically black.

Frantz Fanon, a leading black anti-colonialist writer, did not agree. What is needed after the revolution, Fanon wrote, is "the liberation of the man of color from himself. However painful it may be for me to accept this conclusion, I am obliged to state it: for the black man, there is only one destiny, and it is white." In this Fanon is right: For generations, blacks have attempted to straighten their hair, lighten their skin, and pass for white. But what blacks need to do is to "act white," which is to say, to abandon idiotic back-to-Africa schemes and embrace mainstream cultural norms, so that they can effectively compete with other groups.

There is no self-esteem to be found in Africa or even in dubious ideologies of blackness. "Let the sun be proud of its achievement," Frederick Douglass said.

Instead, African Americans should take genuine pride in their collective moral achievement in this country's history. Blacks as a group have made a vital contribution to the expansion of the franchise of liberty and opportunity in America. Through their struggle over two centuries, blacks have helped to make the principles of the American founding a legal reality not just for themselves but also for other groups. As W.E.B. Du Bois put it, "There are no truer exponents of the pure human spirit of the Declaration of Independence than the American Negroes."

Yet rejection in this country produced what Du Bois termed a "double consciousness," so that blacks experience a kind of schizophrenia between their racial and American identities. Only now, for the first time in history, is it possible for African Americans to transcend this inner polarization and become the first truly modern people, unhyphenated Americans. Black success and social acceptance now are both tied to rebuilding the African American community. If blacks can achieve such a cultural renaissance, they will teach other Americans a valuable lesson in civilizational restoration. Thus they could vindicate both Booker T. Washington's project of cultural empowerment and Du Bois' hope for a unique African American "message" to the world. Even more, it will be blacks themselves who would finally discredit racism, solve the American dilemma, and become the truest and noblest exemplars of Western civilization.

Claims of Lending Discrimination Are Unfounded

by Gene Koprowski

About the author: *Gene Koprowski is a freelance writer who frequently contributes to* Insight *magazine.*

Attorney General Janet Reno, accompanied by her underlings, strides to the podium at the Department of Justice and announces another settlement with a bank for alleged lending discrimination. Reno has reached a number of similar accords with high-profile institutions such as the Chevy Chase Federal Savings Bank in Washington, Shawmut Bank in Boston and the First National Bank of Vicksburg, Miss. "We will tackle lending discrimination wherever it appears," declares Reno. "No loan is exempt; no bank is immune."

[One recent] agreement came in June 1995, when the Justice Department signed a $700,000 settlement with Northern Trust Corp., one of the nation's largest banks, based upon allegations that the Chicago institution discriminated against minority home-loan applicants. The Clinton administration reckons that racial discrimination is rampant in mortgage lending and has stepped up investigations and enhanced regulations.

Is Racism the Real Problem?

But conservatives are questioning whether racism really is the reason that many minorities and low-income individuals have been turned down for loans. Several studies by academics, as well as by the Federal Reserve Bank of Chicago, have detailed how factors other than race are used by bankers when weighing loan applications. And the House Banking and Financial Services Committee, headed by Republican Jim Leach of Iowa, issued a report that said the Justice Department should consult with other federal agencies before bringing civil suits for lending discrimination. . . .

"We're hearing complaints that the Justice Department is overzealous," states Margo Tank, an aide to Leach. "We're planning our oversight agenda. But we think there does need to be some regulatory relief. The Justice Department can't just launch these investigations on its own."

An oft-cited 1992 report by the Federal Reserve Bank of Boston—completed just as Clinton was assembling his administration—influenced the liberal establishment's thinking on race and lending. The study of more than 6 million mortgage applications showed that blacks were rejected for loans 17 percent of the time while whites were turned down 11 percent of the time.

> *"Factors other than race are used by bankers when weighing loan applications."*

The economist responsible for the study, Alicia Munnell, was appointed as an assistant Treasury secretary in the Clinton administration.

Though criticism of the report still resonates, the question remains: If racism is not to blame for blacks getting turned down for mortgages more often than whites, what is? Dinesh D'Souza, author of the controversial book, *The End of Racism,* claims that one reason may be the applicants' net worth.

White households have a median net worth of around $45,000, while black households have a median net worth of $4,200—less than a 10th that of whites, says D'Souza, citing U.S. census data. "Since black incomes have risen dramatically in the last few decades, even blacks and whites who earn roughly the same amount often have vastly different levels of net worth. These gaps in accumulated wealth could influence mortgage-lending decisions."

A study by the Federal Reserve Board, which examined default rates of federally insured housing loans during the late 1980s and early 1990s, sheds further light on the problem. Default rates for blacks averaged around 9 percent—substantially higher than the 4 percent for whites. American Indians defaulted on about 6 percent of their loans, Hispanics a little more than 5 percent. Asians exhibited the lowest default rate, 3.2 percent. "Studies that take credit histories into account fail to demonstrate racism," says Jonathan R. Macey, a professor at Cornell University Law School.

Rational Discrimination

The Federal Reserve Bank of Chicago completed its own study in 1995, examining 1990 data on mortgage lending. According to the study, white applicants often develop an "affinity" with bank loan officers that blacks don't. Banks often ask applicants for further information about themselves, their income or the property they intend to buy. But in many cases, blacks may feel slighted if this information is requested and, as a result, don't provide the extensive documentation required. "It's easier and cheaper for the loan officer to acquire additional information about a white applicant's creditworthiness than a minority applicant's creditworthiness," says Mary Beth Walker, a Georgia State University economist. "These effects are rational responses to costs of information."

D'Souza calls this practice "rational discrimination." Lenders try to lower the information costs of considering the complex circumstances of borderline applicants. Even identically situated individuals could be treated differently for legitimate economic reasons. "Rational discrimination may be difficult to understand in loan practices to racial groups, yet its economic justification is obvious in other areas. Insurance companies have no special dislike for teenage boys, but they charge them higher rates than female and older drivers," notes D'Souza.

Most recently, Harold Black, a professor of finance at the University of Tennessee, found that black-owned banks are more likely to turn down black applicants than their white-owned counterparts. He also found that black-owned banks are less likely to lend in declining neighborhoods, a policy known as redlining.

Advocates for minorities disagree with the above reports. "It is unfair for lenders to take white applicants by the hand and walk them through the loan process while leaving black applicants on their own and then denying their applications," says Assistant Attorney General Deval L. Patrick.

Credit Quotas

But the Cato Institute's Vern McKinley, author of a white paper on the Community Reinvestment Act, or CRA, a statute passed during the Carter administration requiring local banks to give special consideration to loan applications from their communities, says the Clinton administration and its allies want to find racism in lending in order to influence lending decisions. "Banks may one day be forced to make unsound loans to meet credit quotas," states McKinley. "Bankers distribute loan dollars for a living, taking on risks that can get them fired. No similar discipline constrains regulatory agencies."

Political interest groups often employ the CRA to wring concessions from banks. "During the recent high-profile announcements of such commitments from Fleet Financial Group," says McKinley, "activists [such as the Union Neighborhood Assistance Corp.] showed up . . . to praise the commitment. And the group was paid a sum to administer the program, but the exact sum was not disclosed." The settlements also offer televised op-

> *"Studies that take credit histories into account fail to demonstrate racism."*

portunities for politicians such as Reno to ascend the dais and gain publicity.

"Such tactics amount to a tax on lending," claims McKinley. "Even those innocent of discrimination will be willing to pay such a regulatory tax in order to avoid the costs of investigations and adverse publicity." David W. Fox, chief executive officer of Northern Trust, seemed to admit to the practice, noting that his bank may have settled with the Justice Department, but it denied practicing racial prejudice, "which has not been tolerated and never will be tolerated at our banks."

Nevertheless, the strategy seems to work for the Clinton administration—though legislative rebuttals are in the offing. "The administration's radical agenda is succeeding in banking where it has failed so dramatically elsewhere because the administration has persuaded the general public to believe that racism is pervasive among bankers," says Cornell's Macey. "No bank, no matter what it does, is safe from charges of discrimination. And this is true despite the fact that the industry spends over half of its profits to comply with regulations."

> *"No bank, no matter what it does, is safe from charges of discrimination."*

Will Leach and the GOP successfully challenge the conventional wisdom about racism and lending practices? Paul Mondor, director of residential finance and government-agency relations at the Mortgage Bankers Association in Washington, thinks not. Banking regulations and ceaseless investigations are burdensome, he says, "but I don't know if they'll ever repeal all these regulations—even in this environment."

D'Souza offers a broader vision: It is time to foster a separation of race and state. "We need a new vision for a multiracial society," he says. "Racism undoubtedly exists, but it no longer has the power to thwart blacks or any other group in achieving their economic, political or social aspirations."

Claims of Environmental Racism Are Misguided

by Nancie G. Marzulla

About the author: *Nancie G. Marzulla is the president and chief legal counsel of Defenders of Property Rights in Washington, D.C.*

Claims that the poor and minorities are exposed to higher-than-average levels of pollution because they are more likely to live near industrial and waste disposal sites have sparked charges of "environmental racism." These communities allegedly bear the brunt of industrial development while reaping few of its benefits. The Clinton administration has taken this misguided notion and built policy on it, but do not expect this to lead to greater environmental protection.

One of the first studies to allege a correlation among risk, race, and income was the government's own Council of Environmental Quality's 1971 Annual Report to the President. It stated that racial discrimination adversely affected the ability of urban poor to improve the quality of their environment. In 1979, Texas Southern University sociologist Robert Bullard described the futile attempt of a black neighborhood in Houston, Texas, to block the nearby siting of a hazardous waste landfill. He provided evidence that race, not just income status, was a probable factor in this local land-use decision.

"Environmental justice" became a nationally-recognized issue in 1982, when 500 demonstrators protested the siting of a landfill for polychlorinated biphenyls (PCB's) in a black, low-income neighborhood in Warren County, North Carolina. In 1987, the United Church of Christ Commission for Racial Justice released a study which looked at all Environmental Protection Agency regions in the country and concluded that race, not income status, was the factor most strongly correlated to residence near a hazardous waste site. In addition, two major conferences on environmental justice were held in the early 1990s.

In response to these charges, the Office of Environmental Equity was officially established in late 1992, with a specific directive to deal with environ-

Reprinted, by permission of the author, from Nancie G. Marzulla, "Pollution Is an Equal Opportunity Offender," *Ecoworld.com*, issue #3, Summer 1995, at www.ecoworld.com/aaracism.html.

mental impacts affecting minority and low-income communities. In Congress, nine environmental justice bills were introduced in the 103rd Congress. Twenty bills were also introduced in fourteen states during the 1993–94 legislative sessions, with bills signed into law in Arkansas, Florida, Louisiana, Michigan, Tennessee, Virginia, and Washington.

A Problem Rooted in Economics

Linking environmental and racial problems, however, turns the concept of environmental protection on its head. A recent study of the St. Louis (Missouri) area over the past twenty years conducted by Washington University researchers Thomas Lambert and Christopher Boerner found that the location of low-cost housing, as opposed to outright racial discrimination, was the root cause of claims of environmental racism. They note that "[r]acism may have been a factor in the subsequent migration of these residents to communities hosting polluting facilities," but judge the problem to be rooted in economics rather than racial prejudice. To resolve the problem, they suggest that the community and local industries pay reparations to residents and provide more community amenities like parks and playgrounds.

The Clinton administration, on the other hand, chooses to view the problem as a one-dimensional racial issue. As it has acted on previous issues relating to race, it has embarked on an extensive program aimed at achieving only a statistical balance. Executive Order 12898, issued in February of 1994, mandates that all federal agencies "make environmental justice a part of all they do." Agencies were required to have environmental justice strategies in place within a year to "collect, maintain, and analyze information that assesses and compares environmental and human health risks borne by populations identified by race, national origin, or income." Each agency was additionally ordered to determine whether its programs have a "disproportionately high and adverse human health or environmental effects on minority pop-

> *"Environmental harm is color-blind, and pays no heed to financial status."*

ulations and low-income populations." As a result, the Environmental Protection Agency now boasts an Office on Environmental Justice, complete with a 24-hour hotline to record any cases of environmental racism.

A Misguided Premise

But neither of these proposals will lead to the environmental goals they seek. The whole premise that environmental hazards are purposely located in minority and low-income communities, through either economics or racism, is misguided at its core. And reliance on bean-counting measures—which create a quick-fix in areas like employment practices and voting-rights—will not be effective in promoting environmental protection. Environmental harm is color-blind, and pays no heed to financial status. Proposed actions to provide only this statistical balance instead of the strong, informed decisionmaking on health and safety issues that is needed just will not cut it.

"Environmental racism" can be more properly understood as a multidimensional problem commanding the understanding of a variety of environmental, social, and economic factors. The one unifying concern, however, is the health and safety of the residents of affected communities. For example, problems with pollution affect groups as diverse as Hispanic farm workers handling pesticides, Asian immigrants working with toxic chemicals in Silicon Valley, Native Americans living near nuclear waste facilities, or urban Blacks who assert that their neighborhoods serve as dumps for polluting industries. No one plan can handle the needs of all of these people and still be effective.

Due to the local community nature of these issues, broad federal solutions are clearly inappropriate. Fundamentally, the decision of where best to place industrial projects should be left with the industry, and should not be turned into a federal racial or social policy issue. Private industry has itself recognized the need to address these issues recognizing that, if ignored, they can lead to increased inspections, restrictive operating conditions, and increased community pressure. The Chemical Manufacturers Association, for example, has developed specific proposals to address "environmental justice" concerns, and now advocates a program called "Responsible Care." They and other businesses believe that open dialogue between a community and the industries located there can better respond to concerns of safety, health, and the environment than can the federal government.

> *"Toxins do not discriminate, and combating their spread cannot be equated with a racial issue."*

Race Is Not the Issue

Combining "racism" and "pollution" creates a political hand grenade. Attempting to address environmental risks on racial versus environmental grounds misses the point entirely. Toxins do not discriminate, and combating their spread cannot be equated with a racial issue. Threats to public health must be resolved by any means necessary. Policies that are driven solely by statistics are doomed to failure because they will not address the underlying concerns over health and safety.

Whenever the threat of pollution affecting public health is found, we should address that problem head on. If there is a threat to human health or safety, neither the income nor the race of the neighborhood should matter. It should never be acceptable to suggest that environmental hazards or toxic risks be addressed on the basis of someone's race.

Hispanics Have Become Successful

by Linda Chavez

About the author: *Linda Chavez is president of the Center for Equal Opportunity in Washington, D.C., and author of* Out of the Barrio: Toward a New Politics of Hispanic Assimilation.

The more than 21 million Hispanics now living in the United States are fast becoming the nation's largest minority group. Some demographers can already see the day when one of three Americans will be of Hispanic descent. Will this mean a divided nation with millions of unassimilated, Spanish-speaking, poor, uneducated Hispanics living in the barrios? Well, here is one reply: "Each decade offered us hope, but our hopes evaporated into smoke. We became the poorest of the poor, the most segregated minority in schools, the lowest paid group in America and the least educated minority in this nation."

This pessimistic view of Hispanics' progress—offered in 1990 by the president of the National Council of La Raza, one of the country's leading Hispanic civil rights groups—is the prevalent one among Hispanic leaders and is shared by many outside the Hispanic community as well. Hispanics are widely perceived as the dregs of society with little hope of participating in the American Dream.

The trouble with this perception is that it is wrong. The success of Hispanics in the United States has been tremendous. They represent an emerging middle class that is a valuable addition to our culture and our economy. However, their story has been effectively suppressed by Hispanic advocates whose only apparent interest is in spreading the notion that Latinos cannot make it in this society. This has been an easy task since the Hispanic poor, who, although they only constitute about one-fourth of the Hispanic population, are visible to all. These are the Hispanics most likely to be studied, analyzed, and reported on, and certainly they are the ones most likely to be read about. A recent computer search of stories about Hispanics in major newspapers and magazines over a twelve-month period turned up more than 1,800 stories in which the words *Hispanic* or

Reprinted from Linda Chavez, "Hispanics and the American Dream," *Imprimis*, November 1996, by permission.

Latino occurred in close connection with the word *poverty*. In most people's minds, the expression "poor Hispanic" is almost redundant.

Hispanic Progress

Most Hispanics, rather than being poor, lead solidly lower middle- or middle-class lives, but finding evidence to support this thesis is sometimes difficult. Of course, Hispanic groups vary one from another, as do individuals within any group. Most analysts acknowledge, for example, that Cubans are highly successful. Within one generation, they have virtually closed the earnings and education gap with other Americans. Although some analysts claim their success is due exclusively to their higher socioeconomic status when they arrived, many Cuban refugees—especially those who came after the first wave in the 1960s—were in fact skilled or semi-skilled workers with relatively little education. Their accomplishments in the United States mainly are attributable to diligence and hard work.

Cubans have tended to establish enclave economies, in the traditional immigrant mode. Opening restaurants, stores, and other émigré-oriented services. Some Cubans have even formed banks, specializing in international transactions attuned to Latin American as well as local customers, and others have made major investments in real estate development in south Florida. These ventures have provided not only big profits for a few Cubans but jobs for many more. By 1980, there were 18,000 Cuban-owned businesses in Miami, and about 70 percent of all Cubans there owned their own homes.

But Cubans are, as a rule, dismissed as the exception among Hispanics. What about other Hispanic groups? Why has there been no "progress" among them? The largest and most important group is the Mexican American population. Its leaders have driven much of the policy agenda affecting all Hispanics, but the importance of Mexican Americans also stems from the fact that they have had a longer history in the United States than any other Hispanic group. If Mexican Americans whose families have lived in the United States for generations are not yet making it in this society, they may have a legitimate claim to consider themselves a more or less permanently disadvantaged group.

That is precisely what Mexican American leaders suggest is happen-

> *"The success of Hispanics in the United States has been tremendous."*

ing. Their "proof" is that statistical measures of Mexican American achievement in education, earnings, poverty rates, and other social and economic indicators have remained largely unchanged for decades. If Mexican Americans had made progress, it would show up in these areas, so the argument goes. Since it doesn't, progress must be stalled. In the post–civil rights era, it is also assumed that the failure of a minority to close the social and economic gap with whites is the result of persistent discrimination. Progress is perceived not in absolute but in relative terms. The poor may become less poor over time, but so long as those on the upper rungs of the economic ladder are climbing even faster, the poor are believed to have suffered some harm, even if they have made absolute gains and their lives are much improved. But in order for Hispanics (or any group on the lower rungs) to close the gap, they would have to progress at an even greater rate than non-Hispanic whites.

A Changing Population

Is this a fair way to judge Hispanics' progress? No. It makes almost no sense to apply this test today (if it ever did) because the Hispanic population itself is changing so rapidly. In 1959, 85 percent of all persons of Mexican origin living in the United States were native-born. Today, only about two-thirds of the people of Mexican origin were born in the United States, and among adults barely one in two was born here. Increasingly, the Hispanic population, including that of Mexican origin, is made up of new immigrants, who, like immigrants of every era, start off at the bottom of the economic ladder. This infusion of new immigrants is bound to distort our image of progress in the Hispanic population if, each time we measure the group, we include people who have just arrived and have yet to make their way in this society.

"Most Hispanics, rather than being poor, lead solidly lower middle- or middle-class lives."

In 1980, there were about 14.6 million Hispanics living in the United States; in 1990, there were nearly 21 million, representing an increase of 44 percent in one decade. At least one-half of this increase was the result of immigration, legal and illegal. Not surprisingly, when these Hispanics—often poorly educated with minimal or no ability to speak English—are added to the pool being measured, the achievement level of the whole group falls. Yet no major Hispanic organization will acknowledge the validity of this reasonable assumption. Instead, Hispanic leaders complain, "Hispanics are the population that has benefited least from the American economy."

In fact, a careful examination of the voluminous data on the Hispanic population gathered by the Census Bureau and other federal agencies shows that, as a group, Hispanics have made significant progress and that most of them have moved into the social and economic mainstream. In most respects, Hispanics—particularly those born here—are very much like other Americans: They work hard, support their own families without outside assistance, have more education and higher earnings than their parents, and own their own homes. In short, they are pursuing the American Dream with increasing success.

The Hispanic Family

No institution is more important to the success of Hispanics (or any group) than the family. Studies published in the early 1990s reported that 73 percent of all Mexican-origin families and 77 percent of all Cuban-origin families consist of married couples. Only 20 percent of the Mexican-origin and 19 percent of the Cuban-origin families are headed by women with no husband present. While out-of-wedlock births to Mexican-origin women are higher than those to white women generally, they fall considerably short of the number of such births to black women, and Hispanic children born out of wedlock are still likely to grow up in families with two parents.

> *"As a group, Hispanics have made significant progress and . . . most of them have moved into the social and economic mainstream."*

The babies of Mexican-origin women, even those who have received little or no prenatal care, are generally quite healthy. There is also a lower infant mortality rate and smaller incidence of low birth weight, a common predictor of health problems, than among blacks and whites. While researchers are not sure what accounts for the apparent health of even poor Mexican babies, one reason may be that their mothers are less likely to drink, smoke, or use drugs, and they place special emphasis on good nutrition while pregnant.

In general, Hispanic families are somewhat more traditional than non-Hispanic families: Men are expected to work to support their families and women to care for children. Hispanic families tend to be child-centered, which increases the importance of women's role as child bearers. Hispanics are also more likely than other Americans to believe that the demands and needs of the family should take precedence over those of the individual. In an earlier age this attitude was common among other ethnic groups—Italians, for example. Today, however, it runs counter to the dominant culture of individualism characteristic of American life and may even impede individual success. This perhaps explains why so many young Hispanics are starting to drop out of school to take jobs, a decision that has some immediate financial benefits for the family but is detrimental to the individual in the long run. Nonetheless, Hispanics' attachment to family is one of their most positive cultural attributes. Family members are expected to help each other in times of financial or other need, which some analysts believe explains why so many Mexican-origin families shun welfare even when their poverty makes them eligible for assistance.

An Increase in Opportunities

For most Hispanics, especially those born in the United States, the last few decades have brought greater economic opportunity and social mobility. They are building solid lower middle- and middle-class lives that include two-parent households, with a male head who works full-time and earns a wage commensurate with his education and training. Their educational level has been steadily rising, their earnings no longer reflect wide disparities with those of non-Hispanics, and their occupational distribution is coming to resemble more closely that of the general population. They are buying homes—42 percent of all Hispanics owned or were purchasing their homes in 1989, including 47 percent of all Mexican Americans—and moving away from inner cities. Even in areas with very high concentrations of Hispanics, like Los Angeles, the sociologist Douglas Massey reports, "segregation [is] low or moderate on all dimensions." And, in what is perhaps the ultimate test of assimilation, about one-third of all U.S.-born Hispanics under the age of thirty-five are marrying non-Hispanics.

In light of these facts, the policy prescriptions offered by many Hispanic advocacy organizations and by most politicians seem oddly out of sync. They rely too much on government programs of doubtful efficacy like affirmative action, welfare, and bilingual public education. And they perpetuate demeaning stereotypes of the very people they claim they are championing. What they should be doing instead is promoting tax reform, deregulation, enterprise zones, English instruction, and private education—all of which will help Hispanics help themselves.

Groups do not all advance at precisely the same rate in this society—sometimes because of discrimination, sometimes because of other factors. As Thomas Sowell and others have pointed out, no multi-ethnic society in the world exhibits utopian equality of income, education, and occupational status for every one of its ethnic groups. What is important is that opportunities be made available to all persons, regardless of race or ethnicity. Ultimately, however, it will be up to individuals to take advantage of those opportunities. Increasing numbers of Hispanics are doing just that. And no government action can replace the motivation and will to succeed that propels genuine individual achievement.

> *"For most Hispanics, . . . the last few decades have brought greater economic opportunity and social mobility."*

Blacks Do Not Encounter Constant Discrimination from Police

by Thomas Sowell

About the author: *Thomas Sowell is a nationally syndicated columnist and a senior fellow at Stanford University's Hoover Institute.*

Everyone seems to have a racial story that fits the spirit of the times. Let me tell you a couple of mine.

One sunny Sunday afternoon many years ago, I was out driving along Ocean Avenue in Santa Monica, enjoying a view of the Pacific. Suddenly a bicycle rider made a left turn in front of me.

I slammed on the brakes but it was too late. His body bounced off the hood of the car, hit the windshield and ricocheted off into the street, where he landed in a heap.

Horrified, I stopped the car and got out to help him. He had only a few minor bruises but I was more shaken up than he was. Soon a police car stopped at the scene and a white policeman got out.

He had only one question for me: "Are those your skid marks on the street?"

"Yes."

He turned immediately to the bicyclist, who was also white, and asked: "What were you doing out there?"

"I have every right to be there," the cyclist replied.

"No, you don't," the cop said and cited the traffic law that covered the situation. He then turned to me and said, in a reassuring tone: "You guys settle this." Then he got back into his patrol car and drove away.

He never asked to see my driver's license nor even checked the license plate on my car.

Now, suppose that the racial situation was the other way around—that the cyclist was black and the driver white. How would this episode play in the media? What would "community leaders" and civil rights activists have said? What if someone had videotaped the accident?

I keep reading stuff by deep thinkers—black and white—who tell me that every encounter between a black male and the cops is sheer hostility or humiliation. But I keep thinking back over the years to my various encounters with the police and cannot come up with examples to match theirs. Has it all been just dumb luck on my part?

Most of my encounters with the police have involved traffic problems ranging from stop signs I hadn't noticed or speed limits I hadn't observed to an accident that wrecked the car and left me astonished that I was still alive and unhurt. All the policemen and highway patrolmen who became involved were white, but none of these episodes turned into racial incidents.

One night, my car was weaving on the highway, often the sign of a drunk driver. When the patrolman pulled me over, I explained that my little daughter had fallen asleep on the seat beside me and was leaning up against me. In wriggling around to try to get comfortable, I caused the car to weave around. He gave me a warning and sent me on my way.

None of this proves that there are no racist cops. There are racist everything, including economists and media people. The point is that there is a market for only one kind of story.

My kind of experience is of no interest to anybody. It won't sell newspapers or get a television audience excited. It will not provide any bond of racial solidarity or any claims against "society."

Discrimination Is Uncommon

A few years ago, a well-known restaurant chain was sued for gross racial discrimination against some black customers. I was surprised because I had eaten in many restaurants in that chain—either by myself, with my wife or with my children—and nothing like that had ever happened.

Other blacks I asked could not recall having any such experiences either. My sister remembered having eaten in that chain years ago and being treated so nicely that she left an extra large tip.

Do I just lead a charmed life or what? One of the blacks I asked about the restaurant chain pointed out that, while he had never had any trouble with them, he had also not gone into any of their restaurants in or near a ghetto.

He suggested that people who have had bad experiences with black customers may turn around and have some bad attitudes toward other black customers thereafter. Maybe.

Sometimes the way you carry yourself has a lot to do with how other people treat you. Over the past 30 years, a more belligerent style has been promoted by minority activists and others who push racial hype. Could this have something to do with the situation?

Perhaps there is some other explanation. Or maybe there is just a market for one kind of story and not for others.

Chapter 2

Are Race Relations Improving?

Chapter Preface

The 1994 book *Living with Racism: The Black Middle-Class Experience,* by Joe R. Feagin and Melvin P. Sikes, includes excerpts from several interviews with African Americans about their day-to-day encounters with whites. One black male interviewee, a college student residing in a predominantly white neighborhood, describes walking home from work as a consistently painful experience: "Every day . . . you're reminded [of] how you're perceived in society. . . . Just the other day, I was walking down the street, and this white female with a child [passed] a young white male about twenty yards ahead. When she saw me, she quickly dragged the child and herself across the busy street. . . . The police constantly make circles around me as I walk home."

Such experiences, assert Feagin and Sikes, are common for black Americans who venture into public domains that are usually frequented by whites. African Americans report that whites often assume—sometimes unconsciously—that blacks are dangerous, unintelligent, subservient, and not worthy of respect. Furthermore, Feagin and Sikes argue, many whites discount blacks' complaints about discrimination, claiming that blacks misperceive harmless incidents as examples of prejudice. Because whites often treat blacks poorly or deny the credibility of blacks' accounts of discriminatory treatment, blacks are frequently placed on the defensive when encountering and discussing racism, Feagin and Sikes contend. They point out, moreover, that having to maintain "such a constant defensive stance" can cause a great degree of "pain and emotional drain." The fact that minorities still encounter such racism on a daily basis has led many to conclude that race relations in America have not significantly improved in the twentieth century.

On the other hand, several commentators argue that race relations have continued to progress, especially during the last half of the twentieth century. Some contend that the impact of the civil rights movement of the 1960s enabled whites to abandon antiblack sentiments. Others, including law professor Randall Kennedy, point out that the emergence of a thriving black middle class attests to the success of several legal reforms supporting equality and racial justice, including the 1954 Supreme Court decision to desegregate public schools and the 1964 Civil Rights Act. Such reforms would not have been possible without the backing of white and minority champions of racial justice, Kennedy maintains. He asserts, moreover, that although racism still exists, "[Americans] should be told that on the basis of our demonstrated ability to reform ourselves . . . we can realistically expect to build on past accomplishments and press further."

The state of race relations in America continues to be a subject of intense debate. The authors of the following chapter offer various opinions on this much-discussed issue.

Anti-Black Prejudice Persists

by Jerelyn Eddings

About the author: *Jerelyn Eddings is a senior writer for* U.S. News & World Report, *a weekly newsmagazine.*

For Roy Johnson, a senior editor at *Money* magazine, the latest indignity came after a recent dinner at a fancy restaurant in the wealthy New York City suburb where he and his family live. First the parking valet handed him the keys to his Jaguar instead of fetching the car. Then an elderly white couple came out and handed him the keys to their automobile, with the instruction: "It's a black Mercedes-Benz." Johnson responded that his own car was a black Jaguar, but the Mercedes-Benz owner didn't seem to understand. "It took him a while to re- alize that I was not a valet," says Johnson. "It didn't matter that I was dressed for dinner and had paid a handsome price for the meal, just as he had. What mattered was that I didn't fit his idea of someone who could be equal to him."

Such incidents, which are depressingly familiar to African-Americans of all ages, incomes and social classes, help explain why black and white attitudes of- ten differ so starkly—not only toward the O.J. Simpson verdict and Nation of Islam leader Louis Farrakhan but also toward each other, toward the country and toward almost all of America's institutions. A 1995 *Washington Post* survey found that 68 percent of blacks believe racism is still a major problem in Amer- ica. Only 38 percent of whites agreed.

"Stealth Racism"

Many Americans find the gulf between blacks and whites perplexing. After all, official racial segregation is a bad memory and 40 years of laws, policies and court decisions have helped African-Americans make significant progress toward equal opportunity. . . .

But a kind of stealth racism persists, unmistakable to every black but largely invisible to many whites who are appalled by a Mark Fuhrman or a cross burn- ing. It is evident in the everyday encounters African-Americans have with racial prejudice and discrimination, like the valet parking incident. Such encounters often strike whites as trivial misunderstandings. But they remind blacks that they are often dismissed as less intelligent, less industrious, less honest and less likely to succeed. Some insults are patently racist; others may be evidence of insensitivity or bad manners rather than racial prejudice. But the accumulation of affronts feeds the simmering anger described in books such as Nathan McCall's bestseller *Makes Me Wanna Holler* or Ellis Cose's chronicle of the injuries suffered by middle-class blacks, *The Rage of a Privileged Class.*

> *"A kind of stealth racism persists, unmistakable to every black but largely invisible to many whites."*

"What is amazing to me is the number of whites who express surprise that any of this happens," observes Mary Frances Berry, chairperson of the U.S. Commission on Civil Rights, who says she has been kept under surveillance at shopping malls and recently was forced to wait for a table at a restaurant until a group of whites who arrived after she did was seated. "We are not the melting pot we pretend to be."

"There are isolated cases of racism daily for African-Americans. I am not surprised at anything I see or hear," says Myrlie Evers-Williams, chair of the NAACP [National Association for the Advancement of Colored People], who says a white man accidentally bumped into her in a hotel lobby on the day of the Simpson verdict and called her a "black bitch" before stomping off. "This country is saturated with examples of racism—blatant and subtle, and that is nothing new to African-Americans and it is nothing new to me."

Examples of Racism

A few stealth racism staples:

• *Taxis that never stop.* Andrew Barrett, a commissioner of the Federal Communications Commission, says that on days when he's not wearing a suit and tie but needs to catch a cab home he calls the taxi company and identifies himself to the dispatcher as a black man not wearing a suit. "If I stay for dinner late, I walk to a hotel and ask the doorman to get a cab," he says. "Quite often a driver will jump out of line to avoid taking me."

U.S. News & World Report photographer Brian Palmer phoned for a taxi to pick him up at the White House at 2 a.m. after an out-of-town trip with the president. "I called the taxi service from the Secret Service kiosk. They assured me one was coming. I stood out on the street and attempted to hail empty taxis right in front of the White House. Nothing. Over 20 cabs zipped by me," including one from the service Palmer called. Finally Palmer called back to tell the dispatcher the fare is the black man with camera equipment and press credentials around his neck. The next cab stopped.

• *Suspicious shoppers.* Thomas McCrary Jr. and a friend went bargain shopping for a new computer at a strip mall in a predominantly white suburb of Chicago. After comparing prices at different stores, they got the best buys and loaded the equipment into their car, only to be blocked by two police squad cars. The officers checked their licenses, asked about their credit cards and questioned why the two had gone to so many stores. The process took 20 minutes and left McCrary wondering, "When did it become against the law to go shopping?"

Victoria Roberts, a black lawyer from Detroit, tells a similar story about her 16-year-old daughter. A few years ago, Rachel Gehrls and four white and six black girlfriends had a slumber party at a hotel in suburban Detroit. The next morning she and three of the black girls went to the hotel gift shop for candy, but the white owner refused to serve them, complaining that there were too many people in the store and demanding that they leave. Rachel persuaded her four white girlfriends to visit the shop. The owner sold them candy with no problem.

• *Shopping slights.* Bebe Moore Campbell, author of *Brothers and Sisters*, a novel that examines racial tensions among a group of co-workers and friends, says she believes whites are in denial about prejudice in America and instances of subtle racism. "I often run into the 'What are you doing in Saks?' attitude from white salespeople, who watch me as I go around the store," she says. "At a jewelry store, they approach me early on and say, 'Well now, that costs $2,500,' as if it's just assumed that I can't afford to pay for nice things."

Campbell also describes going to a white dentist who refused to let her insurance company pay the bill, demanded payment up front and treated her rudely. "I know these things happen to white people, too, but I doubt with the same frequency or degree of disrespect," she says. "These things begin to have a cumulative effect, until you find yourself angry and perplexed."

• *Fear of black men.* Robert Mackey, a 31-year-old accountant, got into an elevator in an Atlanta office building in August 1995 with two other black men, all on their way to work. In the instant before the door closed, a white office worker on the elevator jumped out, leaving the black men stunned. "We were three well-dressed, well-groomed men going to work, and it is outrageous that this woman would act as if she was unsafe in the presence of three black men going to work," says Mackey. "I'm 5 foot 10 and 240 pounds, and I try to see myself as others see me, but I don't think a white man the same size would have been perceived as threatening."

> *"There are isolated cases of racism daily for African-Americans."*

• *Unequal service.* Margaret Bush-Ware, a professional fund-raiser who recently moved to Washington, D.C., from Los Angeles, was on standby for a TWA flight from St. Louis to Los Angeles. She was next in line but watched helplessly as the airline agents put white passengers on ahead of her and four other black standbys. She missed two flights. "It was only when I finally found a black ticket agent and told her what happened that I got a flight," she says. "But I had been there all day."

• *The unwelcome mat.* Robert Lawrence, 73, is a retired deputy superintendent of education in California and one of the original Tuskegee Airmen, the
first black Army Air Corps pilots. He and his wife, Ernestine, went shopping
for a new home in an upscale subdivision of Santa Fe, N.M., but he says the
agent made it clear they were not welcome. "On more than one occasion during
the visit, we were made to feel, 'Why are you looking here?'" Lawrence says.
"I had the gut feeling they didn't want me there even if I could afford it."

• *No respect.* Carolyn Harraway, a third-year resident at the Medical College
of Virginia, is offended every time she goes to her bank. "They refer to me as
'Carolyn' but they always call white women by their last name," she says. "I'm
young, but I'm still very offended, especially because I've watched very carefully and they always call white women Mrs. or Miss or even Ms. . . . Sometimes I think it's just part of that Southern girl thing where whites think they
can call African-Americans anything."

• *Surprised by success.* Harriet Richardson Michel, who with her husband owns
parking garages and medallion taxicabs in New York, was on vacation in Costa
Rica when she was approached at poolside by a white woman from Idaho. "Oh,
you speak such good English," the woman said. When Michel said she was an
American, the response was amaze-
ment. "I'm just amazed that you could
afford the same vacation as I can," the
woman said. "Maybe being from
Idaho she was less sophisticated, I
don't know," says Michel. "But I
think there are a lot of whites that are
amazed that any of us can afford the

> *"Bebe Moore Campbell . . .
> says she believes whites are in
> denial about prejudice in
> America and instances
> of subtle racism."*

same cars and addresses if we're not entertainers. Some may have no conscious
notion of it, but some others must know how many indignities they visit upon
black people every day because of their attitudes and actions."

"With the aftermath of the Simpson case we have clear documentation that
we are a divided society," says Evers-Williams, whose husband, civil rights
worker Medgar Evers, was murdered in Mississippi three decades ago. "Those
who thought we were doing extremely well . . . are wrong." Indeed, the banality
of prejudice in America today suggests that the battle for equal rights—and for
better communication between whites and blacks—is far from over.

Black-Jewish Unity Is a Myth

by Edward S. Shapiro

About the author: *Edward S. Shapiro is professor of history at Seton Hall University in South Orange, New Jersey, and the author of* A Time for Healing: American Jewry After World War II.

In her 1991 autobiography, *Deborah, Golda, and Me,* Letty Cottin Pogrebin argued that black-Jewish relationships rested on a common history of oppression. "Both blacks and Jews have known Egypt," she wrote. "Jews have known it as certain death (the killing of the firstborn, then the ovens and gas chambers). Blacks have known it as death and terror by bondage." Paul Berman agreed. "It was the past that made the blacks and the Jews almost the same," he wrote in the February 28, 1994 issue of the *New Yorker,* "and the past has the singular inconvenience of never going away." Jewish attitudes toward blacks have developed within the context of this faith in a common history and destiny. Of the many pieties of American Jewry, few have been accepted so readily and widely at face value or have been so influential as the easy assumption that blacks and Jews share vital interests arising out of what the rabbi-historian Arthur Hertzberg termed the "comradeship of excluded peoples."

The dismay of American Jews regarding the current status of black-Jewish relations arises from the presumption that blacks and Jews should stand side by side through thick and thin. "The truth is that Jews do feel different vis-à-vis the black community," Abraham Foxman, national director of the Anti-Defamation League of B'nai Brith, recently stated. "There is a history, there is a kinship, and it goes beyond the rhetoric. Look, there's never going to be a crisis in Irish-black relations or Italian-black relations, because they have no relations. But we do."

Jews have supposed that they, more than any other group, could and did empathize with the plight of blacks, and that blacks recognized this. Jewish newspapers early in the twentieth century compared the black movement out of the

Excerpted from Edward S. Shapiro, "Blacks and Jews Entangled," *First Things*, August/September 1994. Reprinted by permission of the author and *First Things*.

South to the exodus from Egypt, noted that both blacks and Jews lived in ghettos, and described anti-black riots in the South as pogroms. Even European Jews voiced compassion for the American black. *Uncle Tom's Cabin* was translated into both Yiddish and Hebrew. In his 1902 book *Old New Land,* Theodore Herzl wrote:

> There is still one other question arising out of the disaster of the nations which remains unsolved to this day, and whose profound tragedy only a Jew can comprehend. This is the African question. . . . I am not ashamed to say, though I may expose myself to ridicule in saying so, that once I have witnessed the redemption of the Jews, my people, I wish also to assist in the redemption of the Africans.

Assuming Black-Jewish Unity

Among Jewish leaders, if not the Jewish man-in-the-street, it became an article of faith that the fates of blacks and Jews were intertwined. Jews were propelled into the civil rights movement by the belief that Jews and blacks shared the same agenda. Joel and Arthur Spingarn helped found the National Association for the Advancement of Colored People, Jack Greenberg succeeded Thurgood Marshall as head of the NAACP [National Association for the Advancement of Colored People] Legal Defense Fund, and Jewish organizations such as the American Jewish Committee, the American Jewish Congress, and the ADL [Anti-Defamation League] were in the forefront in the campaign against racial prejudice. The financial contributions of Jews were crucial in the work of the NAACP, the Urban League, the Congress of Racial Equality, the Student Non-Violent Coordinating Committee, and other civil rights organizations. More than half of the whites who went to Mississippi in 1964 to challenge Jim Crow were Jews, and about half of the civil rights attorneys in the South during the 1960s were Jews. No white ethnic group voted more readily for blacks than Jews. This was true in Philadelphia and Los Angeles, in Chicago and New York. Tom Bradley, Harold Washington, and David Dinkins would not have been elected the mayors of Los Angeles, Chicago, and New York City had Jews voted the same as Italians, Poles, and the Irish. . . .

Jewish spokesmen emphasized that this affinity of Jews toward blacks stemmed not only from idealism but also from self-interest. Jews would benefit the more America moved toward a society of merit in which religious, ethnic, and racial barriers were unimportant. One year before the

> *"[Jewish] dismay . . . arises from the presumption that blacks and Jews should stand side by side through thick and thin."*

Supreme Court outlawed school segregation in the 1954 *Brown v. Board of Education* decision, the Jewish Community Relations Advisory Council declared, "In a still imperfect society, Jews, together with many other groups, suffer from inequalities of opportunity and other forms of discrimination." Jewish leaders stressed the similarities rather than the differences between the Jewish and black experience in America. Both groups, they asserted, were powerless and victims of persecution. Both included in their ranks martyrs to American intolerance, Leo Frank in the case of Jews and Emmett Till in the case of blacks. The murder of James Chaney, Andrew Goodman, and Michael Schwerner in Mississippi in 1964 strengthened the presumption that the fates of blacks and Jews were intertwined. . . .

Encouraging Anti-Semitism

It is precisely because Jews have presumed that blacks and Jews have common interests that they are so disappointed by the reluctance of Jesse Jackson and other black leaders to strongly condemn the anti-Semitic rantings of Louis Farrakhan and his ilk. This disappointment stems not only from the belief that blacks have not shown the proper gratitude for all that Jews have done for them. More important is the fact that black anti-Semitism throws doubt on an important element of the identity of American Jewish liberals and radicals—the presumption that blacks and Jews comprise a community of the oppressed and that Jews are never acting more true to their religious and ethnic heritage than when they are working side by side with blacks to create a society free of racial and religious prejudice. If anything, this belief of Jews in their special relationship with blacks encourages anti-Semitism.

> *"If anything, this belief of Jews in their special relationship with blacks encourages anti-Semitism."*

As Arch Puddington argued in the April 1994 *Commentary,* anti-Semites such as Farrakhan are encouraged in their anti-Semitism "in the knowledge that Jews, unlike other whites, will react not simply with anger, but with wounded innocence and appeals for 'dialogue' and 'healing.' Abandoning the fiction of the special relationship might thus have the paradoxical effect of contributing to a reduction of racial tensions.". . .

Jews have continued to call for the maintenance of the black-Jewish alliance despite the socioeconomic differences between the two groups. Leonard Fein, the founder of *Moment* magazine, has been among the most eloquent spokesmen for this position. In his 1988 book *Where Are We? The Inner Life of America's Jews,* Fein admitted that American Jews were no longer among the oppressed. Nevertheless, Jews should continue to identify with blacks because of "our continuing need to see ourselves among the miserable—or, at least, the still-threatened." The involvement of Jews in the civil rights movement, Fein concluded, "has helped preserve our sense of ourselves as still, and in spite of all the successes we've known, among the oppressed, hence also among the decent, the just, the virtuous." Those familiar with the history of anti-Semitism in Europe, the Middle East, and even the United States would hesitate before conflating, as does Fein, being oppressed with being decent, just, and virtuous.

Even a cursory examination of the history of black-Jewish relations in the United States reveals that they were never as warm as Pogrebin and Fein would have us believe, nor are they today as frigid as alarmists claim. If support for blacks is an ineluctable result of Jewish values, then one would expect that the most Jewish of American Jews—the Orthodox of Brooklyn— would be the most sympathetic toward blacks. The exact opposite,

> *"No matter how much Jews did for blacks, in black eyes Jews were whites with all the privileges accruing to those with white skins."*

however, is true. Secure in their Jewish identity, they do not require close relations with blacks to define their Jewish identity. Their Jewishness rests on more substantial grounds. . . .

The Myth of Black-Jewish Identity

The myth of black-Jewish identity also mistook the nature of black-Jewish relations and the attitude of blacks toward Jews. It is true that in a variety of ways blacks ever since the time of slavery have modeled their lives on the Jewish experience. As indicated by black spirituals such as "Go Down, Moses," blacks drew parallels between their own situation in the South and that of the Jews in Egypt. Just as Jews escaped from slavery and, in the process, inflicted punishment on their taskmasters, so blacks anticipated flight from slavery and the chastisement of the South. The popularity of "Zion" in the names of black churches shows the extent to which the experience of the exodus resonated among blacks. Black nationalists used the Zionist movement as a model for their own back-to-Africa movement. Finally, blacks used the example of the upward social and economic mobility and bourgeois values of Jews as a model for their own people. For groups such as the Black Jews of Harlem this admiration for Jews led to syncretic religious cults containing Jewish elements.

Despite, however, what affinity they might have felt to Jews, blacks believed that there was still a vast racial gulf separating the two groups. No matter how much Jews did for blacks, in black eyes Jews were whites with all the privileges accruing to those with white skins. For blacks, the great fault line in America was not between the oppressors and the oppressed, including Jews, but between those with white skins and those with black skins. The rapid decline of American anti-Semitism after 1945 combined with the nation's continuing pervasive racism was proof to blacks, if they needed any such proof, that the condition of American Jews bore little resemblance to that of blacks.

Even during the first two decades after World War II—the supposed "golden age" of black-Jewish relations—James Baldwin, Kenneth Clark, and other blacks warned liberal Jews that their image of a close black-Jewish affinity was a fiction of their imagination, and that candor and realism were now required.

69

As Baldwin noted in a famous statement, "Georgia has the Negro and Harlem has the Jew." Whenever the black had to pay rent to a Jewish apartment house owner, or shopped at a Jewish-owned store, or was taught by a Jewish school teacher, or was supervised by a Jewish social worker, or was paid by a Jewish employer, the fact of black subservience to Jews was driven home. The title of one of Baldwin's essays was revealing: "Blacks are Anti-Semitic because They're Anti-white."

The constant advice to blacks to look to the Jewish experience as a model exacerbated the problem. That advice assumed that if Jews could make it in American society then presumably so could blacks; but this assumption ignored the crucial fact that Jews were white. Furthermore, the fact of Jewish social and economic advance was painful to blacks in the face of their own less rapid progress. It was as if Jewish success was a constant insult, drawing continual attention to their own inadequacies and failures. One could hardly think of a more effective way to increase anti-Semitism among blacks than to encourage blacks to emulate Jews and to harp continually on the disparity between black and Jewish economic and social development. If Jews and blacks were really oppressed brothers, how could one account for the disparity in their social and economic conditions?

> *"If Jews and blacks were really oppressed brothers, how could one account for the disparity in their social and economic conditions?"*

One can only imagine the impact on blacks of Eric Hoffer's comparison of blacks and Jews. The example of Jews, Hoffer wrote,

> shows what persistent striving and a passion for education can do . . . even in the teeth of discrimination. This is a fact which the Negro vehemently rejects. It sticks in his gullet. . . . The Jew impairs the authenticity of the Negro's grievances and alibis. He threatens the Negro's most precious possession: the freedom to fail.

From this perspective, the success of the Jew was a continual contradiction of the cult of victimization fostered by black spokesmen. . . .

Black Anti-Semitism

For decades sensitive observers warned Jews that black-Jewish relations were not what they presumed. In 1964, Rabbi Richard C. Hertz discussed the "Rising Tide of Negro-Jewish Tensions" in the black magazine *Ebony,* and two years later the sociologist Dennis Wrong prophesied that "Negro anti-Semitism is not a passing phenomenon." This prediction seemingly has come to pass. Polls have revealed that 63 percent of New York City's blacks believe Jews to have too much influence in the city and that blacks are twice as likely to hold anti-Semitic views as other Americans. Gary E. Rubin of the American Jewish Committee has raised serious doubts about the methodology of these polls, and he insists that they overestimate the extent of overall American anti-Semitism. Still, there seems little question that anti-Semitism is more widespread among blacks than whites. American blacks are the only major American ethnic group that has leaders who are clearly anti-Semitic.

"On every possible social and economic index—and for whatever reasons—blacks have lagged far behind Jews."

Black anti-Semitism seems to have repealed the traditional sociological laws of anti-Semitism. Whereas for whites anti-Semitism is more prevalent among those older, less affluent, less educated, and more religious, among blacks the exact opposite is true. Within the black community there is a positive correlation between youth, schooling, income, and lack of religiosity on the one hand and anti-Semitism on the other. Yet are these results so surprising? Is it really so strange that upwardly mobile blacks would see Jews as part of an undifferentiated mass of whites bent on limiting their advancement? Is it so odd that blacks, after contrasting their economic and social status with that of Jews (or Asians), would hold ambivalent, frustrated, and resentful attitudes toward them? Nevertheless, Jews continue to assume that black anti-Semitism is irrational and transitory. Since blacks and Jews have supposedly been close in times past, black anti-Semitism appears incongruous. Hence Gary Marx's 1967 book, *Protest and Prejudice,* which discounted the presence of black anti-Semitism.

Some Jews on the left would prefer to explain away black anti-Semitism because its existence casts doubt on the myth of black-Jewish comradeship. Thus one participant in a roundtable on "Beyond Crown Heights," published in the January-February 1993 issue of *Tikkun,* asserted, "It's no surprise that we might expect a problem with anti-Semitism after twelve years of Reagan and Bush in which social inequalities have grown." Jews were forced to resort to such bizarre arguments because they consistently misunderstood the history of black-Jewish relations and the relative status of the two communities. Hillel Levine and Lawrence Harmon's *The Death of an American Jewish Community: A Tragedy of Good Intentions* (1992) exemplifies another attempt to hold on to the black-Jewish alliance. This study of the transformation of the Jewish neighborhood of Roxbury-Dorchester-Mattapan in Boston into a black slum blamed the hostility of blacks and Jews on unscrupulous bankers, realtors, and politicians, who presumably were only too happy to pit the two groups against each other.

Disparities Between Jews and Blacks

The problems between Jews and blacks, however, go much deeper. American Jews, whatever their problems with prejudice, never experienced anything remotely resembling the enslavement, discrimination, and racism encountered by blacks, while blacks, whatever their gains in status, never experienced the economic and social prosperity of Jews. Blacks and Jews derived different lessons from American history. "The Jewish travail occurred across the sea and America rescued him from the house of bondage," Baldwin wrote in 1967. "But America *is* the house of bondage for the Negro, and no country can rescue him." Their own experience convinced Jews that America was an open society in which education and merit would eventually win out. Hence their firm opposition to affirmative action. History, however, suggested to blacks that American society was irredeemably stacked against them and that something more than the merit principle was necessary if the legacy of three and a half centuries of racism was to be overcome.

On every possible social and economic index—and for whatever reasons—blacks have lagged far behind Jews. Jews, who comprise less than 3 percent of the American population, made up over 25 percent of the names on a 1994 *Forbes* magazine list of the four hundred richest Americans. By contrast, there was only one black on the list, the entertainer Bill Cosby, even though 12 percent of Americans are black. Blacks are still waiting for one of their number to be selected to head an elite American university, while Jews have already served as presidents of Princeton, Dartmouth, Columbia, Harvard, Yale, the University of Chicago, and the University of Pennsylvania. Blacks have also lagged behind Jews in national politics. . . . Jews are overrepresented in the Senate by a factor of four and in the House by a factor of three. Although blacks comprise roughly 10 percent of the House of Representatives, there is only one black Senator—Carol Mosely Braun of Illinois.

While Jews constitute an economic and social elite group within contemporary America, a significant minority of blacks comprise what sociologists call the "underclass." The disparities between Jews and blacks regarding crime, family breakdown, drug addiction, alcoholism, and educational achievements are well known. There is nothing in the American Jewish experience similar to what exists today in the inner city and what the sociologist Oscar Lewis called "the culture of poverty." Jewish criminality, such as that found on the Lower East Side of New York and in Brownsville, Brooklyn back in the 1920s and 1930s, was largely a one-generation phenomenon, as was the Jewish working class. Jewish membership in the American labor union movement is concentrated in the white collar unions of teachers, government employees, and social workers. While the major problem facing America's Jews today is maintaining Jewish identity in the midst of affluence, acculturation, and declining anti-Semitism, the major problems facing most blacks are the more immediate ones of economic survival, family breakdown, and continuing racial prejudice. If the comradeship of Jews and blacks as victims was not a mirage in times past, it certainly is one today.

> *"If the comradeship of Jews and blacks as victims was not a mirage in times past, it certainly is one today."*

Chapter 2

The Need for Honesty

Black-Jewish relations can never be on a sound footing as long as Jewish leaders remain wedded to romantic notions regarding the links between the two groups. The fact is that on a whole host of issues the interests of Jews and blacks diverge, and there is nothing unusual or surprising about this. It is demeaning to both blacks and Jews to argue that each must reflexively support the other's agenda in order to avoid antagonisms. As Michael Meyers, a black leader in New York City, recently asserted, Jews should face "the tough realities":

> It's true that Jews and Blacks have been allies, but we've also been rivals. To many Jews racial quotas are anathema, for many nonwhites affirmative action must be distinguished from exclusionary quotas. We have rivalry about housing. . . . We have disagreements about how and where there are double standards in the criminal justice system.

Meyers could also have added that Jews and blacks have disagreed as well over Jesse Jackson, Israel, and multiculturalism.

Two centuries ago George Washington in his Farewell Address laid down the standards by which the United States should conduct itself with other nations. Here he warned American citizens not to take sides in European conflicts engendered by the French Revolution.

> In the execution of such a plan nothing is more essential than that permanent, inveterate antipathies against particular nations and passionate attachments for others should be excluded, and that in place of them just and amicable feelings toward all should be cultivated. The nation which indulges toward another an habitual hatred or an habitual fondness is in some degree a slave. It is a slave to its animosity or to its affection, either of which is sufficient to lead it astray from its duty and its interest. . . . Sympathy for the favorite nation, facilitating the illusion of an imaginary common interest in cases where no real common interest exists, . . . gives to ambitious, corrupted, or deluded citizens (who devote themselves to the favorite nation) facility to betray or sacrifice the interests of their own country without odium, sometimes even with popularity. . . . I hold the maxim no less applicable to public than to private affairs that honesty is always the best policy.

Washington's advice—above all that honesty is the best policy—is equally applicable to relations between blacks and Jews.

73

The Burning of Black Churches Reveals Enduring Racism

by Ron Nixon

About the author: *Ron Nixon is a general assignment reporter for the political journal* Southern Exposure.

The 1994 World Trade Center bombing, the bombings at the federal building in Oklahoma City in 1995 and Atlanta's Centennial Park during the 1996 Olympics, as well as the 1996 crash of TWA Flight 800, focused public fear on the vulnerability of the US to terrorist attacks. These tragedies sparked intensive investigations and provoked often strident calls for countermeasures. Although some of the assaults were attributed to foreign fanatics, others brought home the reality that America is capable of producing its own violent extremists.

For many, particularly media pundits, these attacks signal the end of American insouciance: Terrorism has finally penetrated US borders. Yet strangely absent in the public discourse on the perceived upsurge in domestic terrorism is a long pattern of attacks against abortion providers and the recent targeting of a central organization, especially in the South, for much of black culture, political organizing, and life—the church. According to the Atlanta watchdog group, the Center for Democratic Renewal (CDR), more than 80 black churches have been burned or desecrated since 1990. From January 1995 through July 1996, at least 42 have been set on fire. While politicians have paid lip service and passed what many church leaders feel is a meaningless bill to raise the penalty for burning a house of worship, they have refused to classify these attacks as acts of terrorism or even as racially motivated. In a national radio address and in a two-hour meeting with ministers from a number of black churches, President Clinton said that the fires are the result of "racial hostility," but stopped short of calling the burnings acts of terrorism.

"The problem with the Clinton administration is that they have yet to say to

This article was adapted from Ron Nixon, "Ashes of Racism, Fires of Terror" *CAQ* (*Covert Action Quarterly*) #58, Fall 1996, and is reprinted with permission of *CAQ*, 1500 Massachusetts Ave. NW, Washington, DC 20005, USA. Annual subscriptions in the U.S., $22; Canada $27; all other areas $35. The issue of *CAQ* containing the full text of this article with footnotes is available from *CAQ* for $8 (add $4 outside the U.S.).

the nation that this is domestic terrorism and they will not tolerate it," said CDR's research director, Rose Johnson. "Until such time as that comes out of the administration's mouth, I think the nation knows that they're not serious. [The burning of churches] is terrorism by the administration's own definition and it must take a stand."

Racially Motivated Terrorism

According to the Federal Bureau of Investigation (FBI), domestic terrorism is the "unlawful use of force or terror against persons or property to intimidate or coerce the government, civilian population or any segment thereof in further-ance of political or social objectives." Under this definition, at least some of the church fires could be classified as acts of terrorism. Consider the following:

• South Carolina, June 1995. Two white men were convicted of burning two black churches and stabbing a mentally ill black man. Both culprits, Christopher Cox and Timothy Welch, were members of the Christian Knights of the Ku Klux Klan. Police confirmed that they attended a Klan meeting shortly before the burnings at which the speaker stated that black churches instruct African Ameri-cans on how to get on welfare. Several days later Herbert Rowell, a Klansman who had attended the meeting and was a friend of the two suspects, asked re-porters, "Have you ever noticed that when there's free cheese or milk and stuff we [whites] don't know about it, but they [blacks] are the first in line?" Cox and Welch also had contact with another Klansman, Arthur Haley, whose home was raided by Bureau of Alcohol, Tobacco and Firearms (ATF) agents. Guns and Klan paraphernalia were confiscated. The pastor of one of the churches burned by Cox and Welch was threatened after the two were arrested and later charged with conspiracy to violate civil rights. According to the minister, he was ap-proached by an unidentified man who said, "I'm going to get you nigger."

• Bowling Green, Kentucky, 1993. Ernest Pierce, state leader of the Knights of the Ku Klux Klan, and three others were indicted and prosecuted on federal charges for the December 1991 burning of Barren River Baptist Church. Court records show that five days after the church fire, Pierce came to a Klan meeting, threw down a newspaper with coverage of the fire, and congratulated members on a job well done. After a KKK march, the minister of the church had openly criticized Pierce and the Klan. In court, Pierce testified that he torched the church in retaliation for the criticism.

> *"According to . . . the Center for Democratic Renewal (CDR), more than 80 black churches have been burned or desecrated since 1990."*

• Southeastern Arkansas, May 17, 1992. Three black churches in Oak Grove and St. James in Desha County, and Love Rest Baptist Church in Arkansas County, were burned by two white males, Kenneth A. Coates and Perry Moore, both age 23. According to Assistant US Attorney Michael D.

Johnson, the two men wanted to "get African Americans." Moore and Coates pleaded guilty to conspiracy to burn the churches.

• Clarksville, Tennessee, 1995. Shortly after what the Justice Department called a "racially motivated arson spree," a church was burned. During the spree, molotov cocktails had been thrown at the home of an African American family while they were asleep. A Nashville, Tennessee man convicted on federal charges for the string of fires is serving eight years in prison. The man belonged to a white supremacist group, the Aryan Faction, dedicated to driving blacks out of Clarksville. No one has been arrested in the burning of the church.

> *"[A] leader of the Knights of the Ku Klux Klan . . . [was] indicted and prosecuted on federal charges for the December 1991 burning of Barren River Baptist Church."*

These attacks, and many others that followed, share a similar profile: They are racially inspired and are usually preceded by years of intimidation by hate groups and individuals. Nonetheless, federal investigators do not see them as terrorism and rarely acknowledge that they are racially motivated. At the top, Attorney General Janet Reno and Treasury Secretary Robert Rubin have pledged all available resources toward finding the culprits in the church fires. On the local level, however, FBI and ATF agents aren't as enthusiastic.

Says FBI agent Jim Brown with the agency's Birmingham, Alabama office, "Just because you have white people burning black churches doesn't mean that it's racially motivated or domestic terrorism." FBI head Louis Freeh, who testified at a congressional hearing on the terrorism in Atlanta and possibly in the TWA crash, has yet to issue a statement on the church fires. Nor did he testify at the congressional hearings on the subject held in May 1996.

Shifting the Blame

When law enforcement and the media failed to find an organized conspiracy behind the church fires, they sought to characterize the incidents as politically as well as geographically isolated. If the attacks are not linked through a cabal of individuals or organizations, they seemed to be saying, they can have no connection to each other at all. Instead of seeing the arson as a natural byproduct of a pervasive atmosphere of racism, scapegoating, and official neglect, many reports discredited charges of racism or terrorism. In this backlash, the media juggled statistics and focused on the small number of blacks arrested in connection with the church fires.

The Associated Press (AP) weighed in with a July 5, 1996 article that hit the front page of newspapers nationwide. Based on interviews with law enforcement officials, insurance companies, and the National Fire Protection Association (NFPA), which tracks church fires, AP concluded that charges of racism or domestic terrorism were unfounded. "There is no evidence that most of the 73 black church fires recorded since 1995 can be blamed on a conspiracy or a climate of racial hatred," wrote AP reporter Fred Bayles. "There's a lot of feeling out there that these fires are copycat fires," says Richard Gilman of the Insurance Committee for Arson Control, a trade group that uses insurance data to track fires.

Using similar data, *New Yorker* writer Michael Kelly also discounted racism and domestic terror as a motive for the burning of black churches—blaming instead the CDR for causing a crisis to serve its own interests. "An epidemic of church burnings is the sort of crisis that engenders respectful attention from the press, opens wallets of the people on the mailing list, and provides a virtually unassailable vehicle for the advancing of the group's larger agenda," Kelly wrote. He quotes the NFPA as saying the number of fires is actually down.

Also citing the NFPA as well as southern law enforcement officials, Michael Fumento charged in a *Wall Street Journal* op-ed that portraying the church fires as a serious crisis was a deliberate hoax by the Center for Democratic Renewal. "What the Klan could no longer do, a group established to fight the Klan is now doing . . . frightening black churchgoers," the conservative attorney wrote.

> *"These attacks . . . are racially inspired and are usually preceded by years of intimidation by hate groups and individuals."*

The problem with the analysis of these three writers is their over-reliance on data that is likely to be incomplete and misleading. Insurance industry statistics, for example, can omit cases of arson at black churches, especially those in rural poor areas, since they are sometimes uninsured. And using data compiled by the National Fire Protection Association—which Fumento himself admits is limited—is a sure way to dismiss claims of racism. Because the association does not keep statistics by race, it has no way to determine how many black churches burn. Nor are official statistics likely to reveal an accurate count since only about 44 percent of all fires are reported each year. Further limiting the accuracy of information, NFPA gets much of its data from reports filed by state agencies to the Federal Emergency Management Agency. States are not required to file these reports and not all do.

A Legacy of Racism

Finally, all three writers depend on federal and state law enforcement officials to determine if the fires are racially motivated acts of terrorism or simple arson. While both Kelly and Fumento question the motive of civil rights leaders for calling attention to the church fires, they wholeheartedly accept the conclusions of law enforcement officials. This bias ignores the fact that many of these agencies have been accused of racism and, as a matter of record, have led attacks on blacks.

• The FBI assault on black liberation movements is well known. Through its

COINTELPRO (Counterintelligence) program, the bureau targeted black leaders including Martin Luther King, Jr., Malcolm X, the Black Panthers, and Elijah Muhammad of the Nation of Islam. The goal, according to an August 25, 1967 memo from J. Edgar Hoover, who spearheaded the program, was to "expose, disrupt, discredit, or otherwise neutralize the activities" of black groups and leaders. One of the people who helped to implement COINTELPRO was James O. Ingram.

> *"There is a long history by the Klan and other white supremacist groups of targeting churches."*

He is now director of Public Safety in Mississippi and leads the investigation into the black church fires.

• Over the years, the FBI has come under criticism for targeting black elected officials such as Mayor Richard Arrington of Birmingham, Alabama, and many members of the Congressional Black Caucus.

• In the mid-1970s, the ATF was instrumental in framing the "Wilmington 10," a group of North Carolina civil rights activists led by Ben Chavis, wrongfully jailed for racial violence and burning a white store. Instead of going after Klansmen—who were suspected by community members of starting the racial violence and torching the store—the ATF coerced three black prisoners into blaming Chavis and the others. Although the three later admitted lying, the FBI and a federal court refused to reopen the case and the 10 served a number of years in prison before international pressure forced their release.

• In 1995, the ATF again gained attention for its racism when it was discovered that many of its agents had attended a "good-ol' boy roundup" in Tennessee, where racist literature was sold and skits degrading blacks were performed. Some of the agents who attended these roundups were later assigned to the church burnings. They were removed after public outcry from the black community.

• Just recently, ATF settled a lawsuit by 240 current and former African American agents charging racism and overt discrimination.

• The FBI has also been sued numerous times by black agents for discrimination.

The Significance of the Arsons

There *is* a difference between the terrorist attacks on the World Trade Center and in Oklahoma and the attacks on black churches. For one thing, no one has yet been killed in the church arsons. But the number of incidents and the extent of the damage to community is far from insignificant, and the terror they spread is part of a long historical pattern. Different, too, is the reluctance of officials to brand the church burnings as terrorism. Even in the downing of TWA Flight 800, when terrorism was only suspected, the threat to public safety was considered so serious that vast investigatory resources were instantly mobilized. In the church burnings, however, every reason other than political motivation or terrorism is given while the media and official investigators discount or downplay the role of racism. "When it comes to attacks on black people, the terrorist or attacker is always given the benefit of the doubt," says Selma, Alabama attorney Rose Sanders.

And while there is doubt of some overarching conspiracy, that question is largely irrelevant—either to defining the crimes as terrorist or to understanding that they are fundamentally racist. There is a long history by the Klan and other white supremacist groups of targeting churches. These attacks hit at the heart of African American life in the South and, like cross burnings and lynchings, they are designed to show blacks who is in control and to keep them in their place in a white man's world. A government that does not act swiftly to investigate and deter these crimes as good as lays the tinder and provides the matches for the destructive fires of racism.

Uncontrolled Immigration Threatens Race Relations

by Lance T. Izumi

About the author: *Lance T. Izumi is a fellow in California studies with the Pacific Research Institute for Public Policy in San Francisco, California.*

At an Asian American Lawyers convention in 1993, I sat on a panel that, among other things, attempted to predict the future of race relations in post-riot Los Angeles. As the panel's only conservative, it was interesting to watch my liberal counterparts perform all manner of mental and rhetorical gymnastics so as to avoid addressing the obvious reality that their self-created multiculturalist world was in shambles.

The 1992 L.A. riots exposed the fact that multiculturalism is based on a lie. Stripped of its euphemistic cliches, multiculturalism's fundamental characteristic is its hostility to the majority culture of white Americans. The liberal Asian American activists who sat on my panel, like their multiculturalist brethren in other minority communities, still cling to the bizarre belief that this hostility is enough to submerge all differences between the non-white races and unite them all in the liberal crusade.

Multiculturalism Will Not Work

This viewpoint is flawed for several reasons. First, many minorities, especially Asian Americans, have done extremely well in white capitalist America. As opposed to the liberal civil rights leaders who presume to speak for them, most Asian Americans do not spend their entire waking moments thinking about how oppressed they are. In Asian American communities, people are usually more concerned with making the most of the opportunities offered by the free enterprise system than in complaining about imaginary white bogeymen. Little wonder then that Republican candidates have always done well among Asians.

More fundamentally, the multiculturalists ignore the fact that the cultural gulf between various minority groups is often so large and deep that any minor re-

Reprinted from Lance T. Izumi, "Will L.A. Be the Next Bosnia?" *Sacramento Union*, January 2, 1994, by permission of the author.

sentiments they may share against whites are overwhelmed by their differences with each other. The starkest example of this comes from Los Angeles where a recent confidential police report states that "there will be an upcoming race war between blacks and Hispanics."

The reasons for this probable race war are instructive. On one level, the rising conflict will be caused by black and Hispanic gangs warring over turf and drug-trafficking "rights." However, in a front-page article, the *Los Angeles Times* notes that, "Although the battle may be over money, authorities concede that race is intimately woven into the struggle. The prison gangs encouraging the fight are steeped in a separatist mentality forged from years of confrontation behind bars."

Conservatives have warned that the multiculturalist prescription of diversity at the expense of common culture would lead to tribalism and eventually to separatism and violence. Sadly, these predictions are now coming true.

Further, it appears that uncontrolled immigration is playing a key role in the building racial conflict. While black gang membership has slowed in recent years, such has not been the case for Hispanic gangs.

According to the *Times* article, "Latino gangs have been rejuvenated by a new generation of Mexican and Central American immigrants. On the streets and behind bars, they have come to the realization that—if only through sheer numbers—they have the potential to dominate the underworld." As one Los Angeles police officer observed, the Hispanic gang members' attitude is, "Why appease any other group when you can just take things over yourself?"

Uncontrolled immigration must therefore be stopped, not only because of the negative fiscal impact it is having on state and local governments, but also because it is literally tearing apart the social fabric of our society. Indeed, the ultimate effect of uncontrolled immigration has been to turn California's urban areas not into the multicultural fantasy land of brown, black and yellow brotherhood, but into our own budding version of Bosnia.

This disastrous situation has been brought to us courtesy of our liberal elites, both white and minority, who have waged war against the common Western culture that has held our nation together for two centuries.

This common culture, made up of Judeo-Christian tradition, democratic capitalism, and the teachings of a whole slew of politically incorrect dead white males, created an environment that allowed ethnic group members to prosper as long as they were willing to assimilate into the mainstream.

Today, though, liberal elites view assimilation as evil. Consequently, we have become a nation of unconnected racial groups characterized not by what we share in common with our fellow countrymen, but by increasingly hostile ethnocentrism. A race war is therefore the natural, if somewhat ironic, outcome of our current multicultural madness.

It is time for politicians to stop talking about our diversity and start talking, like William Bennett, about the common American culture that we at one time all shared.

There Is Hope for Race Relations

by Randall Kennedy

About the author: *Randall Kennedy is a professor at Harvard Law School and the editor of* Reconstruction, *a quarterly journal focusing on African American politics, society, and culture.*

The attitude with which we approach our democracy is an important feature of it, as real and influential as legislation or the GNP [gross national product]. Thus it is worthwhile to consider the attitudes with which our citizenry approaches the various difficulties that confront our democracy. One of these difficulties is the race issue, or, to be more precise, that aspect involving the black-white relationship.

Two broad traditions encompass reflection on the prospects for that relationship. One is a pessimistic tradition, the other optimistic.

The pessimists say that racial harmony on the basis of racial equality is impossible in America. Many impressive people have embraced this view. Thomas Jefferson, for instance, maintained that it is certain that blacks and whites "can never live in a state of equal freedom under the same Government, so insurmountable are the barriers which nature, habit, and opinion have established between them."

Alexis de Tocqueville, Abraham Lincoln, Malcolm X, and an array of others have voiced similar sentiments. In the words of legal scholar Derrick Bell, we should not expect our society to overcome its racist past because "[r]acism is an integral, permanent and indestructible component of this society."

There are, of course, well documented facts and trends that nourish the pessimistic perspective. Along virtually every significant socioeconomic index of well-being—from lifespan, to income, to wealth, to education—a large gap separates whites and blacks. Globalization of the private sphere and reduction of the public sector will likely exacerbate these divergences.

At the same time, there are facts and trends that reflect and nourish a different

Reprinted from Randall Kennedy, "Race: A Case for Optimism," *Responsive Community*, Summer 1996, by permission of the *Responsive Community*.

tradition, an optimistic tradition. At the level of formal legal change, one can point in this century not only to the legal reforms of the 1950s and 1960s, but also to the fact, often minimized, that at the height of the Reagan Era, statutes were enacted that went considerably beyond anything that could have been enacted even at the high point of the civil rights revolution—for example, the amendments in 1982 to the Voting Rights Act and the amendments in 1991 to the Civil Rights Act. In terms of other indicators, one can point to the dramatically improved position of the upper third of the black population, as well as the attitudinal transformations that have made possible numerous breakthroughs in many areas of American life—breakthroughs epitomized perhaps most dramatically by the ascendancy of Colin Powell to the highest circles of authority and respect.

Choosing Optimism

What we confront, then, is a complex, ambiguous situation with respect to which we can choose to be either pessimistic or optimistic. Facts alone do not compel choosing one or the other. The decision is a matter of politics.

Our democracy can flourish only if the great majority of people adopt an optimistic perspective towards the race question. The optimism I envision does not ignore racism in its numerous guises. Nor does it privatize public matters, shifting blame to individuals for social disasters. Rather, the optimism I envision is one that acknowledges our massive problems but also recognizes that, through intelligent collective action, we can meet and overcome them.

It is important to champion this brand of optimism. For one thing, people are more likely to rally behind calls for progressive political action on racial and other fronts when they sense that what they do has mattered and can matter. A sense of possibility is an essential nourishment for political endeavor. That is why it is worthwhile to recall champions of racial justice and to value the difference that their actions have made and continue to make in the life of the nation. The ferocious ongoing attacks against the monuments of the New Deal ought to put all on notice of the perils of permitting past progressive accomplishments to lose their stature in the public's estimation.

> *"The optimism I envision is one that acknowledges our massive [racial] problems but also recognizes that, through intelligent collective action, we can meet and overcome them."*

Americans should be encouraged to be proud of what they and their forebears have accomplished in terms of transforming a pigmentocracy into a severely flawed multiracial society that is clearly more decent now than it used to be. They should be told that on the basis of our demonstrated ability to reform ourselves for the sake of racial justice we can realistically expect to build on past accomplishments and press further.

At the outset I mentioned that a number of distinguished persons have articulated the pessimistic tradition. By the same token, the optimistic tradition I have sought to sketch briefly has also been enlivened by distinguished persons. I think of Wendell Phillips, Charles Sumner, James Chaney, Andrew Goodman, and Mickey Schwerner. I think of Thurgood Marshall, Martin Luther King Jr., and Lyndon Johnson. My favorite, though, is a man who literally bore on his back the stigmata of racial oppression. Speaking in May 1863, only five months after the Emancipation Proclamation and before the complete abolition of slavery, Frederick Douglass asked whether "the white and colored people of this country can be blended into a common nationality, and enjoy together . . . under the same flag, the inestimable blessings of life, liberty, and the pursuit of happiness, as neighborly citizens of a common country." He answered: "I believe they can." So should we.

Blacks and Jews Can Cooperate to Improve Race Relations

by Michael Lerner and Cornel West

About the authors: *Michael Lerner is editor and publisher of the liberal Jewish journal* Tikkun. *Cornel West is a professor of Afro-American studies and the philosophy of religion at Harvard University. Lerner and West are also coauthors of* Jews and Blacks: Let the Healing Begin.

Michael Lerner: Do African-American progressives have a strategy for how to overcome the anti-Semitism that does exist and how to confront the problems being faced by inner-city Blacks?

Cornel West: As to anti-Semitism, the first step is to get our community to acknowledge that there is a problem. You have to convince people that it is a problem. Black people are facing so many difficult issues today—Blacks don't have enough resources, and food and housing and health care and so forth—that it's not always obvious to African-Americans that alongside of these there's also the problem of anti-Semitism. You can't go into the Black community and say their major problem is Black anti-Semitism because you will be talking to people who have kids who can't get food or education, you see.

But on the other hand, you can't allow the fact that young kids aren't getting enough health care and food to obscure the fact that Black anti-Semitism is a problem.

You've got to acknowledge anti-Semitism, but not make it seem that you think that this is the major moral problem facing our community—which is often the way it is represented in the mainstream media.

Lerner: I entirely agree. The major problem facing the Black community, like the major problem facing the rest of the population, is the dominant ethos of selfishness and reckless disregard for others, an ethos that then allows so many Americans to turn their backs on the poor, a majority of whom are white, but also turn their backs on the concentrated suffering of the Black community. Though I believe that fighting anti-Semitism and every form of racism, sexism, and homophobia is justified in its own terms, and is the morally right thing to do, it's also the prudential thing for Blacks to do. Publicly and systematically fighting anti-Semitism could help Blacks restore the kind of political coalition that would confront the ethos of selfishness that has been growing in America. And that is the only way Blacks will ever succeed in

> *"The major weight of the Black Freedom Movement has been against anti-Semitism."*

ending the hunger and poverty you rightly cite as being at the top of Black people's agenda.

West: Yes, that struggle is important. And part of the way we need to proceed is to indicate that this is not some new opportunistic concern, but that the struggle against anti-Semitism itself has a rich history. You have to accent the ways in which great Black, heroic freedom fighters have been strong critics of anti-Semitism. W.E.B. Du Bois, Frederick Douglass, Martin King, Ella Baker, Malcolm X after Mecca, and many other leaders throughout our history have a legacy that needs to be built upon—people who were critical of anti-Semitism. The major weight of the Black Freedom Movement has been against anti-Semitism—so it's not just West or Henry Louis Gates or bell hooks who are critical of anti-Semitism—no. We're just echoing a richer tradition that came before us. When this history is made more explicit, more Blacks will understand that to engage in anti-Semitic rhetoric or actions runs counter to one of the important trends within our own history.

The Fight Against Racism

Lerner: I also think it needs to be pointed out that one can't successfully fight against racism in the U.S. while simultaneously participating in anti-Semitic racism. In my view, the fight against racism requires an assault on the ways that people split off from their consciousness the needs and concerns of others, legitimating that splitting by finding some aspect of the others that is supposed to be the "basis" for not thinking of these others as equally made in the image of God and hence not equally deserving of one's own immediate attention and caring. That's why I've placed so much emphasis on fighting the ethos of selfishness, because I see this as another way to get into the underlying economic and political framework of American society that encourages this kind of racist or xenophobic nationalist splitting, and hence creates the conditions for people to turn their backs on others and explain to themselves that they have "a right" to take care of themselves without regard to what's happening to others. Yet that turning away from others, shutting one's ears to their cries, runs against what most people really want—it is a depressive reaction, based on having given up their hope that people would be emotionally and spiritually and morally there for us. Such despair is based in part on having become convinced that the underlying message of the competitive marketplace is true, namely the message that tells us that "no one is going to be there for you, nobody is going to take care of you, so you'd better watch out for yourself and do everything you can to advance your own interests at the expense of others, because otherwise others will do that to you and you will be screwed." It is the undermining of that message that is, in my mind, the prerequisite for defeating racism. . . .

What's the actual form in which a Black-Jewish alliance could take place? . . . In our own cases it's amazingly fortuitous that we ran into each other and developed a connection. I must say that the only time I see a Black-Jewish dialogue taking place in some organized structural way is through Jewish mainstream institutions. . . .

As far as I can see, there aren't any serious organizational links between Jewish progressives and Black progressives. Right now there aren't even any mass Jewish or Black progressive organizations. I don't see any institutional structure for an ongoing connection, dialoguing, or strategizing between progressives in these two communities. I wonder if you have any ideas about how we could or should do that?

West: I think that we need to call an emergency meeting of major progressive leaders and progressive intellectuals of our two communities. Not to form just an exchange between talking heads, but to launch a strategy for serious cooperation.

One dimension would be to create links between the grassroot members of neighborhood organizations, and get them involved in dialogue. Dialogue is a form of struggle: it's not just chitchat. Create a dialogue that focuses not just on the vulnerability of both groups, but on these larger issues of justice, democracy, and the crisis in our own communities. Then try to hammer out some programs that relate to the everyday lives of these groups. It could be tutoring, it could be struggling against tenant abuse—it could be a whole host of things. We have to put this on the agenda because we're concerned not solely about the self-interest of the respective groups but about the future of this country. That would serve as one source of the revitalization of public life in the country as a whole.

> *"I . . . have met with . . . Black-Jewish groups in synagogues and churches around this country and you really do have large numbers doing the right thing."*

Doing the Right Thing

West: In the last two years I must have met with thirty to thirty-five Black-Jewish groups in synagogues and churches around this country and you really do have large numbers doing the right thing. These were primarily liberal and progressive Blacks and Jews who engaged in serious, candid dialogue about where the tensions are. These folk realize that we are sliding down a slippery slope, and are willing to do something about it on a personal and a collective level. To that degree I've been inspired. It's a difficult dialogue, but it's still going on among everyday folk. They know they are cutting against the grain, and there's a lot of tension. But I see people willing to say, "Let's engage in conversation that provides an understanding of why we're at an impasse." Opening the forms of communication, and understanding this opening as a prelude to a more substantive struggle. In a large number of these different places where I've met, what's emerged has been living-room dialogues with Blacks and Jews. This is the kind of thing that I think can be one of the spin-offs of what we're calling for. It won't be just at the national level, but at the neighborhood level. The major institutions and community organizations reflect on the possibilities, and from there begin to program the most important needs in light of each neighborhood. I've seen some communities move from under tremendous obstacles. That's the more hopeful side. The less hopeful side is that, once one gets above ground, the conversation becomes more shrill, more sensationalist and polarized, so that the possibilities of bridging the chasm become more difficult.

Grounds for Hope

Lerner: In terms of the transformative voices in the Black world, let me ask you what it is that makes you optimistic or not optimistic? What is your strategy for how a progressive Black force is going to reemerge? Because if there were a progressive Black force that had something of the quality of a Martin Luther King tradition, then it would be a lot easier for us in the Jewish world to connect with. Whereas if the only people who are articulating Black rage are also articulating anti-Semitic rage, it's extremely difficult. What ought to happen?

West: There are a whole host of persons who are part of the same legacy of King's still at work in the Black churches. For example, the United Theological Seminary at Dayton, Ohio, under President Darryl Ward, my Black brother, has the largest program of training for Black preachers. Hundreds of them are part of the legacy of King. They are rarely sought out. Very few people in the white or Jewish world even know them.

Or take Gary Simpson, the pastor of the largest Black Baptist church in America, Concord Baptist Church in Brooklyn. He's a young man; he's the one who preached the sermon against anti-Semitism after brother Yankel Rosenbaum was murdered in 1991, and wrote the letter to the *New York Times.* The council of rabbis had never heard of him. The first thing they did was invite him in, and they

> *"I see people willing to say, 'Let's engage in conversation that provides an understanding of why we're at an impasse.'"*

found they had one of the most visionary, articulate, humane persons they ever knew. There are many thousands of men and women like Gary Simpson in Black America.

Do you think large numbers of people in the white world or in the Jewish world would seek these people out? Not yet. Gary Simpson's got a whole network of people who are building on the legacy of King and Fanny Lou Hamer. There are many many King-like figures on the grassroots level in the Black community, but with the chasm in place we hardly ever hear about them. And so one has to go out to do the kind of thing I was talking about before to bring these folk together.

> *"Even though we don't have any grounds for thoroughgoing optimism, we don't have any grounds for despair."*

For example, brother Rabbi Jacobs, who's up in Westchester county, brought brother Reverend Mark Taylor to speak at his synagogue. They had a fascinating exchange, and now they've hooked up. And these small hookups can take place around the country. Why? Because there are many more progressive Jews than the Black world recognizes, both in and outside of the synagogues: there's many more progressive and prophetic Black folk in and out of the church who are interested in this kind of thing, even though they know that at a higher level, in newspapers and on television, you've got this battle going on. When I'm really down and out I tend to want to go to this grassroots level and see this kind of interaction taking place. And I say, "Even though we don't have any grounds for thoroughgoing optimism, we don't have any grounds for despair. We can at least have some hope." Because this kind of thing is taking place. It's not a movement. I don't think we're at a point now when we can talk about a movement amongst progressives at any level. But we've got some momentum created, and we hope down the road to produce a movement. My work with The New Party—Joel Rogers, Josh Cohen and others—as well as Democratic Socialists of America—is part of this effort.

A Campaign of Healing

Lerner: Let's go back to what our two communities can do together. Building on your idea of a national gathering, I propose a conference aimed at launching a campaign of healing and repair in both communities, aimed at undermining the anti-Semitism in the Black community and the anti-Black racism in the Jewish community.

But then we need to launch an ongoing campaign and an ongoing organization committed to shaping a climate of opposition to racism and anti-Semitism, so that those who wish to reject or combat racism or anti-Semitism in their own communities will find a community of people ready to give them support and to validate their perceptions.

The mechanism for generating a change in consciousness on these issues would involve a balance between a large-scale public assault and smaller efforts individually tailored to the needs of specific communities or subcommunities. On the one hand, we could create a widespread public awareness of the problems, and a climate that supports public repudiation of racist and anti-Semitic ideas and practices.

The focus of the campaign cannot be exclusively against racism or anti-Semitism. We would have to show people how these kinds of sickness are expressions of the dominant selfishness of American society, and we do not believe they can be fully defeated without addressing the need to shift the dominant discourse from an ethos of selfishness to an ethos of caring. This Politics of Meaning goal will be an ingredient in the way that we formulate the discourse in our campaign in both the African-American and the Jewish communities. Demeaning of others is often associated with reactionary forms of meaning-oriented communities, so our task is to provide alternative frameworks of meaning that do not associate to anti-Semitism or racism. In general, our goal is to revalidate a commitment to democratic ideals and to the Jewish notion of *tikkun,* as healing, repair, and transformation of the world. Meanings derived from these commitments can provide an alternative to racist ideologies and world views.

A Politics of Meaning

Lerner: I envision us mobilizing every major culture hero, musician, sports hero, intellectual, artist, television or movie star, disc jockey, talk-show host, preacher or minister or rabbi, teacher, social worker, health care worker, and many more to use their positions to become publicly identified with this campaign and to use their influence to bring these issues into public scrutiny and to fight for a different way of thinking and being together. And I envision the careful fostering of dialogue groups, support activities, and joint education.

Equally important, I envision mobilizing a significant section of the Jewish world to consider using financial resources on a community-to-community aid program designed to provide immediate and substantial assistance to those in the Black community who are seeking to develop their community's resources. But that must be done in a way that does not foster paternalism or resentments. It can't be done as "charity," but it can be done as part of a campaign for a Politics of Meaning, because in that framework people begin to understand that doing acts of caring for others is not a self-denigrating or self-undermining action, but rather a self-fulfillment and self-affirmation of their own most fundamental needs. And that way of thinking has deep roots in the Torah, and in the religious traditions of the Black community.

> *"If the struggle against anti-Semitism . . . and against racism . . . is framed as part of [a] larger struggle, then a real alliance might be possible."*

Ultimately, however, there is no way to defeat the ethos of selfishness in each of our communities without taking on the larger selfishness of the entire society. Black culture and Jewish culture today are both massively shaped by the dominant media and by the assumptions built into the world of work. Those who are most "successful" in material terms in both communities are those who have best mastered the ethos of selfishness of the competitive market, learned to think in those terms, and then become experts. But the corrosive effect of the culture is so powerful that even those who have not been successful blame themselves for not adequately mastering the ethos of selfishness, and so they work at "improving themselves" by learning the latest techniques. Being "cool" is knowing how to "take care of yourself" in these self-interested, materialistic, and manipulative terms, and it is often counterposed to being a shlep or a geek or a fool, namely those who don't know how to maneuver for themselves.

It's utopian to imagine that as long as the larger society rewards this way of being that we are going to be totally successful in undermining these dynamics in our own communities. But if we don't, racism and anti-Semitism will persist. . . .

An Alliance of Blacks and Jews

Lerner: This is a perfect moment for an alliance of Blacks and Jews to advocate a Politics of Meaning that explicitly takes seriously the most fundamental "traditional value": Love your neighbor as yourself. A progressive Politics of Meaning would reclaim the biblical value of caring for others that was central both to the Torah and to Jesus. In fact, these biblical ethics stand in sharp contrast to the ethos of selfishness, enshrined in the politics of Newt Gingrich, Rush Limbaugh, and the very *un-Christian* Christian Right. A Black-Jewish alliance aimed solely at combatting cutbacks of social services won't succeed in either community, because Jews are not going to put themselves in the position of being called "patronizing" or being told that they are really doing this whole thing for their own selfish interests, and Blacks are not likely to want to have Jews in an alliance that is aimed just at improving the material conditions of Blacks. But if the alliance is about this larger social transformative goal, and if the struggle against anti-Semitism in the Black community and against racism in the Jewish community is framed as part of that larger struggle, then a real alliance might be possible. And both groups would rightly feel proud to be bringing to the larger American society a Politics of Meaning perspective that is so badly needed. So a national campaign and national conferences that were focused in this way might be an important new direction for the coming years.

It is precisely because both our communities already have a foundation for this alternative way of thinking, in the Torah, in the New Testament, and in some of the more humanistic trends of Islam, that it becomes possible to imagine a real working together that is neither patronizing nor self-negating. If we can get foundations, corporations, and individual donors to support it, this campaign against racism and anti-Semitism in both communities could be an important direction for healing activity.

West: This is a hell of an idea. Let's see if we can bring other people and some serious resources into such a campaign.

The Burning of Black Churches Does Not Signify Increasing Racism

by Michael Fumento

About the author: *Michael Fumento, a columnist for* Reason *magazine, is an attorney who formerly worked with the U.S. Commission on Civil Rights.*

"Flames of Hate: Racism Blamed in Shock Wave of Church Burnings," read the screaming headline in the *New York Daily News* in the spring of 1996. "The South Is Burning: A Rash of Torchings at Black Churches Has Resurrected the Ugly Specter of Racism," chimed in the *Toronto Star*. *Newsweek* warned of "Terror in the Night Down South," while *USA Today* reported that "Arson at Black Churches Echoes Bigotry of Past." Throughout the media, among public figures, and indeed among most Americans who voiced an opinion on the subject, a consensus had formed by mid-June 1996 that burnings of black churches in the South had so escalated in number over the previous two years as to reach the proportions of an epidemic—an "epidemic of terror," in the words of Deval Patrick, the assistant attorney general in charge of civil rights at the Justice Department.

The cause, it was also agreed, was a terrifying resurgence of white racism. Mac Charles Jones, a board member of the Center for Democratic Rights (CDR), which played a crucial role in bringing the story of the burnings to public attention, initially described them as the handiwork of "a well-organized white-supremacist movement." But when law-enforcement authorities failed to uncover evidence of a conspiracy so specific as that, more generic, more sweeping, and more frightening explanations began to circulate and take root.

After all, asserted Deval Patrick, if the notion of a single conspiracy behind all the incidents was "a chilling thing," the idea "that these are separate acts of racism [is] even worse." Eleanor Holmes Norton, the District of Columbia's delegate to the U.S. House of Representatives and a former chairwoman of the U.S. Commission on Civil Rights, agreed: rather than an identifiable conspiracy, she stated, "we are confronted with something far more dangerous." A CDR staff member summed up the nature of that danger in a dramatic if also vague and cryptic phrase: the "conspiracy," he said, was "racism itself."

A Conspiracy of Racism?

These words were quickly repeated by Al Gore—"for a large number" of the fires, the Vice President proclaimed, "the conspiracy is racism itself"—and soon echoed widely. Indeed, not since the urban riots of the 1960's had a series of events given rise to such apocalyptic talk about the attitudes of American whites toward American blacks. To Jesse Jackson, we were facing "a kind of anti-black mania, a kind of white riot." Representative Maxine Waters (Dem.-California) declared that "never in my wildest dreams did I expect to be refocused on such outright tyranny." President Clinton drew a parallel between the arson attacks and ethnic violence in Bosnia and Rwanda. Visiting Auschwitz, Hillary Clinton (according to Reuters) "compared the motives for the church burnings to the World War II Holocaust." Abraham Foxman, the national director of the Anti-Defamation League, also invoked events leading up to the Holocaust, as did a number of other Jewish leaders.

Given this climate, it was not long before politics of a more mundane kind began to enter in. "The fuel for these fires," wrote Bob Herbert, a columnist for the *New York Times*, "can be traced to a carefully crafted environment of bigotry and hatred that has developed over the past

> *"[There is] no evidence that most of the 73 black-church fires recorded since 1995 can be blamed on a conspiracy or a general climate of racial hatred."*

quarter-century." Bruce Haynes, a professor of sociology at Yale, spelled out some of the components of that "carefully crafted environment": "the [1994] election, the [Newt] Gingrich revolution, the rhetoric from [Pat] Buchanan . . . [which] have helped to create a climate of tolerance of hate." To the Reverend C.T. Vivian, chairman of the board of CDR, the arsonists were clearly allies of the Christian Right: "There's only a slippery slope between conservative religious persons and those who are really doing the burning." And when the Christian Coalition offered to set up a special fund to help rebuild burned churches, Mary Frances Berry, chairwoman of the U.S. Commission on Civil Rights, dismissed the gesture with these words: "You have the very people who created the context for the fires rushing over and saying 'Let us help you put them out.'"

What Are the Facts?

In fact, however, as I and a few others tried to point out, the "epidemic of terror" was a sham.

On July 5, 1996, Fred Bayles of the Associated Press summarized the results of a lengthy "review of federal, state, and local records." Of a total of 409 church fires since 1990, it turned out that about two-thirds were at *white* churches, while of 148 fires since 1995, slightly more than half had also been at white churches; none of these, presumably, could be attributed to white racism. Even more significantly, in the fires at black churches, "only random links to racism" could be found. Bayles's conclusion was unequivocal: there was "no evidence that most of the 73 black-church fires recorded since 1995 can be blamed on a conspiracy or a general climate of racial hatred."

> *"Fires at churches both white and black [have] sharply decreased since 1980."*

In a similar vein, the July 15, 1996, issue of the *New Yorker* (which appeared on July 8) carried a lengthy analysis by Michael Kelly under the title, "Playing With Fire." Kelly reported, among other facts, that fires at churches both white and black had sharply *decreased* since 1980, and that the overall number in 1994 was the lowest in fifteen years. As for the admitted rise in attacks on black churches since 1995, that was attributable in part, Kelly wrote, to "an upsurge in the reporting of arsons," and in part to "copycat arsonists who may have been racist but who also had been inspired by the media attention given to the fires."

From "the evidence to date," Kelly concluded,

> the true picture of black-church fires is less clear, and less apocalyptic, than what the public has been led to believe. . . . Some of the black-church fires were accidents. Racism is strongly indicated in fewer than half of the black-church fires investigated to date. Other motives include mental instability, concealment of theft, and vandalism. . . .

I myself weighed in with an op-ed piece in the *Wall Street Journal* on July 8, 1996, in which I reported the results of my own independent investigation. In many respects my findings paralleled those of Bayles and Kelly, but with differences of emphasis. I was especially interested in how the idea of a racist epidemic—Kelly called it more of a myth than a lie, while to me it was closer to a deliberate hoax—came to be promoted. This had led me to explore in greater depth the role played by various left-wing advocacy groups, in particular the Center for Democratic Renewal.

What I found was that beginning in the winter of 1995 and throughout the spring of 1996, the CDR, in conjunction with the National Council of Churches (NCC), had been feeding the media a steady diet of "news" about black-church burnings in the South. These efforts had been rewarded with considerable attention, but real momentum developed only after another church fire on June 6, 1996, (later revealed to have been set by a disturbed thirteen-year-old girl) galvanized CDR to call a press conference where it re-released a sensational report prepared a few months earlier. Since 1990, the CDR alleged, there had been 90 arson attacks against black churches in nine Southern states; the number had been rising every year; and each and every culprit "arrested and/or detained" was white.

These activities of the CDR were a principal source of the national excitement over the alleged epidemic of burnings, as well as of the hysterical response by journalists and public figures. But as I showed in my *Wall Street Journal* article (and as was confirmed separately by Bayles and Kelly), the CDR's assertions were baseless. By contacting officials in various Southern states, and comparing their figures with those on the CDR list, I established that the CDR had systematically failed to count fires set by blacks in black churches, had labeled as arson a number of fires which responsible authorities insisted were attributable to other causes, and had altogether ignored fires in white churches. Like Kelly, I found that black-church fires had demonstrably increased in number only *after* press reports began to appear, and that the increase could be largely ascribed to a combination of more reliable statistics and copy-cat behavior. In short, by claiming an epidemic of black church burnings, the CDR, I concluded, might actually have helped bring one about.

Partisan Politics and Money

Since my piece was published, more has been learned about CDR, its friends, and its mode of operation. Typically identified in news accounts as a "watchdog" or "anti-hate" group, CDR has, according to its own promotional literature, a rather more explicit agenda than that: namely, working "with progressive activists and organizations to build a movement to counter right-wing rhetoric and public-policy initiatives." One such "progressive organization" is the National Council of Churches, well known for its own partisan support of a variety of left-wing causes. Indeed, Mac Charles Jones, the CDR board member credited with the idea of publicizing the burning of churches, is a full-time "associate for racial justice" on the payroll of the NCC.

Whatever they had in mind when they started their mendacious campaign, the two organizations have certainly struck gold with it. As an August 9, 1996, story in the *Wall Street Journal* revealed, the NCC had been experiencing severe difficulty in raising money for its "ambitious programs designed to combat racism." Jones's brainstorm offered a solution to the problem. In partnership with seven other groups, the CDR and NCC rapidly established a "Burned Churches Fund." Placing full-page advertisements in major newspapers, the coalition solicited contributions that would be used "to restore the damaged churches" as well as "to challenge racism throughout the country."

> *"The CDR had systematically failed to count fires set by blacks in black churches."*

Today the coffers are overflowing. According to the *Journal*, the appeal has enabled the NCC to raise "more money more quickly than it has for any previous cause." By early August it had accumulated $9 million from Americans sincerely alarmed by the specter of burning black churches, and contributions were continuing to pour in at the rate of approximately $100,000 a day. In fact, between insurance coverage and the Burned Churches Fund, enough money is now available to rebuild each church three times over.

A detail not reported by the *Journal* is that the person responsible for overseeing the Burned Churches Fund is an employee of the NCC named Don Rojas, who once served as press secretary to the late Marxist leader of Grenada, Maurice Bishop. In the late 80's, Rojas moved on to the *Amsterdam News*, New York's black weekly, first as a reporter and then as its executive editor; during his tenure the paper outspokenly defended Leonard Jeffries, the chairman of City College's black-studies program, notorious for his racist diatribes against whites and Jews.

> *"The inclination to believe the worst of their country . . . trumped that intrepid sense of skepticism for which journalists are forever congratulating themselves."*

Whether or not Rojas's position is a source of concern to sponsors of the Burned Churches Fund—the coalition includes a number of normally cautious mainstream organizations, Christian and Jewish alike—the fact is that by early August 1996, over a third of the $9 million collected so far had already been earmarked for purposes other than rebuilding churches. Those purposes, according to the *Wall Street Journal*, include what Mac Charles Jones calls "program advocacy"—seminars and other forums to promote "economic justice" and combat "interlocking oppressions from gender to homophobia." Where else the money may be going under Rojas's supervision is, at the moment, anyone's guess.

The Negligence of Journalists

Perhaps the most intriguing aspect of this entire story concerns the public response to those who have raised questions about the alleged epidemic. Although Fred Bayles won an award for his exposé from the Associated Press, only a handful of the hundreds of newspapers which subscribe to that wire service carried his report. Kelly's piece was mentioned in the *Christian Science Monitor* and by a couple of columnists. My *Wall Street Journal* op-ed also drew the attention of a handful of columnists and editorial writers, but apart from a single mention in the *Atlanta Journal and Constitution*, no newspaper examined its claims or even cited it.

The most egregious practitioner of journalistic negligence has been the *New York Times*, which devoted two full-page spreads to the so-called wave of arson and mentioned the church burnings in over 100 news stories, but which never once discussed any of the issues raised in the three dissenting pieces. Needless to say, the *Times* has also carefully refrained from inquiring into the background of the CDR or the operation of the Burned Churches Fund.

But the *Times* is hardly alone. In his June 13, 1996, nationally syndicated column, Clarence Page complained of a "conspiracy of silence" about the church burnings; in fact, by that date, *over 1,400* references to the arson attacks had already appeared in the media since the beginning of the year. If there has been a conspiracy of silence, it is mainly the one that has enveloped the critics.

It might be too much to expect any of the pundits and public figures who seized on the CDR's report as a vehicle for scoring points against their political opponents to register the fact that it was in essence a fabrication, let alone to apologize for the orgy of name-calling in which they participated. But one would think at least some journalists might have been led to wonder what this episode says about the way "news" is manufactured, packaged, and shipped these days, or to reflect on their own role in plunging so many Americans into a paroxysm of utterly baseless recrimination. But in the end, it seems, the inclination to believe the worst of their country once again trumped that intrepid sense of skepticism for which journalists are forever congratulating themselves. As for admitting that they were wrong, and wildly irresponsible, that is a prospect apparently too horrible for them to contemplate.

Chapter 3

Which Policies Benefit Minorities?

Chapter Preface

Affirmative action policies were first implemented in 1965 as part of a federal plan to counter the effects of employment discrimination on minorities and women. These policies typically required employers to actively recruit minority workers or to participate in programs that enlarged the pool of qualified minority job applicants. By the 1990s, however, many people had begun to question the effectiveness and the necessity of such programs. In November 1996, for example, California voters agreed to adopt Proposition 209, a ballot measure that ended affirmative action programs in government hiring and public education in California.

Critics argue that affirmative action has caused many employers to lower their qualifications simply to ensure that minorities are hired. Furthermore, they maintain, affirmative action programs create reverse discrimination by denying jobs and promotions to whites with equal or better capabilities than minorities. According to Steven Yates, author of *Civil Wrongs: What Went Wrong with Affirmative Action,* the ideal of equal employment opportunity through affirmative action has evolved into "equally unjust, equally harmful, and probably unconstitutional practices that give preference to some at the expense of others." Several authorities claim, moreover, that affirmative action actually harms blacks and Latinos because it reinforces negative stereotypes of these minorities as being unable to succeed without preferential treatment.

Supporters of affirmative action, on the other hand, reject the argument that the policies result in the hiring of less qualified workers. Nancy Stein, editor of the progressive journal *Crossroads,* points out that there has always been preferential treatment for white males based on family ties, school connections, and informal friendship networks. However, she argues, "no one ever said [employers] 'lowered quality' until [preferential treatment] began to be applied for the benefit of people of color." In other words, Stein and others maintain, the claim that affirmative action results in the hiring of unqualified people of color is largely based on racist and erroneous assumptions about minorities' abilities. Furthermore, many proponents insist, blacks and Latinos should endorse affirmative action despite the contention that it stigmatizes minorities by encouraging the view that they only succeed because of hiring preferences. According to Stein, "Stereotypes plague people of color and would continue to do so even if [affirmative action] were eliminated." The possibility of negative stereotypes therefore does not justify the elimination of affirmative action, supporters conclude.

The debate over affirmative action reveals a lack of consensus on the best approach to improving the lives of people of color. In the following chapter, the authors present arguments on affirmative action and other governmental and educational policies designed to benefit minorities.

Affirmative Action
Is Beneficial

by Jesse L. Jackson

About the author: *Jesse L. Jackson is president of the National Rainbow Coalition, a social justice organization. He has been active in civil rights issues since the 1960s.*

In the tradition of its predecessors, busing and law and order, the issue of affirmative action became the operative buzzword for racial politics in the 1996 presidential campaign season. While we know that most Americans have benefited from affirmative action programs—Latinos, Asian Americans, Native Americans, African Americans, veterans, the disabled, and women of all races and ethnic backgrounds—current political rhetoric has forced a black face on the issue. This is not only inaccurate but also intellectually dishonest and manipulative.

From statehouses to the halls of Congress, politicians who until very recently lauded the benefits of affirmative action have now commenced a full frontal assault on such programs, the only mechanism proved truly effective for achieving equal opportunity in American workplaces and universities. Senate Majority Leader Bob Dole was right in 1986 when he led the bipartisan fight to maintain the Nixon administration's policy of goals and timetables in the face of Ronald Reagan's attempts to dismantle it.

California Gov. Pete Wilson, as mayor of San Diego, himself championed the city's affirmative action programs as a necessary means to achieve equity. In an eloquent appeal to the city council, he once stated that "it must come from the heart, but we must have goals to do it."

America's Economic Troubles

Americans are anxious. Our fears, while real and justified, are being dangerously misdirected. Politicians who once supported affirmative action as an effective way to level the tilted playing field now would have America believe that affirmative action is at the root of our economic distress. Our jobs have not gone from white to black and brown, from men to women. What workers really

From Jesse L. Jackson, "Affirmative Action: It Benefits Everyone." This article appeared in the November 1995 issue and is reprinted with permission from the *World & I*, a publication of The Washington Times Corporation, ©1995.

feel is the pain of the globalization of the economy.

Where we once exported products, we now export plants and jobs. The real culprits are NAFTA [North American Free Trade Agreement] and GATT [General Agreement on Tariffs and Trade]—destructive economic policies that have sent our jobs across the border and overseas to cheaper labor markets, leaving our plants closed, without a plan to retrain our workers and invest in our economic future.

> *"We must work toward a race-inclusive and race-caring society."*

Affirmative action was never intended to be an antipoverty program. Opponents are using fear, scapegoating, and hysteria to shift the debate from the real issue: jobs. If we had a full-employment economy today, we would not be fighting over minutiae. The affirmative action fight is over what is left, not over what is needed.

Race Consciousness Is Necessary

Opponents of affirmative action would have us turn a blind eye to the past, opting for a scorched-earth approach to history. After 250 years of slavery, 100 years of apartheid, and 40 years of discrimination, we cannot burn the books and start anew at this point by instituting a "color-blind" code of justice.

Race- and gender-conscious programs were crafted precisely because individuals were discriminated against, historically and currently, because of their race or gender. We must not strive to be race neutral. We must work toward a race-inclusive and race-caring society. In the summer of 1995, while the *Adarand* [*Adarand Constructors, Inc. v. Pena*] Court was imposing more stringent requirements for upholding federal affirmative action programs, seven out of nine justices on the most conservative Supreme Court we have had in generations rejected the notion of a color-blind Constitution.

The unbroken record of race and gender discrimination warranted the legal remedy of affirmative action. When we consider what true reparations for past discrimination entail, merely equalizing the laws of competition by leveling the playing field is indeed a conservative form of redress.

Our legal history is replete with the cancer of racism—from the 1857 *Dred Scott* decision, maintaining that blacks at three-fifths human had no rights whites were bound to respect, to the 1896 *Plessy v. Ferguson*'s "separate but equal" mandate of apartheid. The 1954 *Brown v. Board of Education* decision was an effort to heal race cancer with "race cure," to fight exclusion with race inclusion. Title VII of the 1964 Civil Rights Act outlawed discrimination by mandating negative action to offset negative behavior. In 1965, President Lyndon B. Johnson recognized that positive, or affirmative, action was necessary to overcome the vestiges of a discriminatory past.

The current political debate over affirmative action has been based on myth and anecdote rather than data and facts. The American public deserves an honest and informed discussion of the issue rather than a steady stream of divisive and misleading sound bites. Despite typical claims, affirmative action is not quotas or preferential treatment of the unqualified over the qualified. It does not demean merit and is not reverse discrimination.

Contrary to popular opinion, affirmative action does not require quotas. Unless a court imposes them, quotas are illegal. Quotas are used only as a last resort to remedy a manifest imbalance in a company's work force or to compensate for a widespread and persistent pattern of discrimination. All a company must do is prove that it has made a "good-faith effort" to meet flexible goals, targets, and timetables that have been established to diversify its pool of applicants, ensuring that women and people of color are included in the hiring or promotion pool.

Courts may also act affirmatively to root out more subtle forms of discrimination. If a court finds that qualified women and people of color are not sufficiently chosen from the wider pool of applicants, it may impose a quota to bring the employer up to the level of a nondiscriminating employer.

In university admissions, race may be one of several factors that admissions officers use in creating a diverse student body—a benefit that serves all of its students. The Supreme Court has definitively outlawed the use of rigid numerical quotas, while it affirmed the consideration of race and gender along with special talent, geographic origin, athletic ability, or legacy status.

> *"History demonstrates that when [affirmative action] policies were enforced . . . , the employment of women and people of color increased dramatically."*

Furthermore, we must look at the way we define merit. We have yet to see proof of any correlation between standardized test scores and a student's success in his academic or postacademic careers. As I understand it, motivation is the primary predictor of future success.

Can we genuinely believe that the child who was educated in an impoverished farming community without an SAT-preparation course, worked two jobs after school, and still graduated with an "A" average is any less qualified to attend a university than her affluent counterpart who had the benefit of extracurricular activities, honors courses, and training to earn a "competitive" score on the SAT? I think not.

Affirmative action does not mandate reverse discrimination. These policies merely require women and people of color to be included in the applicant pools of universities, workplaces, and unions. If an unqualified applicant is hired or promoted over a qualified one in the name of diversity, this is discrimination, and it is actionable in court just as it is under all other circumstances.

A Rutgers University study commissioned by the Department of Labor found that a majority of claims of reverse discrimination were brought by disgruntled job applicants who were determined by courts to be less qualified than the successful woman or person of color who received the job or promotion. Reverse discrimination is not only illegal; it is rare. Less than 2 percent of the 90,000 employment discrimination cases before the Equal Employment Opportunity Commission are reverse discrimination cases.

White men form 33 percent of the population and 48 percent of the college-educated work force. Yet, they constitute 80 percent of the tenured professors, 80 percent of the House of Representatives, 86 percent of the partners in major law firms, 88 percent of the management-level jobs in advertising, 90 percent of the top positions in media, 90 percent of the officers of major corporations, 90 percent of senators, 92 percent of the *Forbes* 400, 97 percent of school superintendents, 99.9 percent of professional athletic team owners, and 100 percent of U.S. presidents. It is clear that the notion of the "angry white male" is not grounded in reality. Rather, it is an error in perception that has been wrongfully validated by divisive political tactics.

Affirmative Action Works When Enforced

Many opponents concede that our discriminatory past necessitated the need for positive affirmative steps to root out this pervasive evil, yet today they have come to the irrational conclusion that after 30 years on the books, these policies are no longer necessary. History demonstrates that when these policies were enforced as they were during the 1970s, the employment of women and people of color increased dramatically. These gains, however, were offset by the assaults on affirmative action during the Reagan-Bush era.

To say that affirmative action is no longer necessary is to ignore the clear evidence of present-day racism and sexism. The Department of Labor's *Glass Ceiling Report* found that women in the largest corporations hold less than 5 percent of top management posts, while African Americans, Latinos, and Asian Americans hold less than 1 percent of these positions. White males hold 95 percent of these jobs.

The unemployment rates of African Americans and Latinos are twice that of whites. Women are 53 percent of the population, African Americans 13 percent, and Latinos 10 percent. Yet, in the 1994 labor market, 22 percent of all doctors were women, 4 percent African American, and 5 percent Latino. Twenty-four percent of all lawyers were women, 3 percent African American, and 3 percent Latino. Thirty-one percent of all scientists were women, 4 percent African American, and 1 percent Latino.

> *"Affirmative action has not only benefited those who have been historically locked out; it has benefited our nation as a whole."*

The pay differential between white men, white women, and people of color persists. In 1993, for every dollar a white man earned, an African American man made 74 cents, a white woman 70 cents, a Latino man 64 cents, an African American woman 63 cents, and a Latina 54 cents.

The Urban Institute has documented the rampant nature of discrimination in the workplace. Sending equally qualified African Americans and whites to apply for the same jobs, they found that in nearly a quarter of the cases, whites moved further through the hiring process than blacks. The institute likewise found that whites received 33 percent more of the interviews and 52 percent more job offers than equally qualified Latinos. Even when African Americans and Latinos are hired, they are promoted and paid less.

We cannot fall prey to the destructive tactic of "divide and conquer" for the sake of political expediency. Affirmative action has not only benefited those who have been historically locked out; it has benefited our nation as a whole. Two-income-earner households have enabled American families to provide for their children. Race- and gender-inclusive policies turn tax consumers into tax producers. A diversified corporate America is better able to compete in this increasingly globalized economy. Let us not be misled: Increasing the educational and employment opportunities for a majority of Americans is good for the nation and good for our future.

Affirmative Action Is Harmful

by Bill Conti and Brad Stetson

About the authors: *Bill Conti and Brad Stetson are contributing writers for* Destiny, *a monthly magazine of black political opinion and culture.*

Does this seem familiar? Chaos reigns in the classroom at a mostly black inner-city school. The desks have been gouged with knives, classroom walls have been defaced with gang-graffiti and the barely literate "students" are out of control, learning nothing. Surely this is the result of racist neglect by an apathetic white administrator, right?

No, according to Emily Sachar, a teacher and author of *Shut Up and Let the Lady Teach*! This chaos was the result of an affirmative action hire—a black administrator who could not be fired. Tragically, a policy that was meant to help blacks ended up hurting them. This is the new reality of affirmative action—a dark side that hurts the very people it is intended to help.

This story is as old as the victories of Pyrrhus, an ancient general. After a number of costly "victories," in which his troops were slaughtered by the tens of thousands, a wise lieutenant warned him, "One more victory, and we're lost." Many are now wondering if the benefits of affirmative action are as costly.

Opposition to Affirmative Action

Of course, there have long been voices, black and white—crying in the wilderness, warning us about the consequences of an affirmative action culture. But until recently, these voices were muted by regular charges of race betrayal if black and outright racism if white. As columnist John Leo points out, in the past thirty years only a half-dozen serious books on affirmative action have been written. The subject has been, says Leo, "basically off-limits."

But the electoral earthquake of the 1994 political season may have changed all that. The major elements of this political temblor were:

- The overwhelming passage by California voters of Proposition 187, which would deny public benefits to illegal immigrants. This was a bold refutation

Reprinted from Bill Conti and Brad Stetson, "The Dark Side of Affirmative Action," *Destiny*, June 1995, by permission of *Destiny*.

of race-politics.

• Upset victories by Republicans, whose "Contract with America" affirmed the common sense of many politically incorrect views.

• A huge groundswell of advance support for the "California Civil Rights Initiative," a ballot measure which would outlaw race and gender based preferences in public hiring. [The initiative passed in November 1996.]

Like three converging lasers, these events combined to burn away the media-created veneer of public satisfaction with affirmative action. "The taboo has been shattered," observed syndicated columnist Charles Krauthammer. Suddenly, if you were white and voiced your opposition to affirmative action, you were no longer a fringe racist. If you were black and agreed, you were no longer a sellout. . . .

But should blacks take a second look at affirmative action?

Yes, say a growing number of social scientists, who are also becoming uneasy with affirmative action. Sociologists and social critics like Glenn Loury, Frederick Lynch, Nathan Glazer and Dinesh D'Souza have articulated three basic arenas where the destructive dark side of affirmative action policies as they affect everyone—but especially black Americans—is apparent: the moral, the cultural, and the psychological.

A Poisonous Race-Consciousness

But first, how did we get into this mess? The three major steps America took toward its present situation are: 1) There was legal "Jim Crow" discrimination against blacks into the 1960s. 2) Such discriminatory legislation was outlawed by the 1964 Civil Rights Act. 3) Before President Lyndon B. Johnson's signature could even dry, the Federal government—pushed by an impatient black leadership—entered into a race consciousness that was in many ways a flip-side of the biases of the past. The result: the color-blind Civil Rights Act was replaced by color-coded affirmative action court orders and programs. Political philosopher Nathan Glazer comments on the irony of this: "In 1964, we declared that no account should be taken of race, color, national origin or religion in the spheres of voting, jobs, and education. . . . Yet no sooner had we made this national assertion, we entered into an unexampled recording of the records of the color, race and national origin in every significant

"Tragically, a policy that was meant to help blacks ended up hurting them."

sphere of (a person's) life. . . . We entered into a period of color- and group-consciousness with a vengeance."

Before the healing power of racial humanism, expressed in the Civil Rights Act, had a chance to course through the American psyche, it was abandoned for a poisonous race-consciousness. This period of legal color blindness was so short that people today hardly remember it, and so do not see it as a possibility.

Perhaps that is why today we hear exaggerated rhetoric in defense of affirmative action: "Either we keep it the way it is or we go back to the days of Jim Crow," they say. So we see in a recent editorial in the "largest black-owned newspaper in the West," the *Los Angeles Sentinel,* this hyperbole: "Imagine an America without an NAACP [National Association for the Advancement of Colored People]. An American where lynchings are a daily ritual. . . ."

> *"Affirmative action consciousness . . . can also unnecessarily encourage self-doubt and cast a shadow on one's accomplishments."*

Such an obvious and preposterous inflation of American evil irks many blacks. They are proud of the bold, tell-it-like-it-is realism of leaders like Martin Luther King, whose words seared the conscience of America precisely because they were afire with truth. If the French had given the great frame to the Statue of Liberty, these past-masters of social criticism had given America her soul. The current burlesque of black "truth-telling" only sickens them, for it is attacking their nation's soul.

In Defense of Racial Humanism

One such voice unwilling to exchange righteousness for so-called "black advantage" is Errol Smith, a black Los Angeles businessman and former member of the advisory committee for the California Civil Rights Initiative. In defense of this anti-affirmative initiative, Smith wrote in the *Los Angeles Times:* "Is it right to require Chinese applicants to an elite high school in San Francisco to score ten points higher than blacks on entrance exams to qualify for admission? Is it just that white males in certain occupations are precluded from even competing for opportunities because their skin's melanin content roughly approximates that of those who once discriminated against blacks? Is it fair to deem the son of an affluent black family disadvantaged because so many other blacks live in poverty, while declaring a poor young white male privileged because he looks a lot like the CEO of the nearest Fortune 500 firm?"

Smith ends with a moral plea: "We black Americans must lift our heads a bit, look to the horizon and ask ourselves where these policies are leading us. Do we like the world these policies are creating? Are we comfortable with the racial legacy we are leaving for our children?"

The racial humanism of Errol Smith leaps out in stark relief when placed next to the following thoughts of a *Los Angeles Sentinel* columnist—thoughts which reveal the immorality encouraged by the affirmative action consciousness: "Mark Fuhrman looks like a racist! . . . If all the police that were on hand the day that Rodney King was beaten were placed in a lineup beforehand, a lot of minority group members could have picked out the ones who were capable of such inhumanity."

Of course, such moral immaturity and absurd expressions of ethnic defensiveness can be found in every group. Some Italian New Yorkers, for instance, rioted on hearing that John Gotti, the notorious mobster, was sentenced to life. The original civil rights movement knew that ethnic chauvinism and racial hostility damage those who embrace it the most and affirmative action only encourages such ethnic cheerleading.

Psychological Damage

Affirmative action also damages psychologically. Thinkers like Smith realize that when liberals recklessly magnify racist evil in America beyond its true proportions to show the necessity of affirmative action, that monstrous projection intimidates black youth, who subsequently shrink away from big dreams and curtail practical efforts toward fulfilling them. "You cannot cry wolf without the whole village hearing."

The *Wall Street Journal* recently quoted a 17-year-old leader of an Omaha drug-dealing ring who had been neatly fitted with such lenses of racial oppression: "Society is set up so that black people can't get ahead. I'm not supposed to have the American Dream and all that. I'm supposed to be in jail."

Beyond demoralizing black youth, the selling of affirmative action through racial hype and resentment has blinded many to the possibility that they themselves are racist. In *Shut Up and Let the Lady Teach* Emily Sachar illustrates this with a story from her New York City school. Annoyed at the nomination of two Asians to be class leaders, a black youngster stood up in Sachar's classroom and announced, "No way I'm staying here if two slant-eyed kids is running things." Sachar told him he was free to run for the position, too, but that he would have to refrain from racist remarks. The boy seemed truly shocked, and replied softly, "That was racist?" Many blacks are now wondering if the gaudy rhetoric necessary to sustain an affirmative action culture is worth the moral price paid by blacks, especially youth, who become so sensitive to the "racism" of others that they fail to see it in themselves.

Ironically, while the affirmative action consciousness falsely boosts some blacks' "self-esteem" by concealing from them what may be their own moral shortcomings, it can also unnecessarily encourage self-doubt and cast a shadow on one's accomplishments. This happened to a student at the University of Virginia Law School, a young black woman about to become the first black to make the prestigious Law Review when an affirmative action policy went into effect, supplanting a merit-based system of selection.

> *[Affirmative action] policies have been irrelevant to—or have even damaged—the already tenuous vocational hopes of the black underclass.*

When she heard that she had been thrust onto the Law Review as an affirmative action case, she said angrily: "Why are you doing this to me? Students want to be on the Law Review because they know big law firms look to [being on the] Law Review as an imprimatur. . . . But if you have two tracks, one for the white kids and another for minorities, the minority who makes the Law Review is forever having to defend and explain the door he came through. If he came through the door marked 'Minorities Only' the value is gone from it."

Harming Black Communities

Such are the psychological costs borne by the supposed beneficiaries of affirmative action, while other hidden costs inflict direct harm to urban black communities:

• Washington D.C., New Orleans and New York City have all been embarrassed by rogue and criminal police officers who were affirmative action hires with criminal proclivities, if not records. In New Orleans, one newly-hired black officer had to be removed for committing robberies and assaults while on duty—another affirmative action hire, known to be psychologically unfit for police work, was removed after murdering two citizens and a fellow officer while committing a robbery.

> *"The promised advantage of affirmative action is an illusion."*

• Similarly, a paramedic in Stanton, Calif., told one of the authors that affirmative action has torn his department in half. Strife and bitterness brought by affirmative action turned his workplace into an emotional warzone and endangered public welfare by causing less-qualified women and minorities to leap-frog over their more-experienced colleagues. "I have actually seen cases," the paramedic says, "where injured people were harmed by the inadequate performance of someone who was in a position of responsibility simply because of gender or ethnicity."

While supporters of affirmative action use black economic progress as their trump card, such an uncritical position is only part of the story. Obviously preferential treatment has furthered the careers of some blacks, as any policy of favoritism would, but the evidence is mounting that these policies have been irrelevant to—or have even damaged—the already tenuous vocational hopes of the black underclass.

Business owners, reluctant to locate in predominantly black neighborhoods because of preferential treatment standards, are also finding that, while incompetence comes in all colors, firing a minority employee is especially risky. Charges of racism may require too much money for small businesses to refute. The owner of a small factory in Chicago, described by a columnist as "patently innocent of discrimination," was fined $148,000 for employing three blacks instead of the 8.45 blacks federally mandated for companies his size.

"Huge legal liabilities," writes Thomas Sowell, "created by policies that make statistical underrepresentation equivalent to discrimination, create incentives for employers to protect themselves by putting distance between their companies and those communities from which they can expect large numbers of minority applicants." Thus businesses which could help local economies are tidily discouraged from doing so.

What then should morally concerned black Americans think about affirmative action? Many are finally realizing that to oppose affirmative action is not equal to saying that America is racism-free. Rather, it says that there are other morally sound alternatives to fight racism. Many blacks are now unwilling to exchange the high moral birthright handed down by the nation's founders for a mess of preferential pottage, recognizing that the promised advantage of affirmative action is an illusion.

Making English the Official Language Would Benefit Minorities

by the Congressional Committee on Economic and Educational Opportunities

About the authors: *During the 104th Congress, the Committee on Economic and Educational Opportunities was a House Standing Committee chaired by republican representative Bill Goodling of Pennsylvania.*

Editor's Note: The following viewpoint is excerpted from a congressional committee report advocating the passage of the English Language Empowerment Act of 1996, a bill designed to make English the official language of the United States government. The bill did not pass, but was reintroduced into the House of Representatives in January 1997.

We are a nation of immigrants. Our history has been shaped by the contributions of immigrants of different cultures, religions and languages from around the world. We are proud of our nation's ability to assimilate people from around the world into one cohesive society. The purpose of H.R. 123, "The English Language Empowerment Act of 1996," is to build upon our nation's historic tradition as a melting pot of diverse cultures from around the world, and to bind us together through the use of English as a common language.

The Need for Clear Language Policies

Over the past few decades, Congressional action and inaction has resulted in a balkanized national language policy, devoid of any clear, uniform principles. For example, whether documents are published in a foreign language depends in large part upon the particular Federal statute involved. Some Federal statutes require materials to be provided in an individual's native language or mode of communication. In other statutes, Federal law provides for services in the language and cultural context most appropriate to the individuals. While such pro-

Reprinted from the Congressional Committee on Economic and Educational Opportunities, "Committee Report on English Language Empowerment Act of 1996," 104th Congress, July 30, 1996.

visions may initially sound reasonable, they have consequences. As Linda Chavez, former director of the United States Commission on Civil Rights and current President of the Center for Equal Opportunity, stated in testimony before the Subcommittee on Early Childhood, Youth, and Families: "[T]he public policy that has been in place over the last 25 years has discouraged immigrants from learning English, and has made it quite possible for immigrants to function in all aspects of their civic life in their original language."

The Committee on Economic and Educational Opportunities believes it is time for a change; it is time to take stock of the piecemeal policies that have evolved, and replace them with a more uniform policy across all of the Federal government.

Right now, the Bureau of the Census informs us that over 320 different languages are spoken in the United States. Given this fact, it is obvious that Federal taxpayers cannot possibly publish every Federal document of whatever kind in 320 different languages. Furthermore, one might also make the case that [with] the current situation of selectively choosing to sanction a particular foreign language (i.e. publishing a document in Spanish and not the 319 others), the Federal government is implicitly favoring certain languages and peoples over others. It is better to have one common language. . . .

A Common Sense Approach

The Committee believes a new policy consisting of a common sense, common language approach is needed. H.R. 123, the "English Language Empowerment Act of 1996," represents just such an approach. The bill establishes English as the official language of the Federal government and requires the government to conduct its official business in English. It is the language of government, and not the private sector. The Committee emphasizes that the bill has no effect upon the use of foreign languages in homes, neighborhoods, churches, or private businesses. Affirming English as the official language of government ensures that all Americans can count on one language for government actions, policies and documents. That is good, common sense. And it reinforces other national policies, such as the requirement that one be able to read, write and speak English before becoming a United States citizen.

> *"It is our English language which unites us—a nation of diverse immigrants— as one nation."*

Not only does the bill represent good common sense, it also empowers individuals to become successful members of American society. It is our English language which unites us—a nation of diverse immigrants—as one nation. It promotes assimilation, rather than isolation and separatism. In all 50 states and the District of Columbia, it is English and no other language which is consistently written, spoken, and read in a widespread manner. The same cannot be said about other languages.

As earlier alluded to, the English language is a powerful tool. It empowers each new generation of immigrants to access the American dream. Over and over, studies show that people who learn English earn more for their families, are better able to move about and interact in society, and can more easily build a bright future for themselves and their children. In 1994, the Texas Office of Immigration and Refugee Affairs published a study of Southeast Asian refugees in Texas. The study showed individuals proficient in English earned more than 20 times the annual income of those who did not speak English. Furthermore, a 1995 study by the Latino Institute confirmed that the ability to speak English can make the difference between a low-wage job and a high-wage managerial, professional, or technical job.

> *"[The English language] empowers each new generation of immigrants to access the American dream."*

In testimony before the Subcommittee on Early Childhood, Youth, and Families, witnesses spoke first-hand about the significance of learning English, and the need for official English legislation. Ms. Maria Lopez-Otin, Federal liaison officer for the Nuclear Regulatory Commission, who came to this country at age 11 and without either parent, said:

> I have been able, I believe, to participate in the American dream . . . [my] ability to communicate in English is the essential first step in this journey. . . . From the immigrant's standpoint knowledge of English is critically important to success in American society, and discussions about immigration, bilingual education, or English as a second language, are but distractions from the issue at hand, the merits of English as the official language of the United States. And, on that point, on whatever level you consider, education, employment, politics, a social grounding in English is imperative. Now, does this mean rejection of our roots, our heritage, our original language, of course not. What it means is that as Americans we cannot hope to reach our fullest potential unless we speak the language, . . . and that language is English.

H.R. 123 is popular across the nation. As witness Mauro Mujica, Chairman of the Board of U.S. English and immigrant from Chile, recently testified, "Eighty-six percent of Americans and eighty-one percent of immigrants want to make English the official language of this country. The vast majority of citizens in this country are fed up with the present-day situation which has fostered linguistic welfare."

In Support of Official English

Many other individuals and organizations support official English. This legislation enjoys the strong support of the American Legion, the Veterans of Foreign Wars, U.S. English, English First, the National Grange, and many others.

The Committee wishes to note that some have mischaracterized the bill as an

"English only" bill. It's not so. It is an "official language of government" bill. "English only" legislation is commonly understood to be broader and more encompassing, such as the official language of an entire nation, public and private sector—not just of government. H.R. 123 is a more modest approach. This bill simply designates English as the official language for actions, documents and policies of the Federal government.

Further, the "English only" terminology implies English at all times and no others. Such is not the case with this bill. Rather, H.R. 123 provides for several exceptions to the government conducting its official business in English. Those include: (1) teaching of languages; (2) national security issues or international relations, trade, or commerce; (3) public health and safety; (4) actions, documents, or policies that are not enforceable in the United States; (5) actions that protect the rights of victims of crimes or criminal defendants; (6) actions in which the United States has initiated a civil lawsuit; (7) documents that utilize terms of art or phrases from languages other than English; and (8) actions or documents that facilitate the activities of the Bureau of the Census in compiling any census of population. The bill also does not prohibit Members of Congress or employees or officials of the Federal government from communicating orally with other persons in a foreign language. In sum, the most accurate description is "official language of government," not "English only."

Making English the Official Language Would Harm Minorities

by Karen K. Narasaki

About the author: *Karen K. Narasaki is the executive director of the National Asian Pacific American Legal Consortium.*

A battered immigrant spouse is unable to get a restraining order to stop her citizen husband's abuse because she cannot speak English.

A victim of anti-Asian violence is unable to testify against his assailants because he does not speak English.

A refugee calls 911 when her husband has a heart attack, but the operator is not permitted to instruct her in her native tongue.

These are just some of the stories you can expect to hear if English-only legislation and their thinly disguised cousins, English as the Official Language, or English as the Language of Government, become law.

Although these proposals appear to be innocuous on their face, their impact on the Asian Pacific American community and the general public would be devastating. Under most versions of these laws, government employees would be forbidden from speaking any language but English while on the job. Government documents and notices would only be printed in English, and government services would only be offered in English. Bilingual education, bilingual ballots and other government-provided voter education materials would be outlawed.

Flawed Assertions

English-only supporters claim that these laws only acknowledge English as the common language of the United States and argue that without this, immigrants will seek to abolish English in favor of Spanish, Chinese or some other language. They argue that these laws are necessary to encourage non-English speaking immigrants to learn English so they can successfully integrate eco-

Reprinted from Karen K. Narasaki, "Double Talk," *A. Magazine*, February/March 1996, by permission of the publisher.

nomically and socially in the U.S. They add that it is unfair to American tax payers to provide government information in more than one language.

Their assertions and perceptions are fatally flawed. The primacy of English in America has survived for over 200 years despite waves of immigration from different parts of the non–English speaking world. According to the last census, 97 per cent of Americans speak English well. Studies show that immigrants are assimilating even faster now than previous generations. With English rapidly becoming the language of international commerce, it is absurd to believe that English is threatened by extinction in the U.S.

> *"Rather than serving to integrate immigrants, the bills being proposed in Congress . . . would foster a second class of Americans based on language proficiency."*

Immigrants already understand the importance of learning English. With only limited proficiency in English, even professionally trained immigrants have trouble finding appropriate jobs and find themselves working as convenience store owners, janitors, restaurant workers, garment workers and gardeners. They are exploited by landlords, employers and scam artists and are vulnerable targets for crime. That is why there are long waiting lists for English classes. In Washington, D.C., an estimated 5,000 immigrants were turned away from English as a Second Language classes last year. In New York, the schools now conduct a lottery system to determine enrollment in classes. In Los Angeles, 40 to 50 thousand immigrants are on waiting lists for classes.

For those who are sincere in their desire for more immigrants to learn English, their energies would be put to much better use in supporting increased resources for English training. But, not surprisingly, most of the members of Congress who back English-only laws have also voted this year to slash the bilingual education budget in half and to drastically cut funding for community colleges, the major provider of English classes.

Limiting Immigrants' Rights

Rather than serving to integrate immigrants, the bills being proposed in Congress and in various states would foster a second class of Americans based on language proficiency. The bills would limit the ability of certain Americans to exercise their legal rights and to use the government services for which they pay taxes.

English-only supporters are fond of citing the popularity of these proposals. However, any of the laws and government actions that we condemn today as bigoted and heinous were also popular in their day. The Chinese Exclusion Act and the internment of Japanese Americans during World War II were wildly popular, as were the Alien Land laws which prohibited Japanese immigrant farmers from owning property in 13 states. All of these laws were driven by the same forces that motivate the English-only movement: xenophobia, racism and resentment. It is no accident that these laws will have a disproportionate impact on Asians and Latinos, who have constituted over 80 per cent of this country's immigrants over the past two decades.

Ultimately, English-only bills are outlandishly myopic, for it is far more costly in the long run to deny adequate education and health care to immigrant children—and to deny their parents equal protection under the law or the ability to fully participate in the democratic process—than it is to accommodate Americans at *all* levels of English proficiency.

Imagine an America in which the use of languages other than English were penalized. Public school administrators, teachers, counselors, and nurses would be breaking the law if they provided information to students or parents in any language but English, even if they themselves were fluent in that student's or parent's primary language. At a time when educators are working to get parents more involved in their children's education, these laws would make it impossible for many Asian parents.

Immigrant Asian convenience store owners who have been robbed or assaulted would not be able to receive appropriate police protection, use 911 emergency services, or testify in court in criminal cases. Immigrant small business owners with contract disputes or conflicts with regulatory agencies would be hampered because courts would not be allowed to provide translators.

Moreover, doctors and nurses in public hospitals would be barred from effectively communicating with their patients. Many public health hospitals and clinics already underserve the Asian Pacific American community. All too often, treatment is delayed or denied because a hospital tells the patient they must find their own translator. Immigrant rape victims are often too embarrassed to describe an incident or go through the required physical exam when forced to rely on a son or neighbor to translate for them. Illnesses can be misdiagnosed when doctors rely on translation by untrained friends or volunteers.

> *"Isolating those who cannot fluently speak English will not help to integrate immigrants into our society, nor will it . . . reduce ethnic and racial friction."*

Immigrant workers subjected to discrimination, sexual harassment, unfair labor practices or unsafe working conditions would be unable to report and assist in enforcement of the laws by agencies such as the Equal Employment Opportunity Commission, the Office of Safety and Health Administration or the Department of Labor.

Political candidates would be prohibited from greeting voters in other languages, much less engaging in substantive communications or debates. In addition, election debates and election materials cover complex issues and measures that even native-born English speakers find difficult to understand. In the November 1994 elections, 31 per cent of Chinese American voters polled by the Asian American Legal Defense and Education Fund indicated they used election materials translated into Chinese and 14 per cent of the Chinese American voters polled in San Francisco by the Asian Law Caucus indicated they used such materials. Voting is not only a right, but a responsibility, yet these laws would severely inhibit participation by members of our communities.

The Absurdity of the English-Only Debate

English-only bills are not only extremely divisive, they are absurd in light of the fact that English, like any other modern language, is an ever-evolving amalgamation of words from different languages. (It is estimated that three out of four words in the English dictionary are non-Anglo in origin.) The government will have to set up a new bureaucracy and millions of dollars will be wasted in litigation over which words are English, or whether a government official was allowed to use them.

Isolating those who cannot fluently speak English will not help to integrate immigrants into our society, nor will it, as its proponents naively suggest, reduce ethnic and racial friction. English proficiency has certainly not immunized Jewish Americans from religious bigotry, or African Americans and whites from tension or misunderstanding.

What binds American people together is the shared quest for equality, justice, and freedom—including the freedom to be different. The absurdity of the English-only debate was best illustrated during Senate and House hearings, when both committee chairmen referred to the hope that English-only laws would finally make a reality of the national motto, *E Pluribus Unum*, a Latin phrase meaning "out of many, one."

Ebonics in the Classroom Could Benefit Black Children

by Toni Cook, interviewed by Nanette Asimov

About the author: *Toni Cook, president of the Oakland, California, Board of Education, works at the San Francisco Housing Authority. She is interviewed by Nanette Asimov, a staff writer for the* San Francisco Chronicle.

Toni Cook never expected to be at the center of a national uproar, but she's not intimidated by it. On December 18, 1996, Cook, president of the Oakland Board of Education, inspired her colleagues to pass a resolution recognizing black English—known as ebonics, from *ebony* and *phonics*—as the primary language of the school district's majority African-American population. That decision propelled the wiry 53-year-old woman into a national debate about language, race, and the education of African-American children. Jesse Jackson came out against the resolution, then shifted to enthusiastic support of it. But other prominent African-Americans, such as NAACP [National Association for the Advancement of Colored People] chair Kweisi Mfume, a liberal, and Shelby Steele, a conservative intellectual, oppose the idea of ebonics. Editorial writers and columnists nationwide have weighed in on the school board's action, most with a tone of incredulity and outrage.

The response was, perhaps, inevitable. After all, the school board's resolution did not simply say that teachers need to understand black English in order to help black students speak standard English. It said that ebonics is an "African-language system" that is "genetically based" and that teachers should instruct African-American students "in their primary language": ebonics. Under pressure, the board subsequently qualified the latter two phrases, then deleted them altogether.

A former organizer for Jesse Jackson who was first elected to the school board in 1990, Cook works at the San Francisco Housing Authority. "I'm a little black woman going down the street trying to keep her humility," she says of the controversy. But she's not backing away from the board's resolution, even if the board is. Cook insists that all she cares about is helping black children—and to her, that means talking about ebonics.

Nanette Asimov: You've got about half the country mad at you, don't you?

> **"Communication and language are critical elements to being able to compete."**

Toni Cook: I've sounded a bell that everyone is talking about. Some people are mad. Some are curious. More are becoming anywhere from supportive to understanding.

Were you surprised by the controversy?

I got broadsided. The school board met on this [ebonics resolution] between telling two former colleagues good-bye and going back into closed session on the school superintendent's evaluation. It was 2 A.M. before I got home. So all I'm thinking about is, what kind of illness will I have for my eight o'clock day job? You know—"Just screw it, I'm tired."

Shortly after your school board vote, Richard Riley, the secretary of education, came out against spending federal money on ebonics programs. What was your reaction to that?

Riley—he was as stupid as the rest. He never called us to ask what we were doing. He just read the newspaper. The school board never intended to ask for bilingual funds.

A Response to Low Achievement

How did the resolution come up for a vote?

In September 1996, I asked the superintendent to form a task force that would look at the performance and achievement issues of African-American kids. In the six years I've been on the board, every index of performance and achievement has gone down for African-American kids. And those that you wanted to go down were going up.

Dropout rates? Teen pregnancies?

You name it. Suspensions, expulsions, truancy—all of them.

What about special education for learning-disabled children?

Disproportionately represented. Of the 5,000 and something students in special ed here, 71 percent are African-American. And even there, what you found was that most of the African-American students, who were disproportionately male, were in there for a category called "causing disruption," or something like that.

So they were placed in special ed because of their behavior?

Yes. And the referrals were also beginning to say ". . . because of a language deficiency."

Which was what?

The inability to write or speak standard English. And it wasn't because the teacher was old or racist or didn't live in Oakland or wasn't black. It wasn't any of those simplistic answers. There were both white and black teachers who made the referrals. In every instance, the pattern that the task force found traced back to the inability of students to master the language because they weren't comfortable with it.

Give me an example.

Some kid was cutting up in class, and the teacher wanted to know if his grandmother was home. So it was like, "Rashid, is your grandmother at home?" And the kid said, "Yeah, my grandmother be at home." But the teacher called, and she wasn't. So the teacher said, "Rashid, you said your grandmother is at home." And he said, "She be at home, but she went to go take my mama to work." So not only did he not conjugate the verb *to be* right, he had a different sense of time. The teacher thought "is" meant now, and for the kid it was that his grandmother does not work.

The Importance of Standard English

So you want to teach African-American students standard English?

Yes. Communication and language are critical elements to being able to compete. So if we get the competitive language right, there will be an increase of African-Americans in the college-bound courses.

You seem to be agreeing with your critics that standard English is the way to go.

What I'm saying is, in my village we'd better call it a survival tool. If this is the key to filling out a résumé, getting your next union card, or going to college, then we'd better make darn sure that we've given you the survival tool.

But the resolution says that you're going to give people more money to teach "in ebonics."

We don't have to teach them what they already know. We will train teachers to use ebonics to get the children to understand the difference between what the teachers are trying to teach and what the children are saying, reading, or writing.

Okay. So what did the task force do next?

I gave an overview of what I didn't want. I did not want a report that basically said "racism." I did not want a report that put the burden of problem

> *"We will train teachers to use ebonics to get the children to understand the difference between what the teachers are trying to teach and what the children are saying."*

solving on government. We've got to say to our village, it's about time we took some responsibility. *We're* supposed to educate these kids.

How do you teach a kid who's not listening to you or is shouting across the room or even pulls a weapon on a teacher? These things happen in urban public schools.

Maybe you haven't been given the training and learning tools to know how to communicate. We do have some teachers who have kids sitting on the edge of their seats.

Some teachers are better than others.

But the pattern I began to see was that these teachers knew how to communicate. How to hear the child, correct the child, and make the child feel good about being corrected. These are teachers who have been through [the state's] Standard English Proficiency Program.

> *"[Many] African languages had no verb* to be. *So when a youngster here has difficulty conjugating the verb* to be— *maybe there is some connection there."*

Why wouldn't these kids pick up standard English from television?

Yeah, they're watching television—MTV, The Box. The unfortunate thing is that vulgar language is mostly sung by African-Americans. And that is an element [in this controversy] that has scared people.

Black English

So people don't know what black English really is?

That's right. It's a rhythm style. It's like reading [the nineteenth-century poet] Paul Laurence Dunbar—he writes in ebonics. Maya Angelou writes in a language pattern that is ensconced in culture, that takes on the same rhythmic form, same syntax, and we say yes!

I'm not sure how many kids are talking the way Maya Angelou writes.

The kids take on the same melodious sound.

Ain't *is not melodious.*

Right. That's a no-no. In my day *ain't* was a no-no, and if we said it we were told "are not." But we said it enough, and it became acceptable.

Why don't some black parents teach their children standard English? Is there a resentment of "talking like white folks?"

People say, "You talk like a white girl!"

Right. It's an insult. So how do you overcome that?

A lot of it is about economics—you can't adopt that which you've never been exposed to. Also, I was talking to a lady who said to me, "Do you realize you said 'ax' instead of 'ask'?" And I said, "Yeah, because I'm an African-American."

I have African-American friends who would take great offense at the notion that they would say "ax" because they're black.

Talk long enough and your friends may say "ax." Even though they may have been exposed to the finest training, education, whatever.

You're saying that this is because the language pattern is genetic?

We all know only one definition of that—in the genes. But is not the root of the word *genesis*? It doesn't say in your blood. It says in the beginning! Ancestral! We believe that the language pattern that our young people bring to class is rooted in poverty. But in the beginning there was something else: the African part of me. The linguists say that in the African areas from which most of the slaves were taken, the African languages had no verb *to be*. So when a youngster here has difficulty conjugating the verb *to be*—maybe there is some connection there.

My grandparents didn't speak any English, and I can conjugate to be.

There cannot be comparisons. You were always allowed to grope with the new language. It was not illegal for your grandmother, wherever she came from, to learn how to read, write, and speak in English. Up until 1865, for my great granddaddy it was illegal. So you self-taught. Understand where I'm coming from: I am teaching myself another language.

You apply this to all African-Americans?

We all sprang from that. After 1865, the bulk of the [black] population was still in the South. The irony is, when we were in a segregated system those old black teachers knew how to take [potential black leaders such as] Andy Young and make sure that he was comfortable speaking standard English.

You're talking about class.

Those who were oppressed and kept down, they held on to the old language. You could hear it more. If the truth be known, even in black communities today it's all about class.

You came from a family of educators, including your grandparents. But you never spoke ebonics, did you?

> **"Why aren't we as mad about the products of our public schools as we are at this resolution [to recognize black English]?"**

But I heard it, from relatives. My family had southern roots.

What's the connection between your mother's being a linguist and your own recognition of ebonics?

My mom was a linguist with the National Security Agency. It was she who told me the story that the more kids adopt standard English, white folk's English, the more they begin to be ashamed of their parents. My mom always reminded us that we stand on the backs of others—you never had the right to snub your nose at anybody based on speech patterns. She mastered the "twoness" of language. So when the bridge club was coming over, you heard a slight alteration of language style.

Focusing on the Right Thing

How did you get into politics?

My grandmother on my father's side was in the NAACP. But I'm from the black power era. I was at UCLA. I became very out front in the Black Student Union, coming to the defense of [black activist] Angela Davis, out front on student government, in the thick of the '60s. We were championing equity, black studies—education was the key to freedom.

Now you have this resolution to help today's students. I've got a copy of it, but the Oakland schools won't give it out in press packets or put it on the Web site. Why not?

I honestly don't know why they won't do it. I think they should. I don't know what the strategy is. I'm not ashamed of the resolution. If you ask me for it, I'll give it to you.

Then why has the school board issued several clarifications about it?

It obviously needs clarification. Everyone is confused.

What good is a resolution that isn't clear?

Most of the resolutions we adopt aren't clear.

Maybe you should change your style.

We ain't changing nothing. Resolutions are not for Joe Blow Public. Resolutions are a legislative means from the hallowed walls of school boards in which you use legalese and educationese to move a program or policy. They are not written for my next-door neighbor to understand.

This resolution contains nine "whereas" clauses, six "be it resolved" clauses, typographical errors, run-on sentences, and questionable facts—not to mention phrases that have angered blacks and whites alike.

So what? If you watered it down and made it grammatically correct, that's not my thing. That's not going to do anything for what I'm focused on, which is raising the performance of African-American students.

While, apparently, making everyone in America mad.

Well, it's about time we got mad—about the education of our kids. I don't mean to be simple, but why aren't we as mad about the products of our public schools as we are at this resolution? Until this came along, nobody gave a shit.

It's just that your resolution seems to be getting in the way of the message. After reading the phrase about how ebonics is "genetically based," an African-American attorney told me, "The grand wizard of the Ku Klux Klan couldn't have put it any better."

I guess my response would be that the grand wizard of the KKK couldn't be any more satisfied, given the performance of our kids.

But I'll tell you what. You can beat the shit out of me over a poor language choice if I can get something out of you for these kids. If I can get you to work for these kids—to write a letter, go to a classroom, take a kid to work. We've got kids who've never been across the bridge to see San Francisco.

We have not had a good conversation about education and African-American children since *Brown v. Board of Education* in 1954, when it was being talked about in everybody's house. So if we accomplish that goal, as pissed off as everyone may be, I think we'll be focusing on the right thing—our kids.

Ebonics in the Classroom Harms Black Children

by Jacob Heilbrunn

About the author: *Jacob Heilbrunn is an associate editor of the* New Republic, *a weekly journal of opinion.*

On December 18, 1996, the Oakland school board unanimously approved a two-page resolution declaring black English a formal language. The resolution stated that the district's 28,000 African American students are bilingual and need to be taught in their mother tongue: Ebonics. "African Language Systems," the resolution noted, "are genetically based and not a dialect of English." After the vote, Board Director Toni Cook said: "I think we made a hell of a good beginning. What we did was go offensive and quit saying there's something wrong with a majority of the children."

A chorus of voices quickly denounced the Oakland school board. On NBC's "Meet the Press," Jesse Jackson said, "This is an unacceptable surrender, borderlining on disgrace. It's teaching down to our children." In a December 24 editorial, *The New York Times* decried "LINGUISTIC CONFUSION." Secretary of Education Richard Riley declared that using federal funds for "black English or Ebonics is not permitted."

Ebonics Programs Already Exist

In all the uproar, however, one detail is being overlooked: when the Oakland school board announced Ebonics was the "primary language" of African Americans, it was simply codifying accepted practice. Ebonics programs have for years been an official and widespread part of the education of black children in California. What the Oakland school board did may be appalling, but it was in no way novel. Ebonics programs have been a feature of California schools attended by black students since 1989, when Thomas Payzant, then superintendent of schools in San Diego and later an assistant education secretary under Bill Clinton, approved the creation of four pilot schools that taught Ebonics. Payzant's test program has since been expanded to include all San Diego schools. The Pomona Unified School District endorses the teaching of Ebonics. In the Los Angeles Unified School District, Noma LeMoine, who is writing a text book of Ebonics and has instructed over 2,000 teachers, is director of L.A.'s Ebonics program. LeMoine's Ebonics program is called the Language Development Program for African American students; it receives $3 million a year from the L.A. School District, is used at thirty-one schools, and reaches around 25,000 students. In the San Francisco Bay area, Oakland already has programs in twenty-six schools that train teachers to understand black English; and Wade W. Nobles runs a College of Ethnic Studies on the San Francisco State University campus that trains teachers from around California in Ebonics epistemology. The methods used in all of these programs are outlined in Evelyn Baker Dandy's 1991 *Black Communications:* they include using "call-response" techniques, in which the OnT (time) method encourages students to praise the teacher for being timely in his or her recitation by affirming "shon-uff," "ooooo-weeee!"; and favors group "mumble reading" so as to avoid embarrassing individual children about pronunciation.

Ebonics is not just a bit of amateur crackpotism. It is professional crackpotism, well within the pedagogical mainstream. And Ebonics was not schemed up by a few opportunistic, marginal pols in a desperately poor city but stems from decades of scholarship conducted at America's most distinguished universities. The Oakland School District can point to a rich corpus of academic work on which to base its decision.

The linguist Robert L. Williams coined the term in his 1975 book *Ebonics: the true language of Black folks* by combining the words ebony and phonics. Williams and his fellow Ebonologists—who include John Baugh, John R. Rickford, Peter Sells and Tom Wasow of the Stanford University linguistics department, William Labov of the University of Pennsylvania, Ralph Fasold of Georgetown University, Walt Wolfram of North Carolina State University, Geneva Smitherman of Michigan State University, Lisa Green of the University of Texas at Austin and Orlando Taylor of Howard University, who is a consultant to the Oakland school board—trace the origins of Ebonics to African languages such as Yoruba, Ewe, Fula, Igbo and Mandinka. The consensus among these linguists is that black English is a legitimate linguistic system with a highly complex grammar and syntax that can be identified as coming out of Africa and the Caribbean.

> *"Ebonics programs have for years been an official and widespread part of the education of black children in California."*

Over the past decade, as these theories of African culture have moved from the university into the public school, the consequences have been profound. By providing Ebonics with a patina of legitimacy, these scholars have bolstered the efforts of a number of black educators to utilize what are viewed as the skills of "rap" and "playin' the dozens" (black male verbal confrontation) in the class-room. The purveyors of Ebonics have picked up enough academic argot to maintain that, since all reality is socially constructed, there is no such thing as a "good" or a "bad" version of English. On the contrary, demands that black children conform to white bourgeois notions of "good" English amount to an attempt to destroy African American identity and culture.

The Foundations of Ebonics

The historical work that laid the foundations for Ebonics began in the 1960s. The key issue was, and remains, whether Africans acquired the English of other groups they came into contact with, or whether an African- and Caribbean-based black English emerged among the slaves. In other words, did the slaves adapt the language of the oppressor or did they outwit him by creating their own language based on their own traditions? The contemporary political implications are clear enough.

Until the 1960s, the first view was dominant: black Americans learned their English from the English. In his still-standard 1925 two-volume work *English Language in America,* the linguist George Philip Krapp ascribed black English to Old English: "As the Negroes imported into America came from many unrelated tribes . . . it is reasonably safe to say that not a single detail of Negro pronunciation or Negro syntax can be proved to have any other than an English origin." Black English was seen as an embarrassing relic of

> *"Ebonics is not just a bit of amateur crackpotism. It is professional crackpotism."*

the past, and linguists devised remedial programs to correct it.

With the rise of Black Power, a new generation of linguists who might be called "creolists" set about overturning the received wisdom. In 1967, William Stewart asserted that the pidgin English slaves had learned on the west African coast evolved into its own language on Caribbean and American soil: "this form of language," wrote Stewart, "became so well established as the principal medium of communication between Negro slaves in the British colonies that it was passed on as a creole language to succeeding generations of the New World Negroes, for whom it was their native tongue."

The idea is that a common "bridge-language" had developed in eighteenth-century coastal west Africa itself—between languages such as Ewe, Twi, Mende, Mandingo, Igbo, Nupe, Mossi and Kanuri. Since slaves were isolated when brought to America, they maintained this indigenous language to create a secret code behind the backs of their masters. "Needless to say, didn't nobody sit down and decide, consciously and deliberately," wrote Geneva Smitherman of Michigan State in her 1977 *Talkin and Testifyin,* "that this was the way it was gon be—languages, pidgins, creoles, dialects was all like Topsy: they jes grew." The language that emerged from pidgin is known among linguists as Creole.

Though it adopted English words, it retained the structure of west African languages. Hence the special patterns of Ebonics.

Features of Black English

Some of the west African features governing black English cited by Smitherman are: repetition of noun subject with pronoun—"My father, he work there"—no tense indicated in verb—"I know it good when he ask me"—and no consonant pairs—"jus" for "just" and "men" for "mend." The linguist John R. Rickford, who was born in Guyana and who teaches a course at Stanford University titled "African-American Vernacular English," agrees. According to Rickford, "I found that people are using as a habitual marker 'does' and 'does be' which are precisely forms used in the Caribbean. People would say, 'He does be sick,' 'He does be walkin.' A lot of times it was highly reduced. 'He be sick. He be walkin.' I hypothesized a series of reductions starting with 'does be,' then losing 'be,' then reinterpreting 'be.' What's crucial, though, is I started to look at rules that allow 'does' to be lost. You want to get from 'does be' to rules for the reduction of 'does.' All over Creole you find a rule that can delete 'be.' 'I'm a do it.' This is far more correct than people realize who think this is lazy slang."

One of the first attempts to link "Creole" scholarship with the teaching of African American children came in a special June 1979 issue of the *Journal of Black Studies.* The issue was devoted to "Ebonics (Black English): Implications For Education." The editor of the journal then and now is Temple University professor Molefi Kete Asante, one of America's leading, and most controversial, Afrocentrists. In one article, "Ebonics: A Legitimate System of Oral Communication," Jean Wofford complained that "black children continue to be subjected to teachers who label the Ebonics system as bad, substandard, incorrect, impoverished, deprived, and nonlanguage." In fact, the ability of black children to switch back and forth between language "suggests that their total linguistic resources are greater than that of monolingual white children."

That same year, a group of black Michigan parents sued the local school district in *Martin Luther King Jr. Elementary School Children* v. *Ann Arbor School District Board* to have the right to have their children educated in Ebonics. In a limited decision, U.S. District Court Judge Charles W. Joiner relied on the testimony of scholars such as Geneva Smitherman

> *"The purveyors of Ebonics . . . maintain that, since all reality is socially constructed, there is no such thing as a 'good' or a 'bad' version of English."*

and William Labov on the Creole origins of black English to rule in favor of the parents. Joiner ordered Ann Arbor to institute special language programs for black students.

But Ebonics did not really take off until the late 1980s, when black parents saw that new waves of immigrants were receiving federal funds for bilingual language education. "Black parents feel that the schools validate the language of the Cuban, Puerto Rican and Mexican students," Gwendolyn Cooke, director of Urban Services at the National Association of Secondary School Principals, said in the December 23, 1996, *Chicago Tribune.* "They wonder: Why can't the schools apply the same teaching methods to the black child?"

> *"There is no evidence that Ebonics has improved the English of black students."*

California, as so often is the case, became the testing ground. Seeking to address the problem of San Diego black students' chronically poor academic performance, Thomas Payzant turned to Agin Shaheed, an instructor at the Timbuktu Learning Academy at San Diego's Fulton Elementary School, one of Payzant's original pilot schools. Shaheed says that in eight years the program has become institutionalized. "We're right on the cutting edge," Shaheed says, "which has been to introduce to schools the idea that African American students do come with a home culture orientation to a majority culture, European American. The Ebonics is that there is a west African dialect that causes them to speak in a way that makes English almost a second language." The aim of the program is to boost the "self-validation" of students. To this end, Ebonics-trained teachers stress what is called the oral tradition of call-response. The students listen to poems and then give each other "skin" or respond in slang to the teacher. If they agree with the speaker, this is called "cosigning."

The argument of Ebonics advocates is that their unique programs will permit black children to excel at what critics of Ebonics say they want black children to learn: regular English. By reading and conversing in both, Ebonologists say, they will become bilingual in both Ebonics and "standard" English. This assertion has already prompted previous critics of Ebonics such as Jesse Jackson to beat a retreat. Even a cursory look at how Ebonics actually is being taught, however, suggests that this rationale cannot be sustained. As Ebonics programs are administered, they seem to be little more than a means to allow black youngsters to pass through the school system without ever mastering the basics of grammar, spelling and punctuation. Consider San Diego. "At our school," says Agin Shaheed, "if a writing assignment is handed in, written in the home language, the teacher will say, 'I like this. This is good. How would it look otherwise?' They will not say, 'This is incorrect.'"

And Shaheen's views do not seem particularly unusual in the California system. In Los Angeles, where LeMoine is running the Ebonics program, teachers apparently employ Ebonics not merely as a bridge to English, but teach it as a language in its own right. According to the February 16, 1995, *Los Angeles Times,* in Pomona at the Roosevelt Elementary School, teacher Vicky Rasshan explained to her fifth-graders that as slaves "picked up English, it blended with their African languages, creating Ebonics."

Ebonics-trained teachers rely on books such as The *Hundred Penny Box* (published by Scholastic), which is written in dialect: "The ice cream be melted fore you get home." Then the students discuss whether black English dialect or standard English dialect is superior.

Ebonics Does Not Work

There is no evidence that Ebonics has improved the English of black students. In San Diego, the effects of Ebonics teaching on standardized test scores have, as Shaheed reluctantly put it, been "spotty." Grades are up, he notes. But on what criteria? In Los Angeles, where the school district spends considerable sums on Ebonics, the latest Comprehensive Test of Basic Skills showed, according to the December 23, 1996, *Sacramento Bee,* that scores at the Ebonics-infused Normandie Elementary School have, in fact, dropped in reading and language skills.

But Ebonics continues to gain legitimacy. In December 1996 in Washington, the nation's arbiters of language, the members of The Modern Language Association, met for their annual conference. In a December 28, 1996, session on the "'I' Construction in African American Discourse" William Cook of Dartmouth made a stirring case for what might be called the classical view: he used the poetry of the freed slave Phyllis Wheatley to show how her love of Roman and Greek literature allowed her to transcend ephemeral concerns about race, and the limitations imposed upon her by slavery, to write poems such as "To Maecenas." But the classicist Cook cut a lonely figure. Far more representative of the panelists was English professor Demetrice A. Worley of Bradley University, who veered between offering poems and anecdotes about herself and reciting Swahili. "My ancestors are forcing me to make new sounds," Worley cried out. New sounds for the votaries of Ebonics as they enslave a new generation in the chains of ignorance.

> *"In Los Angeles, . . . scores at the Ebonics-infused Normandie Elementary School have, in fact, dropped in reading and language skills."*

A Multiracial Census Category Would Be Beneficial

by Amitai Etzioni

About the author: *Amitai Etzioni, a professor at George Washington University, is the founder and director of the Communitarian Network.*

In 1990, the Census Bureau offered Americans the choice of 16 racial categories. The main groupings were white and black, which 92 percent of the population chose. The remaining categories were Native American, Aleut and Eskimo, 10 variations of Asian and Pacific Islanders, and "Other." Some 9.8 million Americans, or 4 percent of the total population, chose "Other" rather than one of the established mono-racial categories—compared with fewer than 1 million in 1970.

This number will continue to expand. Since 1970, the number of mixed-race children in the United States has quadrupled to reach the 2 million mark. And there are six times as many intermarriages today as there were in 1960. Indeed, some sociologists predict that, even within a generation, Americans will begin to look more like Hawaii's blended racial mix.

It's time to acknowledge the increasing number of multiracial Americans—not only because doing so gives us a more accurate portrait of the population, but also because it will help to break down the racial barriers that now divide this country. And the place to recognize these new All-Americans is with the next census in the year 2000. . . .

Many people feel they don't belong in one of the existing mono-racial categories. Some simply reject the notion of being categorized. Others, especially Hispanics, are viewed as members of one race but wish to be considered as members of another, or change their minds as to which race they belong to over their lifetime. The great variation in skin color and other racial features within all racial groups makes the question of who is "in" versus who is "out" far more

Reprinted from Amitai Etzioni, "The Place of Race in the Census," Commentary, *Washington Post National Weekly Edition*, June 16–22, 1997, by permission of the author.

flexible than it sometimes seems. For example, many Hispanics have dark skin but do not consider themselves black, just as many light-skinned African Americans do not wish to pass as white.

The "Other" Category

The "Other" category, which many of these people chose, has never been fully recognized as an independent grouping. When the Census Bureau released its 1990 data for use by the government, it "modified" the figures by eliminating the "Other" category and reclassifying its members according to the monoracial categories by a process known as "hot-decking," a standard means of imputing missing data in surveys. The Census Bureau argues that it allowed for better comparisons with past data, when the "Other" category did not exist. But this does not explain why government agencies that deal with the distribution of funds by racial categories chose to use the modified data rather than the original, which was also available.

The "Other" category is not satisfactory, and dropping the whole social construction of race does not seem to be in the cards, however persuasive the arguments for a colorblind society are. So why not introduce a new "multiracial" category?

Objections to the Multiracial Category

The very idea infuriates some leaders of the African American community. Ibrahim K. Sundiata, chairman of the African and Afro-American Studies Department at Brandeis University argues that it reflects a drive to undermine black solidarity. He fears that in cities where blacks now hold majorities, the new category will divide them and undermine their dominance. But his argument overlooks the fact that nobody will be forced to give up their racial allegiances; citizens will still be free to check the box of their choice, even if the new category is added.

African American leaders also object to a multiracial category because race data is used to enforce civil-rights legislation in employment, voting rights, housing and mortgage lending, health-care services and educational opportunities. They worry that the category could decrease the number of blacks in the nation's official statistics, and thus undermine efforts to enforce anti-discrimination statutes, as well as undercutting numerous social programs based on racial quotas.

> *"Since 1970, the number of mixed-race children in the United States has quadrupled to reach the 2 million mark."*

It's a concern that Democratic Rep. Carrie Meek of Florida voiced clearly during congressional hearings early in 1997: "I understand how Tiger Woods and the rest of them [mixed-race Americans] feel. But no matter how they feel from a personal standpoint, we're thinking about the census and reporting accuracy. . . . The multiracial category would cloud the count of discrete minorities who are assigned to a lower track in public schools . . . kept out of certain occupations and whose progress toward seniority or promotion has been skewered . . . multiracial categories will reduce the level of political representation for minorities."

Meek is probably correct in predicting that if large numbers of Americans remove themselves from recognized minority categories in favor of a multiracial category, there would be some loss of public funds, set-asides in federal contracts and affirmative-action jobs for certain groups. But the

> *"Introducing a multiracial category would help soften the racial lines that now divide America by making them more like transitory economic differences."*

social costs of encouraging people to define themselves by their race are even greater. And the political gimmick of assigning people to a racial category that they have avoided by choosing "Other" is downright dishonest.

Softening Racial Lines

In addition, there are strong sociological reasons to favor the creation of a multiracial category in the census, as well as abandoning the practice of modifying racial numbers.

Introducing a multiracial category would help soften the racial lines that now divide America by making them more like transitory economic differences rather than harsh, immutable caste lines. Sociologists have long observed that a major reason the United States experiences few confrontations along lines of class is that people in this country believe they can move from one economic stratum to another—and regularly do so. For instance, workers become foremen, and foremen become small businessmen, who are considered middle-class. There are no sharp class demarcation lines here, based on heredity, as there are in Britain. In the United States, many manual workers consider themselves middle-class, dress up to go to work, with their tools and lunches in their briefcases.

But confrontations do occur along racial lines in America because color lines currently seem rather rigid: Many members of one racial group simply couldn't imagine belonging to another.

If the new category is adopted and, if more and more Americans choose it in future decades, it will help make America look more like Hawaii, where races mix freely, and less like India where castes still divide the population sharply. And the blurring of racial lines will encourage greater social cohesiveness overall.

Perhaps how one marks a tiny box on the census form is between oneself and the keepers of statistics. But, if the multiracial concept becomes part of the census—the nation's main source of statistics—it will soon break out and enter the social vocabulary.

Early indications that the country is ready for more widespread changes in our social categories and social thinking is supported by the fact that in some states these processes have already begun to unfold. In California, there is an Association for Multi-Ethnic Americans, and several states have introduced legislation to create a multiracial category on school and college application forms. At least two states, Georgia and Indiana, have already required government agencies to use the multiracial category.

At stake is the question of what kind of America we envision for the future. Some imagine a blur of racial distinctions, with Americans constituting some kind of new hybrid race. In the fall of 1993, *Time* magazine ran a cover story on the subject, featuring a computer composite of a future American incorporating characteristics of several races—a new, rather handsome breed with almond-shaped eyes, straight, dark hair and honey-colored skin.

That vision is often confronted by those who are keen to maintain strict racial lines and oppose intermarriage (especially between white men and black women), in order to maintain the races as separate "nations." (The term nation is significant because it indicates a high level of tribalism.) In a world full of interracial strife, this attitude, however understandable it is as a response to racial prejudice and discrimination, is troubling. I'd rather see a situation in which those who seek to uphold their separate group identities will do so (ideally viewing themselves and being seen as subgroups of a more encompassing community rather than as separate nations), but those who

> *"If the multiracial concept becomes part of the census—the nation's main source of statistics—it will soon break out and enter the social vocabulary."*

wish to redefine themselves will be able to do so, gradually creating an ever larger group that is free from racial categorization.

If a multiracial category is included in Census 2000, in the future we might think of adding one more category, that of "multi-ethnic" origin, which most Americans might wish to check. Then we would have recognized the full importance of my favorite African American saying: We came in many ships, but we now ride in the same boat.

A Multiracial Census Category Would Not Benefit Mixed-Race People

by Kenya Mayfield

About the author: *Kenya Mayfield is a freelance writer.*

Not so long ago, life for most mixed-race individuals was a painful experience of second-guessing one's "true" identity. In a society constructed of opposing sides in which one is either "one (of us)" or the "other," it was virtually impossible to happily exist betwixt and between categories. Further, if G.W.F. Hegel is correct and one's identity is determined by one's interaction with others, it would seem very difficult for a "mixed" person to gain a secure sense of self when he or she is constantly forced to choose to identify with one race over another. By doing so, the mixed person is asked to deny his biological reality.

Today, however, life for mixed-race people is changing, slowly but surely. The significant increase in the number of interracial sexual relations and mixed-race births has required that we rethink traditional notions of race. Some key issues include: racial classification on census forms, participation in identity politics, and mixed-race identity as a negation of the entire presupposition that race has any real substantive meaning at all.

Rather than rehashing old arguments about race, here are new possibilities and arguments. My focus is on the positive realities of being mixed.

A Racially Mixed Heritage

I am the only child in my family. My father is an American of Scottish and English descent—born and raised in Oklahoma. My mother is an American of predominantly African descent as well as Cherokee. Her parents were both Evangelical ministers in Texas, but now she is a devout Presbyterian living in Oklahoma City. My parents were divorced when I was two but have remained very good friends. My mother remarried my father's best friend (who is Irish),

Reprinted from Kenya Mayfield, "Mixed-Race: The Next Generation," *Interrace*, January 1996, by permission of *Interrace*.

yet all three of my parents remained such good friends that they were partners in a small business for quite some time. My father has been dating a woman, who is black, for nearly six years.

Growing up, I attended public schools that were predominantly comprised of black students and attended a Presbyterian church that is predominantly comprised of white worshippers. Currently, I attend an Ivy League university and study social anthropology. My boyfriend of three years is Jewish.

When I was younger, my father involved me in many cultural events. He runs an agency that addresses social topics from DWIs to alcoholic women and their children, to juvenile delinquents, to therapeutic foster care, and finally to the crises among young black men. All three of my parents are avid Democrats and my mother is an administrator at the Supreme Court of Oklahoma. My stepfather is active in our church and works for the State Department of Agriculture.

All of my parents are well-educated and are very supportive of my own academic pursuits.

Of course, I am not suggesting that my life is by any means typical of that of mixed-race people in general. I offer this sketch to explain my overly optimistic and relentlessly stubborn views on both interracial issues and racial issues in general.

> *"I have no desire to identify politically with any group nor to validate my ethnicity."*

As a cultural product of the United States, I have been conditioned to assert myself as an individual in just about every aspect of my life. Traditionally, such assertions excluded race; however, the chance to exert one's choice in matter of race is arising.

The Proposed Multiracial Category

The U.S. census team is considering adding a "multiracial" category to the 2000 census. This possibility has been introduced in large part to respond to complaints that the previous census forms did not adequately represent the population of the United States. Since this proposal, several camps offering very different opinions have surfaced. One such camp claims that such a category is essential because it would provide representation for the multitude of Americans who do not claim one race. Further, it is believed that this new category would in effect validate mixed-race people, politically and socially.

However, some political activists are concerned that a "multiracial" category would result in the shrinking of the African American community by reclassifying individuals who were formerly considered part of the black population as members of a new mixed-race people. Consequently, social and political programs designed to advance black people would diminish because the size of that community would technically be smaller. This new category can thus be understood as an effort to further subjugate blacks by dividing the population.

Many mixed-race people question their identity throughout their lives, wrestling with feelings of alienation from one group and feelings of unfamiliarity with another.

For those in favor of the "multiracial" category, the identity of mixed-race individuals becomes, in many respects, less ambiguous through the creation of such a category.

"Us," "Them," or "Other"?

Personally, I have no desire to identify politically with any group nor to validate my ethnicity. My disdain for a "multiracial" category is inspired by a dogged attempt to maintain my own position of ambiguity within society. Though the dynamics of racial classification have changed within the last few decades, these dynamics still demand that individuals have specific, immutable characteristics by which their place in society can be determined.

Both blacks and whites are more than eager to pigeon-hole me into one category or another. However, their interest in my identity is, most often, not rooted in their concern for my well-being, but their own need to construct their social relationships. In other words, in order to determine whether I am an "us" or a "them," my identity cannot be ambiguous. When my mother demanded that my primary and secondary school records list my race as "Black/White/Native American" rather than just "Black," she was met with resistance and even hostility. Likewise, my own refusal to be coerced or bullied by other students into claiming one group over another has been met with blatant hostility and resentment.

Most of this resentment has come from black students, but this is not to say that whites have accepted my ambiguity with ease. On the contrary. When asked "what are you?" I have

> *"If we refuse to be lumped into one 'multiracial' category . . . others will grow very weary of trying to accurately label us at all."*

always responded by reciting my ethnic make-up in glorious detail. However, it seems that despite my description, I have already been cast into the "other" category. For whites, my exact composition is of trivial interest but of no real consequence—despite having a father who is white, I am black. For the most part, whites have removed themselves entirely from the racial discourse. Indeed, identity questions for mixed-race people are perceived by whites as a dilemma between blacks and other mixed-race people. I am an anomaly, not a threat.

Embracing Ambiguity

I suggest a new way of thinking for the next generation of mixed individuals. I propose that we all REFUSE to relinquish our position of racial ambiguity. Others will continue to pigeon-hole us, but with the support of family, friends and each other, I am convinced the outcome will be far more significant than if we adopt a "single-race" or "multiracial" identity. If enough of us refuse to identify with established racial classifications, the "social reality" will be forced to change.

In an interview, golfer Tiger Woods commented that he refuses to claim only one race. Woods' father is African American and his mother is Thai. Rightly so, Woods is unwilling to negate any part of his family to accommodate others. People who ask "what are you *really*?" acknowledge the ambiguity of mixed-race lineage. Similarly, if we refuse to be lumped into one "multiracial" category, despite the dramatically different composition among us, others will grow very weary of trying to accurately label us at all. Perhaps through this frustration people will finally recognize that race is completely irrelevant as a divider of individuals.

Forget for a moment my desire for universal abandonment of racial categories. Embracing ambiguity offers a great deal to individuals as well. Rather than being restricted to one world, racial ambiguity is a license to "travel playfully" through many worlds. For instance, if someone challenges my authority to express myself as a "black" woman, I can respond by claiming that the black experience is not monolithic. Depending on socioeconomic status, education, and upbringing, no two African Americans have the same experience. I have no desire to deny my blackness. To deny my blackness is to deny my mother, my grandparents, my aunts and uncles, and cousins who have undoubtedly contributed to the person that I am. Likewise, to deny that I am also white, is to deny my father, my grandparents, my aunts and uncles and my cousins who have supported me every day throughout my life.

Indeed, I have no need to deny any part of my family to "fit in." Further, this ambiguity has provided me with a wonderful sense of empowerment concerning my identity. My identity is constantly being defined by everything other than my perceived race.

So, while I (and hopefully others) continue to cling to this ambiguity in hopes of negating racial classifications altogether, I cannot reasonably support a "multiracial" category. Though I have been endowed with various ethnicities, for the most part, society presumes I am black. For instance, Tiger Woods is widely known as a "black" golfer despite his personal identity. And that will not change with the inclusion of a "multiracial" category. Indeed, I have felt the eyes follow me as I proceed through my all-white church or as I walk with my white boyfriend. That unique sense of isolation among many people is not alien to me at all. However, the environment in which I grew up was full of unquestioning love and respect. And I

> *"I . . . continue to cling to [racial] ambiguity in hopes of negating racial classifications altogether."*

have always presumed that I have the best of both worlds. I, and others like me, represent the harmony that can be achieved through a combination of many groups, and it is for this reason that I refuse to identify with only one race. I would like to be a conduit through which racial discourse travels. Too often, the discussion of race is not about "us" and "them," but about "us" and more of "us."

Can "Race" Be Debunked?

But what about the eventual debunking of "race" altogether? Clearly, there are racial inequities in this country, and it would be a mistake to "sweep them under the carpet" by suddenly removing the word "race" from our vocabulary. How then can we fight these problems without perpetuating what we are trying to combat? For mixed-race people, this offers a particular challenge.

Recently, I applied for a minority summer fellowship program. On the application form, I had to indicate my ethnicity by checking a box. As is my standard practice to such demands, I began to mark the boxes for "black," "Native American," and "white." In this case, however, there was no "white" box to check. Since there was an "other" category, I wrote in "English" and "Scottish," in addition to marking the other boxes. The next day, I turned in the application and the woman in charge informed me that I would be dropped from the applicant pool if the "English" and "Scottish" remained on my application. After I protested, she responded flatly, "well honey, we're all mixed with something." This condescending attitude is typical of "single-race" people when discussing mixed-race issues. Such comments also indicate how pervasive the "one-drop" rule really is. Despite the fact that my father is white, and *especially* because by mother is predominantly black, I am nothing other than black to society-at-large.

> *"Mixed-race people must think very carefully about the repercussions of a 'multiracial' category."*

Mixed-race people must think very carefully about the repercussions of a "multiracial" category. It is not so simple to identify as "multiracial" in every instance. Our ambiguity allows us to "change" our identity. Though our long-term goal is to eradicate racial classifications, there should never be a time when racial inequities are dismissed or ignored. In the case of the fellowship I applied for, I decided that the goal of the program was to diversify the pool of students entering graduate schools and teaching positions, so I agreed to the terms of the application. The opportunities provided by the program outweighed any detriment to my long-term goal. The program will allow me to have a greater influence on this issue than if I had held out, and lost this opportunity for advancement. Such careful reasoning for specific instances is a realistic and effective way to deal with short-term dilemmas.

The tone of this analysis has been very optimistic. The changing dynamics within the social atmosphere of this country dictates that new narratives be heard and read about what it means to grow up mixed-race in America.

Chapter 4

How Are Changing Racial Demographics Affecting America?

America's Changing Racial Demographics: An Overview

by Steven A. Holmes

About the author: *Steven A. Holmes is a staff writer for the* New York Times.

Fueled by immigration and higher birth rates among Hispanic women, the United States is undergoing a profound demographic shift, and by the middle of the twenty-first century only about half of the population will be non-Hispanic whites, the Census Bureau predicted in March 1996.

By 2050, the bureau said, immigration patterns and differences in birth rates, combined with an overall slowdown in growth of the country's population, will produce a United States in which 53 percent of the people will be non-Hispanic whites, down from 74 percent in the mid-1990s.

In contrast, Hispanic people will make up 24.5 percent of the population, up from the current 10.2 percent, and Asians will make up 8.2 percent, an increase from the current 3.3 percent. The percentage of the black population will remain relatively stable, rising to about 13.6 percent by the year 2050 from the current 12 percent.

The population as a whole will rise to about 394 million from 262 million, an increase of 50 percent, the bureau said. Even with that increase, it added, the country would be going through some of the most sluggish population growth in its history.

A Dramatic Ethnic Shift

Overall, the report suggests that the United States is experiencing one of the most dramatic shifts in its racial and ethnic makeup since the trade in slaves transformed the racial composition of the South and the waves of immigration from Eastern and Southern Europe in the late 19th and early 20th centuries gave an ethnic flavor to industrialized urban areas of the Northeast and Midwest.

"The world is not going to be the same in 30 years as it is now," said Gregory Spencer, director of the Population Projections Branch at the bureau. To put the growth rates of the Asian and Hispanic population in perspective, the report noted that the two groups were expected to have annual growth rates of 2 percent to the year 2030. In comparison, even at the zenith of the Baby Boom, the country as a whole never grew by 2 percent a year.

The report, "Population Projections of the United States by Age, Sex, Race and Hispanic Origin: 1995 to 2050," noted that its projections were simply projections. Changes in legislation regarding immigration, changes in fertility rates, and breakthroughs in medical care that could extend life expectancy could alter future estimates.

> *"[Anti-immigration organizations] argue that immigration should be curbed because the country is approaching its limit in terms of a manageable population."*

Though the United States is the fastest-growing country in the industrialized world, the report indicated that the nation was about to embark on a sharp slowdown in the rate of its population increases. Indeed, the report said that after 2025, the United States would grow at a slower rate than any time in its history, mainly because of declining birth rates and an increased number of deaths as the population ages.

But with that slowdown will come more diversity, a phenomenon that will present a host of new economic, business, and social issues. For example, the report noted that by the year 2030, the non-Hispanic white population would make up less than half of the people under the age of 18, but three-fourths of those over 65.

Given this, questions of the mix of tax revenues distributed to public education or Social Security or Medicare could easily take on a racial and ethnic tinge.

"You might have somewhat poorer Hispanics being asked to pay for the benefits of relatively well-off white Baby Boomers," said William H. Frey, a research scientist with the Population Studies Center at the University of Michigan. "It's not clear what the political dynamic of that will be. It may not just be the boomers versus the busters."

The Debate over Immigration

The Census Bureau report is likely to fuel the debate over immigration.

The report's population-growth projections are, in part, based on an annual net increase in immigrants—both legal and illegal—of 820,000. Both the Clinton Administration and Republican sponsors of bills being debated in Congress support changes in the immigration law that would reduce legal immigration by about one-third. Leaders of both parties advocate vigorous efforts against illegal immigration.

Much of the debate has focused on whether immigrants take jobs from unemployed citizens but its subtext concerns population growth in general and ethnic diversity in particular.

Organizations such as the Carrying Capacity Network and Negative Population Growth and the Federation for American Immigration Reform argue that immigration should be curbed because the country is approaching its limit in terms of a manageable population.

Dan Stein, executive director of the federation group, said: "The most important part of the story is that this is happening and no one has asked the country is this what we want. Do we really want another 100 million people?"

For their part, pro-immigration organizations say the country can accommodate a higher population with little difficulty. They say they fear their opponents are worried not about the number of added residents, but rather their ethnic backgrounds. "We are all against illegal immigration," said Lisa Navarete, a spokeswoman for the National Council of La Raza, a Hispanic civil rights group.

"And when it comes to legal immigration, we are not being flooded with people."

> *"[Pro-immigration organizations] fear their opponents are worried not about the number of added residents, but rather their ethnic backgrounds."*

The Census Bureau reports indicate that the number of births to non-Hispanic whites is expected to drop throughout the rest of the 1990s and begin a slow rise in the twenty-first century. In contrast, births to women of Hispanic and Asian descent are projected to more than triple by the year 2050.

In addition to higher birth rates, the median age for these groups is younger than for non-Hispanic whites and, as a result, they have more women of childbearing age. Cultural mores relating to family size also come into play. For example, the fertility rate of Hispanic-American women born in Mexico is 147 births per 1,000 women, much higher than that of non-Hispanic whites and of Hispanic women born elsewhere in Latin America.

Immigration Is Creating a Hybrid Nation

by Guillermo Gómez-Peña

About the author: *Guillermo Gómez-Peña is a writer and performance artist living in San Francisco, California.*

From 1978 to 1991, I lived and worked in and among the cities of Tijuana, San Diego, and Los Angeles. Like hundreds of thousands of Mexicans, I was a binational commuter. I crossed that dangerous border regularly, by plane, by car, and by foot. The border became my home, my base of operations, and my laboratory of social and artistic experimentation. My art, my dreams, my family and friends, and my psyche were literally and conceptually divided by the border. But the border was not a straight line; it was more like a Möbius strip. No matter where I was, I was always on "the other side," feeling ruptured and incomplete, ever longing for my other selves, my other home and tribe.

Thanks to my Chicano colleagues I learned to perceive California as an extension of Mexico and the city of Los Angeles as the northernmost barrio of Mexico City. And in spite of many California residents' denial of the state's Mexican past and their bittersweet relationship with contemporary Mexicans, I never quite felt like an immigrant. As a mestizo with a thick accent and an even thicker moustache, I knew I wasn't exactly welcome; but I also knew that millions of Latinos, "legal" and "illegal," shared that border experience with me.

Then in 1991 I moved to New York City, and my umbilical cord finally snapped. For the first time in my life, I felt like a true immigrant. From my Brooklyn apartment, Mexico and Chicanolandia seemed a million light-years away.

I decided to return to Southern California in 1993. Since the 1992 riots, Los Angeles had become the epicenter of America's social, racial, and cultural crisis. It was, unwillingly, the capital of a growing "Third World" within the shrinking "First World." I wanted to be both a witness and a chronicler of this wonderful madness.

Reprinted from Guillermo Gómez-Peña, "Beyond the Tortilla Curtain," *Utne Reader*, September/October 1995, courtesy of the author.

Chapter 4

Social Tensions

I found a city at war with itself; a city gravely punished by natural and social forces; a city that is experiencing in a more concentrated manner what the rest of the country is undergoing. Its political structures are dysfunctional and its economy is in shambles; cutbacks in the defense budget have resulted in increased unemployment; and racial tensions are the focus of daily news reports. Crime rates and poverty levels can be compared to those of a Third World city. All this coincides with an acute crisis of national identity. Post–Cold War America is having a very hard time shedding its imperial nostalgia,

> *"[The United States] is rapidly becoming a huge border zone, a hybrid society, a mestizo race."*

embracing its multiracial soul, and accepting its new status as the first "developed" country to become a member of the Third World.

Perhaps what scared me more than anything was to realize who was being blamed for all the turmoil. The Mexican/Latino immigrant community was the scapegoat and was being singled out by both Republican and Democratic politicians, fanatic citizen groups like SOS (Save Our State), and sectors of the mainstream media as the main cause of our social ills. The racist Proposition 187, which denies nonemergency medical services and education to illegal aliens, passed with 60 percent of the vote on November 8, 1994, and turns every doctor, nurse, pharmacist, police officer, schoolteacher, and "concerned citizen" into a de facto border patrolman. Furthermore, the very same people who supported Prop 187 [now held up in court] also opposed women's and gay rights, affirmative action, bilingual education, freedom of expression, and the existence of the National Endowment for the Arts. Why? What does this mean? What are we all losing?

The Fear of the "Other"

Despite the fact that the United States has always been a nation of immigrants and border crossers, nativism has periodically reared its head. American identity has historically depended on opposing an "other," be it cultural, racial, or ideological. Americans need enemies against whom to define their personal and national boundaries. From the original indigenous inhabitants of this land to the former Soviets, an evil "other" has always been stalking and ready to strike.

Fear is at the core of xenophobia. This fear is particularly disturbing when it is directed at the most vulnerable victims: migrant workers. They become the "invaders" from the south, the human incarnation of the Mexican fly, the subhuman "wetbacks," the "aliens" from another (cultural) planet. They are always suspected of stealing "our jobs," of shrinking "our budget," of taking advantage of the welfare system, of not paying taxes, and of bringing disease, drugs, street violence, foreign thoughts, pagan rites, primitive customs, and alien sounds. Their indigenous features and rough clothes remind uninformed citizens of an unpleasant pre-European American past and of mythical lands to the south immersed in poverty and political turmoil, where innocent gringos could be attacked for no apparent reason. Yet these invaders no longer inhabit the remote past, a banana republic, or a Hollywood film. They actually live down the block, and their children go to the same schools as do the Anglo kids.

Nothing is scarier than the blurring of the border between them and us; between the Dantesque South and the prosperous North; between paganism and Christianity. For many Americans, the border has failed to stop chaos and crisis from creeping in (the origin of crisis and chaos is strangely always located outside). Their worst nightmare is finally coming true: The United States is no longer a fictional extension of Europe, or the wholesome suburb imagined by the screenwriter of *Lassie*. It is rapidly becoming a huge border zone, a hybrid society, a mestizo race, and, worst of all, this process seems to be irreversible. America shrinks day by day as the pungent smell of enchiladas and the volume of *quebradita* music rise.

We Are All Here to Stay

Authoritarian solutions to "the problem" of immigration can only make things worse. Further militarizing the border while dismantling the social, medical, and educational support systems that serve the immigrant population will only worsen social tensions. Denying medical services to undocumented immigrants will result in more disease and more teenage pregnancy. Throwing 300,000 kids out of the schools and into the streets will only contribute to crime and social disintegration. Not only will these proposals backfire, they also will contribute to a growing nationalism in the Latino and Asian communities and repoliticize entire communities that were dormant in the past decade.

So what to do with "the problem" of immigration? First of all, we need to stop characterizing it as a unilateral "problem." Let's be honest. The end of the twentieth century appears scary to both Anglos and Latinos, to legal and illegal immigrants. Both sides feel threatened, uprooted, and displaced, to different degrees and for different reasons. We all fear deep inside that there won't be enough jobs, food, air, and housing for everybody. Yet we cannot deny the processes of interdependence that define our contemporary experience as North Americans. In a post-NAFTA [North American Free Trade Agreement], post–Cold War America, the binary models of us/them, North/ South, and Third World/First World are no longer useful in understanding our complicated border dynamics, our transnational identities, and our multiracial communities.

> *"We all are here to stay. For better or for worse, our destinies and aspirations are in one another's hands."*

It is time to face the facts: Anglos won't go back to Europe, and Mexicans and Latinos (legal or illegal) won't go back to Latin America. We all are here to stay. For better or for worse, our destinies and aspirations are in one another's hands.

A New Social Order

For me, the only solution lies in a paradigm shift: the recognition that we all are protagonists in the creation of a new cultural topography and a new social order, one in which we all are "others" and we need the other "others" to exist. Hybridity is no longer up for discussion. It is a demographic, racial, social, and cultural fact. The real tasks ahead of us are to embrace more fluid and tolerant notions of personal and national identity and to develop models of peaceful co-existence and multilateral cooperation across boundaries of nationality, race, gender, and religion. To this end, rather than more border patrols, border walls, and punitive laws, we need more and better information about one another. Culture and education are at the core of the solution. We need to learn each other's languages, histories, art, and cultural traditions. We need to educate our children and teenagers about the dangers of racism and the complexities of living in a multiracial borderless society, the inevitable society of the twenty-first century.

Immigration Is Creating a Balkanized Nation

by The American Immigration Control Foundation

About the author: *The American Immigration Control Foundation is an independent research and education organization that advocates stricter controls on legal and illegal immigration.*

Immigration enthusiasts have a remarkable ability to portray the questionable consequences of their policies in the most favorable lights. Thus when immigration overwhelms American communities with clashing values and cultures, the enthusiasts describe it as "the enrichment of multiculturalism and diversity." Packs of journalists reinforce this impression with happy-face articles about the new ethnic restaurants in town and the colorful holidays and festivals of the newcomers. At the same time, packs of economists produce "studies" proclaiming the economic bonanza that mass immigration allegedly brings communities.

In short, according to the enthusiasts, immigration is the pathway to utopia—the paradise of endless enrichment of culture and cash. Some even suggest that immigrants are a superior breed of people—a virtual master race—which we need to replace the decadent washed-out stocks of native-born Americans.

The Problem with Utopia

The problem with utopia is the very definition of the word. It means "no place." Thus one is wise to question schemes which promise perfection on earth, especially when those schemes fly directly in the face of wisdom, prudence, and common sense.

To weigh the claims of the immigration utopians, it is useful to reflect on the history of the socialist utopians of this century. In successive experiments in Russia, China, Cuba and elsewhere, they and their propagandists claimed to have remade human nature and brought happiness and prosperity for everyone. Many Western economists pointed to the "successes" of socialism in those countries as examples to follow.

Significantly, many of these socialist utopians did not live in the societies

Reprinted from the American Immigration Control Foundation, "Immigration Balkanizing America," AICF Special Report, December 1996, by permission.

they were praising. Similarly today, most immigration utopians live far from the maddening multicultural crowds of new arrivals.

The failure of the socialist utopias—long hidden—is now plain for all to see. Nevertheless, from the very beginning, something should have led more people to see through the deception. It was the fact that the citizens of these utopias commonly fled them whenever they could. Denied any democratic right to control their lives, they voted with their feet to leave.

> *"Many Americans . . . are leaving metropolitan areas—and indeed entire regions—to escape massive immigration and its consequences."*

Similarly today, Americans are denied the democratic right to determine the future character and culture of their country. Despite numerous opinion polls showing overwhelming popular support for immigration control, politicians simply ignore the will of the majority. Former New York Mayor Ed Koch summed up their attitude in 1995 when he suggested that political leaders should back immigration and ignore "the mob."

The Flight from Immigration

Faced with an unresponsive political system, many Americans, too, are voting with their feet. They are leaving metropolitan areas—and indeed entire regions—to escape massive immigration and its consequences. Their destinations generally are to areas which still retain a traditional American character.

This trend is well known among Americans who compose the nation's immigration control movement. Many of its members are themselves fugitives from multicultural America or are friends of such fugitives. Until recently, however, the flight from immigration lacked scholarly documentation. Today, this situation is changing, thanks in large part to the work of William H. Frey, Ph.D., a demographer and research scientist at the Population Studies Center at the University of Michigan (Ann Arbor).

What follows is a summary of Dr. Frey's methodology and conclusions. Quotations from Frey come from his 1996 paper, *Immigration, Internal Out-Movement, and Demographic Balkanization in America: New Evidence for the 1990s.*

The Findings of Dr. Frey

Dr. William Frey began his study of displacement of native-born Americans by immigrants by analyzing population movements in ten major cities which have received nearly 70 percent of all immigrants who have arrived during the 1980s and 90s. Approximately three-quarters came from Latin America and Asia, areas culturally distinct from earlier major sources of immigration and from the Western and European culture of the United States.

The ten cities Frey surveyed were Los Angeles, New York, San Francisco, Chicago, Miami, Washington, Houston, San Diego, Boston, and Dallas. He began his research with a study of data from the 1990 Census and continued it with analysis of new Census estimates for 1990 through 1995.

"An . . . important impact," Frey found, "involves the social and demographic division that this immigration is creating across the geographic landscape . . . which indicate that: (1) Most recent immigrants still locate in a small number of traditional port-of-entry states and metropolitan areas; (2) Most internal, domestic migrants locate in different destinations [from] those attracting recent immigrants; and (3) There is an accentuated out-migration 'flight' of less-skilled internal migrants away from high immigration areas."

In terms of specific numbers, notes journalist Jonathon Tilove in the May 19, 1996, *Detroit News*, "What Frey discovered is that between 1985 and 1990, while 2.7 million immigrants entered those 10 metros, another 1.5 million existing residents left. And . . . that between 1990 and 1995, another 2.6 million immigrants entered these same metros, even as 3 million more existing residents left. That includes more than a million each out of metro New York and metro Los Angeles. . . ." Tilove quotes one man saying, who moved from Long Island to North Carolina, "This is America. . . . I lived on Long Island. Now, for the first time in my life I live in America."

Frey continues, "These migration patterns portend an emergent 'demographic balkanization' of the country. Under the scenario, areas where the immigration components dominate demographic change will become increasingly multicultural, younger and

"People choose a new location . . . with an eye to finding a community with a lot of other people, racially and ethnically, like themselves."

more bifurcated in their race and class structures. Other parts of the country, whose growth is more dependent on internal migration flows, will become far less multicultural in their demographic makeup and become separated, as well, in other social, demographic and political dimensions.

"What is new about this balkanization scenario is its geographic scope. Historically, new immigrant and other race and ethnic groups have become segregated across neighborhoods or between central cities and suburbs. However, the emergence of entire metropolitan area or labor market regions that are distinct in their race, ethnic and demographic makeup—from the rest of the country—introduces a new dimension."

Impending Balkanization

What might be the outcome of these trends? Frey observes, "A 1995 statistical portrait and projections to the year 2020 illustrate the impending 'balkanization' scenario. The 10 High Immigration areas are already distinct in their multicultural profile and in their highly bifurcated race-class structure. The remainder of the country is becoming divided into largely black-white areas in the South Atlantic region, growing via internal migration; and older, whiter, more stagnant areas scattered elsewhere. These distinctions will become sharp if current immigration and domestic migration patterns continue. They will re-shape social, racial and political cleavages in fundamental ways. Hence, greater attention to these consequences in the current immigration debate would be well advised."

Frey's critics have tried to cast doubt on his research by claiming that depar-ture of Americans from big cities is a long-standing trend motivated by many causes other than immigration. Frey, in fact, concedes that immigration is not the only reason for native-born flight, but he maintains that key indicators re-veal that it is a very significant cause.

In the past, as many researchers agree, the typical reason for internal migra-tion from a metropolitan area was declining economic opportunities for the people with higher levels of education and ambition.

Recent migration patterns of Americans, notes Frey, are different. In many cases, people are moving from high immigration areas, even when the economy is doing well. Often too, it is poorer, less educated segments of the population that are leaving—the segment of the population most likely to come into actual contact and competition with the newly arrived foreign immigrants.

Frey observes, "While it is clear that the trends in domestic migration for the High Immigration Metros are shaped by changing economic circumstances im-posed by recessions and industry-specific growth patterns, the most dominant of these areas (Los Angeles, New York, San Francisco, Chicago) show a consistent net out-immigration vis-à-vis other parts of the U.S. over the 1985–95 period; and the rest (with the exception of San Diego prior to the 1990s defense cut-backs) display fluctuating levels of either declines or modest gains. These pat-terns are in accordance with the view that immigration itself exerts some impact on domestic migration patterns, irrespective of the current economic conditions."

Particularly in California and Texas, he notes, people have been leaving irre-spective of economic conditions: "It is noteworthy to compare the selectivity pat-terns of California with those of Texas because, as mentioned earlier, these states underwent somewhat divergent economic circumstances between the late 1980s and early 1990s. That is, during the first period, California's economy was still relatively robust, while Texas was undergoing severe employment declines—con-ditions which reversed for the early 1990s. Nevertheless, over both periods, each state's migrant patterns displayed an accentuated net out-migration. . . ."

As previously noted, a large share of the Americans were poor and working class people. Says Frey, "It is, in fact, the uniqueness of the pop-

"Low-skilled Americans simply move rather than even try to compete with immigrants."

ulation groups that move away from High Immigration states and metros that strongly suggest an 'immigrant push' effect is working. Unlike more conven-tional migration which tends to overly select college graduates to areas with well-paying or fast-growing employment opportunities, there was a unique and fairly consistent pattern of out-migration among high school graduates, high school dropouts, and lower income residents away from High Immigration Metropolitan areas and High Immigration States. . . ."

> *"Current evidence and projections . . . point to greater demographic divisions across the nation's broad regions."*

Comments Tilove, ". . . Frey found that the exodus from the metros with the most immigration is even more pronounced for the less affluent and educated. The people who are moving are the most vulnerable for jobs, for scarce public resources and control of their community's cultural symbols, and who are touched by sudden shifts in the racial and ethnic make-up of their neighborhoods and schools.

"What's more, Frey found that people choose a new location not only with an eye to the economy but also with an eye to finding a community with a lot of other people, racially and ethnically, like themselves."

Job Competition

Definitely it appears that immigrants are taking the jobs in the 10 metro areas that blue collar Americans were doing until recent years. Says Frey, "For the 10 metros, the 1995 foreign-born population comprises a disproportionate share of persons without high school degrees, in the lower quartile of family income, and of workers in service and unskilled blue collar occupations. The imbalance is even more pronounced in the Los Angeles metropolitan area where, for example, foreign-born residents comprise three-fifths of all persons whose family incomes fall in the bottom quartile. . . ."

This situation helps explain the outcome of studies conducted by pro-immigration economists which claim that immigrants are not taking a significant number of jobs from low-skilled Americans, or lowering wages for those jobs, in high immigration areas. What happens, as Cornell University labor specialist Vernon Briggs has long maintained, is that low-skilled Americans simply move rather than even try to compete with immigrants. Frey's findings help substantiate his viewpoint.

What, aside from culture clash and job competition, are some other reasons for Americans moving away? Frey speculates that "longer term residents may hold the perception, correctly or not, that the new immigrants contribute to a variety of social costs including higher crime rates, reduced services or increased taxes which imply greater out-of-pocket expenses for middle class residents."

Interestingly, Frey has found a small but noteworthy movement of well-educated and skilled Americans *to* areas of high immigration. Some analysts suggest that these are people who may actually benefit from the inflow of immigrants, such as managers of businesses which profit from immigrants' cheap labor. These same people, however, generally have the means to live in areas not affected by multiculturalism. Such a trend suggests a stark re-creation of a common Third World pattern in our largest metro areas: small islands of wealth and privilege in a sea of dispossession and poverty.

Frey concludes his paper with the following statement: "Current evidence and projections, associated with the present immigration to the U.S., point to greater demographic divisions across the nation's broad regions. These long-term population distribution impacts of immigration on the nation's social and political geography are just as important to evaluate in current immigration policy debates as its short-term economic consequences."

A Country Divided

Dr. Frey affirms that he does not want to become involved in partisan political battles. As one who aims to be an objective scholar, he hopes to present research and thereby provide policy-makers with knowledge to make intelligent decisions.

His findings, however, are certain to intensify the national debate on immigration by highlighting the clear connection between in-flow of large numbers of immigrants and significant out-flow of native-born citizens—and increased balkanization by region, ethnicity, and culture.

Confronted with this information, policy-makers may retreat further into denial, reciting ever more fervently the utopian cliches about "a nation of immigrants." Or, for the first time, they may seriously consider the likely prospects for a country divided by divisions that no Melting Pot can melt.

The Threat of a Racially Diverse America

by Jared Taylor

About the author: *Jared Taylor is a journalist and author of* Paved with Good Intentions: The Failure of Race Relations in Contemporary America.

Editor's note: The following viewpoint is excerpted from a speech delivered at a 1996 conference sponsored by American Renaissance, *a conservative monthly journal.*

I would like to talk to you today about the demographic future of the United States, specifically about what the shifting racial makeup means for the future of our country.

In March 1996, the Census Bureau released its periodic projection of the ethnic makeup of the United States during the next few decades. It reported that if current immigration and birth rates hold steady, by the year 2050 the percentage of Hispanics will have increased from 10 to 25 percent, Asians from three to eight percent, and blacks from 12 to 14 percent. All these increases will come at the expense of whites, who are projected to fall from 74 percent to about 50 percent.

Within 54 years, therefore, whites will be on the brink of becoming just one more racial minority. And because whites are having so few children, they will be an *old* minority. Within just 34 years they will already account for less than half the population under age 18, but will be three-quarters of the population over 65. . . .

As usual, the Census Bureau's projections didn't stir much interest, but let us be frank: if this demographic shift takes place it will transform America. It will transform America because race makes a difference. Race matters.

Seeing the Future

Predictions are usually tricky but when it comes to this transformation, there are a number of things we can say with complete confidence. To know what the

Reprinted from Jared Taylor, "If We Do Nothing," *American Renaissance*, June 1996, by permission of the author and *American Renaissance*, Box 527, Oakton, VA 22124.

future will be like, just visit those places where the transformation has already taken place—places like Miami or Detroit or Monterey Park, California.

The details of what happens when the population shifts from white to non-white are interesting, but let us set them aside for a moment and consider something else that is profoundly important—something that everyone knows but rarely says—and that is this: Once the number of non-whites in an area reaches a certain level, whites cannot or will not stay. They refuse to be a minority; they move to some place where they are once again the majority. This is an empirical, utterly dependable fact and everyone—I mean everyone—knows it.

> *"One certain effect of demographic change will be that whites will withdraw from more and more parts of the United States."*

The process does not work the other way. Not even the most ardent integrationists are willing to take the obvious, simplest first step to make integration happen, which is to buy a house in a black neighborhood. Or move into a Mexican neighborhood. Or even, in many cases, send their children to public school.

As far as whites are concerned, once a school or part of a city goes black or Hispanic or sometimes even Asian, it might as well have disappeared from the map. It becomes *terra incognita*, like those parts of ancient maps that say "Here be dragons." What was once part of our civilization slips its leash and is lost.

Therefore, one certain effect of demographic change will be that whites will withdraw from more and more parts of the United States. It will be *physically possible* for them to live with the Mexicans of Brownsville, Texas, or the blacks of Camden, New Jersey, but whites will do just about anything to avoid it. After all, whites can think of dozens of places where they would like to live—and they are all likely to have large white majorities. By the same token, most whites cannot name a single majority non-white neighborhood in which they could stand to live.

Of course, much of the racial shift the Census Bureau predicts would be caused by third-world immigration. Every year about 800,000 legal immigrants and who knows how many illegal immigrants come to live in this country. Ninety percent of them are non-white. Now immigration is not a force of nature. It is the result of a national policy, which Congress could change. The United States has therefore chosen, in effect, to make more and more parts of itself essentially off-limits for whites.

Race Makes a Difference

You often hear that today's non-white immigrants will assimilate just as the European ethnics did at the turn of the century. This view is hopelessly wrong because it avoids the fundamental question of race. Germans, Swedes, the Irish, Poles and Italians have assimilated. Blacks and American Indians have been here since colonial times but most are still at the margins of society. Why? Because race largely governs assimilation. Sure, some non-whites fully embrace European civilization but large numbers do not. Why should they? Their loyalty is, quite naturally, to their own people and their own culture.

Part of today's orthodoxy holds that the reason whites move out of changing neighborhoods is because whites are uniquely racist. I'll return to this question later, but in fact other races are not keen on living with each other, either. There are now plenty of places in America where blacks and Hispanics make up most of the public school population. They have race riots and race rivalries in which whites play no part whatsoever. From Manhattan to Texas to California, high schools and even junior high schools are sometimes shut down because of black versus Hispanic violence and tension.

Likewise, there are prison blocks in Texas and California that are in a constant state of lockdown because whenever the prisoners are allowed to leave their cells the blacks and Hispanics go at each other's throats. Racial segregation would, of course, solve this problem instantly, but no one dares propose it.

As far as black-Hispanic relations are concerned, I was particularly interested to read the remarks of the president of a black home-owners association in Los Angeles about why she didn't want Mexicans moving into her neighborhood. In 1991, she said to reporters: "It's a different culture, a different breed of people. They don't have the same values. You can't get together with them. It's like mixing oil and water." I sympathize 100 percent

> *"The United States has therefore chosen, in effect, to make more and more parts of itself essentially off-limits for whites."*

with that black lady. Race matters. Needless to say, when the now long forgotten whites moved out of South Central Los Angeles, they no doubt said similar things about blacks.

What happens when Asians arrive in large numbers? The effect is more ambiguous. Some North Asians commit fewer crimes than whites, make more money, and do better in school. Then there are others like the Hmong from Cambodia, 60 percent of whom are on welfare. However, and this is a point I wish to emphasize, it doesn't matter whether Japanese or Chinese build societies that are, in some respects, objectively superior to those of Europeans. It matters only that they are *different*.

When large numbers of North Asian immigrants moved into Monterey Park, California, whites didn't leave because the newcomers were rioting or opening crack houses. They moved out because Monterey Park, in countless ways, simply ceased to be the town they had grown up in or the town they had moved to. They didn't care that these Asians probably had an average IQ of 105, were responsible parents and law-abiding people. Whites saw their way of life melting away beneath their feet, and they moved away in the hope of finding it again elsewhere.

Once again, the particulars don't matter. It is unwelcome, irreversible racial change that matters.

The Effects of Demographic Change

I think one significant sign of the times is what is happening on college campuses all around the country. Today's young people have been reared in the most relentlessly anti-racist atmosphere in the history of the world. Over and over they are told that everybody's beautiful, that distinctions don't matter, that diversity is wonderful, etc., etc. And what do they do as soon as they arrive on campus? They sort themselves out by race. They segregate themselves in social clubs, ethnic dormitories, and all kinds of student activity groups that are defined by race. Race matters, and all the yelling society does makes no difference.

What will demographic change be like at the national level? That's harder to say. A white majority has already established laws and regulations that discriminate against whites. Many non-whites have convinced themselves that this is equal treatment. If non-whites become the majority, I suspect that they will have no trouble convincing themselves that all kinds of new anti-white measures are necessary.

Besides that, what sort of foreign policy would a non-white America have? What would it do—or not do—with nuclear weapons? What sort of government would it have? In the long term, I'm not sure a non-white America would even maintain democracy or the rule of law. The record of non-white nations is not encouraging in this respect.

Even if our forms of government survive, what fanciful readings of the Constitution will emerge from a Supreme Court on which people like Lani Guinier are justices? I suspect that in a non-white America, the First Amendment would go the way of the Tenth, and dissent from racial orthodoxy would be a criminal offense. . . .

Hypocrisy About Racial Integration

But to return to the present, in the United States today, there is not a drop of public sympathy for whites who are being displaced by non-whites. We're all supposed to feel morally superior to anyone who escapes to the suburbs when the neighborhood begins to turn black or Mexican. The theory is that only ignorant bigots do this, but the fact is that people with money never even have to face the problem. As someone once put it, the purpose of a

> *"Race matters, and all the yelling society does makes no difference."*

college education is to give people the right attitudes about minorities and the means to live as far away from them as possible.

This orthodoxy about racial integration has therefore developed a completely transparent set of hypocrisies. Just about every elected official in America, every talking head on television, every self-righteous editorial writer has chanted the mantra of integration so many times he can recite it in his sleep. But where do they live? Where do their children go to school? Whom do they invite to their dinner parties? Whom do they marry and urge their children to marry?

> **"There is not one multi-racial anything in America that doesn't suffer from racial friction."**

No, no, they don't actually live and go to school and socialize with these wonderful black people and wonderful Mexicans and Nigerians and Pakistanis. No, integration is a splendid thing—so splendid that they insist that others should enjoy it while they nobly forgo the benefits. This is the smelly little consensus that our country's elites have quietly arrived at. Integration is our goal—but not for me, and my friends, and my children.

And, in fact, these self-righteous, college-educated, properly socialized folks have come up with a whole set of mental exercises for ordinary Americans who don't have the money to live in the suburbs or send their children to private school. The first exercise is to believe that aliens and strangers are bearers of a special gift called diversity. We are not being displaced; we are being enriched and strengthened.

Of course, the idea that racial diversity is a strength is so obviously stupid that only very intelligent people could have thought it up. There is not one multi-racial anything in America that doesn't suffer from racial friction. Our country has established a gigantic, convoluted system of laws, diversity commissions, racial watchdog groups, EEO [Equal Employment Opportunity] officers, and outreach committees as part of a huge, clanking mechanism to regulate and try to control racial diversity—something that was supposed to be a great source of strength but has turned out to be horribly volatile and difficult to manage. People are so exhausted by this alleged source of strength that they run from it the first chance they get. That is why families, churches, clubs, and private parties—anything not yet regulated by the government—are so racially homogeneous.

Nothing, therefore, could be more obvious: Diversity of race or tribe or language or religion are the main reasons people are at each other's throats all around the world. Just pick up a newspaper. Diversity—within the same territory—is strife, not strength. . . .

The Gift of Diversity?

Whites and North Asians build successful societies that other races cannot build. That is why non-whites want to come. Nicaraguans and Haitians don't come [to the United States] out of generosity, eager to share the gift of "diversity" with poor, benighted white people who are about to choke to death on their own homogeneity. They come because their societies don't work and they know life is better here.

If Europeans had turned North America into a giant pesthole no one would want to come. No one would then have to think up crazy reasons why everyone had the right to come, or why whites actually benefit from being outnumbered and pushed aside by people unlike themselves.

The same process, the same migratory dynamic is at work on a smaller scale. In the United States, virtually every desirable place to live, work, or go to school is desirable because whites made it that way. Non-whites, who do not make things desirable in the same way, want in. This is why it is always non-whites who are pushing their way into white institutions—never the other way around—and why all the phony dramas of "exclusion," "tolerance," "justice," and "racism" are always played out on white territory and put whites on the defensive.

Whites are not clamoring to get into Howard University or to live in South Central L.A. or to move to Guatemala. But if there were something rare and desirable in those places, and non-whites had made them rare and desirable, I can promise you that the proprietors would fight like crazy to keep others—including whites—out.

Of course, generally speaking, once non-whites have gotten what they want, and have arrived in large numbers in what were previously white institutions or neighborhoods, those institutions and neighborhoods lose the qualities that made them desirable and attracted non-whites in the first place. Whites leave, and we are right back where we started. For the most part, blacks and third-world immigrants re-create in their new locations the places they left behind—complete with all the shortcomings that prompted them to leave in the first place.

> *"Diversity of race or tribe or language or religion are the main reasons people are at each other's throats all around the world."*

Now, so far, I have not said anything that everyone in America, at some level, doesn't already know. No school or neighborhood has improved by going from white to black or Hispanic, and whites do not stick around to see whether this time, just this once, water is going to flow uphill.

What is the message of all this white flight? It is, quite simply, that the deepest underlying assumption about race that has directed American policies for the last 40 or 50 years is wrong. The theory—almost always unstated—was that if we work at it hard enough race can be made not to matter. This was something that many people thought noble and idealistic, but it was a misreading of human nature. Race matters. It is a brute, biological fact and wishing will not make it go away. . . .

A Perversion of White Morality

At some point, nature will reassert itself, and whites will decide not to commit racial and cultural suicide. But in the meantime, the real question is why are whites letting this happen to their country. Why do they still pay lip service to ideals of integration that they, themselves, consistently violate? Why are they ensuring that their children and grandchildren will be racial minorities—probably hated racial minorities—in their own land?

My answer is admittedly speculative, but the reason, I believe, has to do with the perversion of something that is good and characteristic of whites, and that is their sense of reciprocity, of morality. When one thinks of the unique characteristics of Western Civilization that set it off from the civilizations of other races, many boil down to a rooted conviction that can be expressed in very simple terms: That the other fellow has a point of view.

Democracy, for example, is based on the truly heroic proposition that not only does the other fellow have a point of view, but that he is theoretically just as likely to be right as I am. For the most part, only whites have been able to make democracy work. The rule of law is likewise based on the same assumption, that power is not self-justifying, that the other fellow has a point of view.

European culture is suffused with this notion. The ideals of sportsmanship are designed to ensure fair play and to prevent humiliation of the loser. Freedom of speech and press ensure that the other fellow can express his point of view. The elimination of hereditary class status lets the other fellow rise or fall on his own merits. It was Europeans and Americans who pioneered and perfected these things—most of the rest of the world has yet to come close. . . .

According to orthodoxy whites are, of course, uniquely evil, and certainly not very concerned about the other fellow's point of view. And, indeed, whites have done a lot of killing, particularly in [the twentieth] century. However, the scale of their killing merely reflected their technological genius. Far more remarkable than the things whites have done is what they did not do. They could have kept non-whites in slavery but freed them for moral reasons. For the same reasons they forced non-white people to free their slaves. Whites had the power to colonize the entire world but voluntarily dismantled their empires. Whites still have the power to establish a purely exploitative regimen for the non-white world, but they do not—because the other fellow has a point of view.

> *"No school or neighborhood has improved by going from white to black or Hispanic."*

Not only does the other fellow have a point of view, this way of thinking has been perverted by current racial orthodoxy to imply that every point of view expressed by non-whites is somehow superior to any expressed by whites. When faced with an explicitly racial demand from any non-white group, whites are terrified and demoralized and have lost the argument before it even begins. Robert Frost used to say that the definition of a liberal is someone who can't take his own side in an argument. The same is true for whites: They cannot or dare not take their own side in any kind of racial discussion. They feel they are not even allowed to have a side.

I think, therefore, that the reason whites are paralyzed in the face of national, cultural and racial dispossession is because they are convinced that it would be immoral to resist. Respect for the other fellow's point of view requires that we do nothing to prevent the country from turning into a colony of the third world. The same impulse that makes them save the snail darter or the spotted owl, or to protect the ozone layer, or believe so fervently in democracy—it is this impulse that prevents whites from acting in their own legitimate group interests.

Loss of Euro-American Culture

White people reveal what they really think about race, immigration, and the future of their country every time they move to the suburbs. In their bones they know that it will be a calamity if America begins to look (and act) exactly like those places where whites refuse to live, like those parts on the map that say "Here be dragons." Whites are deeply, deeply pessimistic and very much afraid of a non-white future for their children. But they dare not say so. They have convinced themselves that to speak would be immoral, that nothing is worse than to open themselves to the charge of racism.

I believe that this is a perversion of what is in fact one of the hallmarks of Western man—this abiding sense of reciprocity. However, when every other race is conscious of its racial interests and works round the clock to advance them, any race that does not do so has committed unilateral disarmament in a war-like world.

> *"Whites are deeply, deeply pessimistic and very much afraid of a non-white future for their children."*

The moral question can be put this way. Let us imagine that Mexico invaded and conquered the southeastern part of the United States. What would the Mexicans do with their new territory? They would establish Spanish as the official language. They would expel much of the white population and replace it with Mexicans. They would abolish American holidays and celebrate Mexican ones. Music, food, education, work habits, religion, primary loyalties, and the very texture of life—all would become Mexican rather than American.

Of course, as I suggested earlier, this is exactly what has already happened in many parts of California and Texas. And a similar invasion from Central America has, in 30 years, reduced the percentage of whites in Miami from 90 percent to 10 percent. Ninety percent to 10 percent in just 30 years! The inner cities of our great metropolises have, in effect, been conquered by Liberia.

Those parts of the country are lost to Euro-American culture and even nationality. America has therefore given up the very thing nations go to war to preserve, the very thing they send their young men into battle to die for. The integrity of a people, race, or nation is so important that sometimes millions of men are sacrificed in their name. Why? Because the preservation of the nation of one's forefathers is more important than life itself.

Obviously, it would be moral to stop an armed invasion by Mexico. Why is it wrong to resist an unarmed process that produces the same results? Why is it wrong to take peaceful measures to forestall the catastrophe that nations wage all-out war in order to prevent?

Before he was assassinated, Yitzhak Rabin explained that what mattered most to him as an Israeli was that Israel remain at least 80 percent Jewish. So far as I know, no one called Mr. Rabin a hatemonger or a bigot. But we know what would be said about any white who advocated that America stay at least 80 percent white. And yet, the reasoning and morality of an American white and an Israeli Jew are identical. Israel will change in countless unacceptable ways if it ceases to be Jewish, just as America will change in countless unacceptable ways if it ceases to be white.

> *"The forms of civility, the folkways, the demeanor and the texture of life that whites take for granted cannot survive the embrace of large numbers of aliens."*

A Great Tragedy

The forms of civility, the folkways, the demeanor and the texture of life that whites take for granted cannot survive the embrace of large numbers of aliens. The things that I love most about culture and human society have not survived in Detroit and Miami. That is why the whites have left. It may not be "nice" to say these things. But for fear of being thought not "nice" whites are preparing to leave to their grandchildren a third-world nation. I can scarcely think of a greater act of collective cowardice and irresponsibility.

Americans have known for hundreds of years that multi-racialism of the kind we are supposed to be practicing today would be disastrous. You may remember the American Colonization Society. Its purpose was to free blacks from slavery and persuade them to go to Africa. A list of some of its officers—and these were officers, not just supporters—reads like an honor roll from American history: James Madison, Andrew Jackson, Daniel Webster, Stephen Douglas, William Seward, Francis Scott Key, General Winfield Scott, two Chief Justices of the U.S. Supreme Court, John Marshall and Roger Taney.

The Liberians named their capital Monrovia, in recognition of James Monroe's efforts to encourage colonization. Abraham Lincoln and Thomas Jefferson also favored colonization; both believed it was impossible for blacks and whites to live together as free men in the same society.

The intellectual antecedents for racial disengagement therefore include many of the genuinely great men of our past. This suicidal fad of multi-racialism is only a few decades old. Not one great American ever advocated it. We are supposed to believe that Jefferson and Lincoln and John Marshall were great men but when it came to race they somehow got it wrong. Well who got it right? Ted Kennedy? Bill Clinton? What a joke.

In conclusion, the Americans of the past would look with horror upon what we are doing. I am quite certain that my ancestors didn't fight for independence from Britain in order for our generation to turn the country over to Mexicans and Haitians. The Founders didn't frame the Constitution to celebrate diversity. Americans didn't spill their blood at Gettysburg or in Europe or the Pacific for multiculturalism. And yet, the rightful heirs to what could have been a shining beacon of Western Civilization are giving up their country without a struggle.

What we are witnessing is one of the great tragedies in human history. Powerful forces are in motion that, if left unchecked, will slowly push aside European man and European civilization and then dance a victory jig on their collective grave. If we do nothing, the nation we leave to our children will be a desolated, third-world failure, in which whites will be a despised minority. Western Civilization will be a faint echo, vilified if it is even audible. I cannot think of a tragedy that is at once so great, so unnatural, and so unnecessary.

The Promise of a Racially Diverse America

by Bill Clinton

About the author: *Bill Clinton is the forty-second president of the United States.*

Editor's note: The following viewpoint was originally delivered as a speech to the graduating class of the University of California at San Diego on June 14, 1997.

Today we celebrate your achievements at a truly golden moment for America. The Cold War is over and freedom is now ascendant around the globe, with more than half of the people in this whole world living under governments of their choosing for the very first time. Our economy is the healthiest in a generation and the strongest in the world. Our culture, our science, our technology promise unimagined advances and exciting new careers. Our social problems, from crime to poverty, are finally bending to our efforts.

Of course, there are still challenges for you out there. Beyond our borders, we must battle terrorism, organized crime and drug trafficking, the spread of weapons of mass destruction, the prospect of new diseases and environmental disaster. Here at home, we must ensure that every child has the chance you have had to develop your God-given capacities. We cannot wait for them to get in trouble to notice them.

We must continue to fight the scourge of gangs and crime and drugs. We must prepare for the retirement of the baby boom generation so that we can reduce [the] child poverty rate. . . . We must harness the forces of science and technology for the public good, the entire American public.

But I believe the greatest challenge we face . . . is also our greatest opportunity. Of all the questions of discrimination and prejudice that still exist in our society, the most perplexing one is the oldest, and in some ways today the newest, the problem of race.

Can we fulfill the promise of America by embracing all our citizens of all

Reprinted from Bill Clinton's commencement speech to the graduates of the University of California at San Diego, June 14, 1997.

races, not just at a university, where people have the benefit of enlightened teachers and the time to think and grow and get to know each other, but in the daily life of every American community? In short, can we become one America in the 21st century?

I know and I've said before that money cannot buy this goal. Power cannot compel it. Technology cannot create it. This is something that can come only from the human spirit. . . . Today the state of Hawaii . . . has no majority racial or ethnic group. It is a wonderful place of exuberance and friendship and patriotism.

[By the year 2000] here in California, no single race or ethnic group will make up a majority of the state's

> *"Today the state of Hawaii . . . has no majority racial or ethnic group. It is a wonderful place of exuberance and friendship and patriotism."*

population. Already five of our largest school districts draw students from over 100 different racial and ethnic groups. At this campus, 12 Nobel Prize winners have taught or studied from nine different countries. A half-century from now, when your own grandchildren are in college, there will be no majority race in America.

Now, we know what we will look like. But what will we be like? Can we be one America, respecting, even celebrating our differences, but embracing even more what we have in common? Can we define what it means to be an American, not just in terms of the hyphens showing our ethnic origins, but in terms of our primary allegiance to the values America stands for and values we really live by?

Our hearts long to answer yes, but our history reminds us that it will be hard. The ideals that bind us together are as old as our nation, but so are the forces that pull us apart. Our founders sought to form a more perfect union. The humility and hope of that phrase is the story of America, and it is our mission today.

Much Work to Be Done

Consider this: We were born with the Declaration of Independence, which asserted that we were all created equal, and a Constitution that enshrined slavery. We fought a bloody civil war to abolish slavery and preserve the union, but we remained a house divided and unequal by law for another century. We advanced across the continent in the name of freedom, yet in so doing we pushed Native Americans off their land, often crushing their culture and their livelihood. Our Statue of Liberty welcomes poor, tired, huddled masses of immigrants to our borders, but each new wave has felt the sting of discrimination.

In World War II, Japanese-Americans fought valiantly for freedom in Europe, taking great casualties, while at home their families were herded into internment camps. The famed Tuskegee airmen lost none of the bombers they guarded during the war, but their African-American heritage cost them a lot of rights when they came back home in peace.

Though minorities have more opportunities than ever today, we still see evidence of bigotry, from the desecration of houses of worship, whether they be churches, synagogues or mosques, to demeaning talk in corporate suites. There is still much work to be done by you, members of the class of 1997.

But those who say we cannot transform the problem of prejudice into the promise of unity forget how far we have come, and I cannot believe they have ever seen a crowd like you. When I look at you, it is almost impossible for me even to remember my own life. I grew up in the high drama of the Cold War in the patriotic South. Black and white Southerners alike wore our nation's uniform in defense of freedom against communism, and they fought and died together from Korea to Vietnam. But back home, I went to segregated schools, swam in segregated public pools, sat in all-white sections at the movies, and traveled through small towns in my state that still marked restrooms and water fountains "White" and "Colored."

By the grace of God, I had a grandfather with just a grade-school education, but the heart of a true American, who taught me that it was wrong. And by the grace of God, there were brave African-Americans like Congressman John Lewis, who risked their lives time and time again to make it right. And there were white Americans like Congressman Bob Filner, a freedom rider on the bus with John Lewis, in the long, noble struggle for civil rights, who knew that it was a struggle to free white people, too.

The Dilemmas of Race and Ethnicity

To be sure, there is old, unfinished business between black and white Americans. But the classic American dilemma has now become many dilemmas of race and ethnicity. We see it in the tension between black and Hispanic customers and their Korean or Arab grocers; and a resurgent anti-Semitism, even on some college campuses; and a hostility toward new immigrants from Asia to the Middle East to the former communist countries to Latin America and the Caribbean, even those whose hard work and strong families have brought them success in the American way.

We see a disturbing tendency to wrongly attribute to entire groups, including the white majority, the objectionable conduct of a few members. If a black American commits a crime, condemn the act. But remember that most African-Americans are hard-working, law-abiding citizens. If a Latino gang member deals drugs, condemn the act. But remember, the vast majority of Hispanics are responsible citizens who also deplore the scourge of drugs in our lives. If white teen-agers beat a young African-American boy almost to death just because of his race, for God's sakes condemn

> *"Those who say we cannot transform the problem of prejudice into the promise of unity forget how far we have come."*

the act. But remember, the overwhelming majority of white people will find it just as hateful. If an Asian merchant discriminates against her customers of another minority group, call her on it. But remember, too, that many, many Asians have borne the burden of prejudice and do not want anyone else to feel it.

An Enriching Diversity

Remember, too, in spite of the persistence of prejudice, we are more integrated than ever. More of us share neighborhoods and work and school and social activities, religious life, even love and marriage, across racial lines than ever before. More of us enjoy each other's company and distinctive cultures than ever before. And more than ever we understand the benefits of our racial, linguistic and cultural diversity in a global society, where networks of commerce and communications draw us closer and bring rich rewards to those who truly understand life beyond their nation's borders.

With just a twentieth of the world's population but a fifth of the world's income, we in America simply have to sell to the other 95 percent of the world's consumers just to maintain our standard of living. Because we are drawn from every culture on earth, we are uniquely positioned to do it. Beyond commerce, the diverse backgrounds and talents of our citizens can help America to light the globe, showing nations deeply divided by race, religion and tribe that there is a better way.

> *"More of us share neighborhoods and work and school and social activities, religious life, even love and marriage, across racial lines than ever before."*

Finally, as you have shown us today, our diversity will enrich our lives in non-material ways, deepening our understanding of human nature and human differences, making our communities more exciting, more enjoyable, more meaningful.

That is why I have come here today, to ask the American people to join me in a great national effort to perfect the promise of America for this new time as we seek to build our more perfect union. Now, when there is more cause for hope than fear, when we are not driven to it by some emergency or social cataclysm, now is the time we should learn together, talk together and act together to build one America.

Let me say that I know that for many white Americans, this conversation may seem to exclude them or threaten them. That must not be so. I believe white Americans have just as much to gain as anybody else from being a part of this endeavor, much to gain from an America where we finally take responsibility for all our children, so that they at last can be judged, as Martin Luther King hoped, not by the color of their skin but by the content of their character.

What is it that we must do? For 4½ years now, I have worked to prepare America for the 21st century, with a strategy of opportunity for all, responsibility from all, and an American community of all our citizens. To succeed in each of these areas, we must deal with the realities and the perceptions affecting all racial groups in America.

First, we must continue to expand opportunity. Full participation in our strong and growing economy is the best antidote to envy, despair and racism. We must press forward to move millions more from poverty and welfare to work, to bring the spark of enterprise to inner cities, to redouble our efforts to reach those rural communities prosperity has passed by. And most important of all, we simply must give our young people the finest education in the world.

"America [could] light the globe, showing nations deeply divided by race, religion and tribe that there is a better way."

There are no children who, because of their ethnic or racial background, cannot meet the highest academic standards if we set them and measure our students against them, if we give them well-trained teachers and well-equipped classrooms, and if we continue to support reasoned reforms to achieve excellence like the charter school movement.

At a time when college education means stability, a good job, a passport to the middle class, we must open the doors of college to all Americans. And we must make at least two years of college as universal at the dawn of the next century as a high school diploma is today.

The Role of Affirmative Action

In our efforts to extend economic and educational opportunity to all our citizens, we must consider the role of affirmative action. I know affirmative action has not been perfect in America. That's why, in 1995, we began an effort to fix the things that are wrong with it. But when used in the right way, it has worked.

It has given us a whole generation of professionals in fields that used to be exclusive clubs, where people like me got the benefit of 100 percent affirmative action. There are now more women-owned businesses than ever before. There are more African-American, Latino and Asian-American lawyers and judges, scientists and engineers, accountants and executives than ever before.

But the best example of successful affirmative action is our military. Our armed forces are diverse from top to bottom, perhaps the most integrated institution in our society, and certainly the most integrated in the world. And more important, no one questions that they are the best in the world. So much for the argument that excellence and diversity do not go hand in hand.

There are those who argue that scores on standardized tests should be the sole measure of qualification for admissions to colleges and universities. But many would not apply the same standard to the children of alumni or those with athletic ability. I believe a student body that reflects the excellence and the diversity of the people we will live and work with has independent educational value. Look around this crowd today. Don't you think you have learned a lot more than you would have if everybody sitting around you looked just like you? I think you have.

And beyond the educational value to you, it has a public interest, because you will learn to live and work in the world you will live in better. When young people sit side by side with people of many different backgrounds, they do learn something that they can take out into the world, and they will be more effective citizens.

Many affirmative action students excel. They work hard. They achieve. They go out and serve the communities that need them for their expertise and role models. If we close the door on them, we will weaken our greatest universities and it will be more difficult to build the society we need in the 21st century.

Let me say, I know that the people of California voted to repeal affirmative action [in 1996] without any ill motive. The vast majority of them simply did it with a conviction that discrimination and isolation are no longer barriers to achievement. But consider the results. Minority enrollments in law school and other graduate programs are plummeting for the first time in decades. Soon the same will likely happen in undergraduate education.

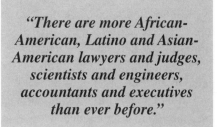

"There are more African-American, Latino and Asian-American lawyers and judges, scientists and engineers, accountants and executives than ever before."

We must not resegregate higher education or leave it to the private universities to do the public's work. At the very time when we need to do a better job of living and learning together, we should not stop trying to equalize economic opportunity.

To those who oppose affirmative action, I ask you to come up with an alternative. I would embrace it if I could find a better way. And to those of us who still support it, I say we should continue to stand for it. We should reach out to those who disagree or are uncertain and talk about the practical impact of these issues. And we should never be unwilling to work with those who disagree with us to find new ways to lift people up and bring people together.

Responsibility from Every American

Beyond opportunity, we must demand responsibility from every American. Our strength as a society depends upon both, upon people taking responsibility for themselves and their families, teaching their children good values, working hard and obeying the law, and giving back to those around us. The new economy offers fewer guarantees, more risks and more rewards. It calls upon all of us to take even greater responsibility for our own education than ever before.

In the current economic boom, only one racial or ethnic group in America has actually experienced a decline in income—Hispanic-Americans. One big reason is that Hispanic high school dropout rates are well above, indeed, far above those of whites and blacks. Some of the dropouts actually reflect a strong commitment to work. We admire the legendary willingness to take the hard job at long hours for low pay. In the old economy, that was a responsible thing to do.

But in the new economy, where education is the key, responsibility means staying in school.

> *"When young people sit side by side with people of many different backgrounds, they do learn something that they can take out into the world."*

No responsibility is more fundamental than obeying the law. It is not racist to insist that every American do so. The fight against crime and drugs is a fight for the freedom of all our people, including those, perhaps especially those minorities living in our poorest neighborhoods. But respect for the law must run both ways. The shocking difference in perceptions of the fairness of our criminal justice system grows out of the real experiences that too many minorities have had with law enforcement officers. Part of the answer is to have all our citizens respect the law. But the basic rule must be that the law must respect all our citizens.

And that applies, too, to the enforcement of our civil rights laws. For example, the Equal Employment Opportunity Commission has a huge backlog of cases with discrimination claims, though we have reduced it by 25 percent [since 1993]. We cannot do much better without more resources. It is imperative that Congress, especially those members who say they're for civil rights but against affirmative action, at least give us the money necessary to enforce the law of the land, and do it soon.

Building One American Community

Our third imperative is perhaps the most difficult of all. We must build one American community based on respect for one another and our shared values. We must begin with a candid conversation on the state of race relations today and the implications of Americans of so many different races living and working together as we approach a new century. We must be honest with each other. We have talked at each other and about each other for a long time. It's high time we all began talking with each other.

Over the coming year [1997–1998], I want to lead the American people in a great and unprecedented conversation about race. In community efforts from Lima, Ohio, to Billings, Montana, in remarkable experiments in cross-racial communications like the uniquely named Eracism, I have seen what Americans can do if they let down their guards and reach out their hands.

I have asked one of America's greatest scholars, Dr. John Hope Franklin, to chair an advisory panel of seven distinguished Americans to help me in this endeavor. He will be joined by former Governors Thomas Kean of New Jersey and William Winter of Mississippi, both great champions of civil rights; by

Linda Chavez-Thompson, the executive vice president of the AFL-CIO; by Reverend Susan Johnson Cook, a minister from the Bronx and former White House fellow; by Angela Oh, an attorney and Los Angeles community leader; and Robert Thompson, the CEO of Nissan USA; distinguished leaders, leaders in their community.

I want this panel to help educate Americans about the facts surrounding issues of race, to promote a dialogue in every community in the land to confront and work through these issues, to recruit and encourage leadership at all levels to help breach racial divides, and to find, develop, and recommend how to implement concrete

> *"Whatever else [immigrants have] found, even bigotry and violence, most of them never gave up on America."*

solutions to our problems, solutions that will involve all of us in government, business, communities, and as individual citizens. . . .

Honest dialogue will not be easy at first. We'll all have to get past defensiveness and fear and political correctness and other barriers to honesty. Emotions may be rubbed raw, but we must begin. What do I really hope we will achieve as a country? If we do nothing more than talk, it will be interesting, but it won't be enough. If we do nothing more than propose disconnected acts of policy, it will be helpful, but it won't be enough. But if, 10 years from now, people can look back and see that this year of honest dialogue and concerted action helped to lift the heavy burden of race from our children's future, we will have given a precious gift to America.

The Face of the Real America

I ask you all to remember, just for a moment, as we have come through the difficult trial on the [1995] Oklahoma City bombing, remember that terrible day when we saw and wept for Americans and forgot for a moment that there were a lot of them from different races than we are. Remember the many faces and races of the Americans who did not sleep and put their lives at risk to engage in the rescue, the helping and the healing.

Remember how you have seen things like that during the natural disasters here in California. That is the face of the real America. That is the face I have seen over and over again. That is the America somehow, some way, we have to make real in daily American life.

Members of the graduating class, you will have a greater opportunity to live your dreams than any generation in our history if we can make of our many different strands one America, a nation at peace with itself, bound together by shared values and aspirations and opportunities, and real respect for our differences.

I am a Scotch-Irish Southern Baptist, and I'm proud of it. But my life has been immeasurably enriched by the power of the Torah, the beauty of the Koran, the piercing wisdom of the religions of East and South Asia, all embraced by my fellow Americans. I have felt indescribable joy and peace in black and Pentecostal churches. I have come to love the intensity and selflessness of my Hispanic fellow Americans toward *la familia.*

As a Southerner, I grew up on country music and county fairs, and I still like them. But I have also reveled in the festivals and the food, the music and the art and the culture of Native Americans and Americans from every region in the world. In each land I have visited as your president, I have felt more at home because some of their people have found a home in America.

For two centuries, wave upon wave of immigrants have come to our shores to build a new life, drawn by the promise of freedom and a fair chance. Whatever else they've found, even bigotry and violence, most of them never gave up on America. Even African-Americans, the first of whom were brought here in chains, never gave up on America.

It is up to you to prove that their abiding faith was well-placed. Living in islands of isolation, some splendid and some sordid, is not the American way. Basing our self-esteem on the ability to look down on others is not the American way. Being satisfied that we have what we want and heedless of others who don't even have what they need and deserve is not the American way.

We have torn down the barriers in our laws. Now we must break down the barriers in our lives, our minds and our hearts. More than 30 years ago, at the high tide of the civil rights movement, the Kerner Commission said we were becoming two Americas, one white, one black, separate and unequal. Today we face a different choice. Will we become not two, but many Americas, separate, unequal and isolated? Or will we draw strength from all our people and our ancient faith in equality and human dignity, to become the world's first truly multiracial democracy? That is the unfinished work of our times, to lift the burden of race and redeem the promise of America.

> *"The unfinished work of our times [is] to lift the burden of race and redeem the promise of America."*

Class of 1997, I grew up in the shadows of a divided America, but I have seen glimpses of one America. You have shown me one today. That is the America you must make. It begins with your dreams. So dream large. Live your dreams. Challenge your parents. And teach your children well. God bless you and good luck.

Multiculturalism Endangers American Values

by Alvin J. Schmidt

About the author: *Alvin J. Schmidt is a professor of sociology at Illinois College in Jacksonville and author of* The Menace of Multiculturalism: Trojan Horse in America.

The French philosopher Ernest Renan once observed that "A nation is a soul, a spiritual principle" and that two things constitute its soul. One is "its common possession of a rich legacy of memories; the other is the present consensus, the desire to live together, the will to continue to value the heritage that has been received undivided. . . . To have shared glories in the past, a common will in the present, to have done great things together, to want to do them still."

This description has especially been true of the United States for at least 200 years. To Renan's definition I would add that America's soul also reflects strong spiritual values and beliefs, undergirded by Judeo-Christian norms and morality that have been largely interpreted and applied in the light of Christian principles.

In 1787, the Continental Congress passed the Northwest Ordinance Act which, among other things, required the teaching of religion and morality in its schools. Article III stated: "Religion, morality, and knowledge being necessary to good government and the happiness of mankind, schools and the means of education shall be forever encouraged." Every student of American history knows that "religion" in Article III meant the Christian religion, not just any religion.

The multiculturalist attack on America's culture, which seeks to reject the natural/moral law, biblical values, and Christian symbols, is an attack not just on the nation's long-standing morality but also on its soul. Thus America is not merely competing with some alternative cultural values but is engaged in an all-out war to preserve its soul. For inspiration and courage to fight and win the war against multiculturalism, the nation needs to restore its long-held beliefs and values. . . .

Attacks on America's National Symbols

During the last 200 years, the United States not only developed impressive national symbols, but its citizens have also deeply internalized their meanings. These symbols are being attacked by multiculturalists directly and indirectly in ways that the public often does not recognize.

For two centuries every school child has been taught the words, "We, the people," the first three words of their nation's Constitution. These words proclaim that the nation is a republic, that public thing (*res publica*) whose people rule themselves by giving consent to those who govern them, as opposed to being ruled by a monarch or dictator who lacks such consent.

In the currently rabid quest for multiculturalism, not only is there the desire to reject America's Western culture, but also there is the goal to undermine what Americans have always meant by the words "We, the people"—namely, a majority of the people rule. But now some want to replace the rule of the majority with weighted voting rights for racial and minority groups, or "peoples," as the multiculturalists say. Weighted voting gives a minority voter more than one vote for a candidate or issue.

The widespread furor over President Clinton's nomination of Lani Guinier in 1993 to a government post resulted largely over this issue. Guinier favored weighted voting. Clinton's nomination of Guinier was an example of what he meant in his inauguration speech when, like a true multiculturalist, he said: "Each generation of Americans must define what it means to be an American." It appears that one way to redefine America is to replace the first three words, "We, the people," of the country's Constitution, with "We, the peoples."

So when multiculturalists say they want to introduce cultural diversity by giving special attention to different "peoples," much more is involved here than what many might think. The eventual goal is to attack the very nerve center of the nation, its Constitution. This historical, and longest continually functioning, constitution spells out the republican concept of "We, the people," not "peoples," as sovereign, and many multiculturalists aim to change it.

If multiculturalists should someday succeed in replacing the word "people" in the Constitution with "peoples," America will become an arena of unassimilated tribal groups primed for racial and ethnic conflicts. The very thing multiculturalists fault America for, namely, racism and discrimination, would inevitably get worse, not better.

> *"America is not merely competing with some alternative cultural values but is engaged in an all-out war to preserve its soul."*

Shortly before his death in 1994, Russell Kirk warned: "Should the multiculturalists have their way, culture, with us Americans a century and a half later, would end in heartache—and anarchy." This may well be an understatement because if the current growth of multiculturalism is not checked and reversed, the heartache and anarchy that Kirk talks about will happen much sooner.

E Pluribus Unum

In 1782, when the United States officially accepted these Latin words that Thomas Jefferson borrowed from Virgil's poem, *Moretum,* as its motto, it did more than merely adopt a slogan. It reflected its identity. The slogan *E Pluribus Unum* declared that out of many people—immigrants from all over the world—the nation formed one united people. *E Pluribus Unum* has been such an integral part of the United States that the phrase is embossed on every American coin. The many became one by means of America's melting pot.

For 200 years Americans took *E Pluribus Unum* for granted. It was an American thing. But then came the multiculturalists in the 1980s and 1990s. Despising cultural assimilation, they long for *E Pluribus Plures* (keeping the many as many). They want "diversity," so that every immigrant group can retain its culture and language. *E Pluribus Unum is* "cultural oppression."

If there are any doubts regarding the good *E Pluribus Unum* has done for America, one only needs to remember Canada's tragic experience. The country is unraveling as its leadership bows to all kinds of demands of its cultural and subcultural groups. No institution has been left untouched. A few years ago, the Royal Canadian Mounted Police (RCMP), of which I was once proudly a member, even capitulated to Canada's multiculturalist mania.

> *"[America's] symbols are being attacked by multiculturalists directly and indirectly in ways that the public often does not recognize."*

One of its regular members, a Sikh, demanded the right to wear a turban in place of the stetson hat that accompanies this police force's famous scarlet tunic. The Sikh won his case in the name of multiculturalist diversity. More than a century of the RCMP's pride and honor was sacrificed on the altar of multiculturalism. One person's deviancy (now called "diversity") was more important than the *esprit de corps* of thousands of other Mounties, which for more than a century was a hallmark of this world-renowned police force. This Canadian example illustrates a common stance of multiculturalists; namely, that when non-Western cultures impose their cultural customs on their host countries, it is only being multicultural, but when the assimilated citizens reject such customs, it is "oppression" or "bigotry."

If America loses the ability to assimilate the many *(plures)* into one united nation, it will become like Canada and other divided countries. When that happens, America will have lost its soul. It will then be a tribalistic country in which each group will selfishly seek its own ethnocentric norms, mores, and other foreign interests, eventually producing serious social and cultural conflicts, and probably even physical violence. . . .

Hyphenating All Americans

In recent years, multiculturalists have done a good job of hyphenating Americans. While this is not a new practice, in the past governmental entities did not encourage or promote it, as it does today, in keeping with the spirit of multiculturalism. In some instances, bureaucrats in the federal government have recently coined new hyphens. The designation "Hispanic-American" came into being in 1978 when the Office of Management and Budget (OMB) in Washington, D.C., came up with this classification. Another recent coinage is the hyphen "Asian-American." And an even more recent one is today's "African-American" designation for American blacks. This hyphen was first launched at the African-American Summit in New Orleans in April 1989 by Ramona H. Edelin, the president of the National Urban Coalition.

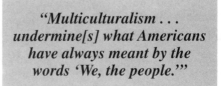

"Multiculturalism ... undermine[s] what Americans have always meant by the words 'We, the people.'"

The mass media insist on hyphenating Americans, especially those from minority cultures. They rigidly refer to blacks as "African-Americans," in spite of research showing that most blacks in the United States prefer to be called black if a distinction must be made. One survey in 1991, conducted by the Joint Center for Political and Economic Studies, a group that focuses on black issues, found that 72 percent of America's blacks preferred to be known as black and only 15 percent preferred African-American. This preference makes a lot of sense because for most black Americans, their ancestors came here 200 to 300 years ago. Thus they know little about African cultures. Moreover, Africa is a continent with 53 countries and some 800 different languages.

Hyphenating Americans does not bind Americans together. Instead, it segregates them into groups, and it also qualifies people's commitment to America. This is why President Theodore Roosevelt in the early 1900s opposed the practice. Unequivocally, he said:

> A hyphenated American is no American at all. This is just as true of the man who puts "native" before the hyphen as of the man who puts German or Irish or English or French before the hyphen. American is a matter of the spirit of the soul. Our allegiance must be purely to the United States. We must unsparingly condemn any man who holds any other allegiance.

Hyphenating Americans runs counter to long-established American practice. No one during World War I called General Pershing a German-American, and no one during World War II referred to General Eisenhower as a German-American. And America was the better for it.

When General Norm Schwartzkopf led the American troops in the Gulf War of 1992, he was not referred to as a German-American, and rightly so. His German descent was of no consequence. Similarly, when General John Shalikashvili, President Clinton's chairman of the Joint Chiefs of Staff, appears on television he is not identified as a Polish-American. Then why do the media refer to General Colin Powell as African-American whenever it's convenient? After all, he is as much an American as is Schwartzkopf or Shalikashvili. To ask the question is not to be insensitive, as many multiculturalists are quick to respond. To the contrary, it is probably insensitive not to accord Powell, or any other noteworthy member of an American minority group, the same degree of American status that is given to other Americans.

There are additional reasons for not hyphenating Americans. They are not identified as hyphenated Americans on their passports. Also, when American soldiers go overseas, they are not referred to as African-American, German-American, or Irish-American but as American soldiers. The sooner the hyphenating ends, the better it will be for all Americans and for the continuing unity of the nation.

Attacks on America's National Pride

Multiculturalists are dedicated to expunging all references to the nation's glorious accomplishments, and this includes the country's national pride. They detest America's national pride, which they regard as "chauvinistic," and are succeeding in many of their attempts to erase American pride. In Portland, Oregon, in March 1994, they persuaded the city to reject a newly fashioned sculpture of a pioneer family on the Oregon Trail that depicted a white pioneer husband pointing confidently to the horizon ahead, a mother holding her deceased daughter's doll, and their son clutching a Bible. The sculpture, *Promised Land*, by David Manuel illustrated American pride.

An editorial in the *Seattle Post-Intelligencer* cited the opinion of an art professor from Oregon State University who saw the sculpture as an affront to multiculturalism. He stated: "I'm not sure we need any more memorials to the dominant culture." So the sculpture had to go.

> *"If America loses the ability to assimilate the many (plures) into one united nation . . . America will have lost its soul."*

Efforts to diminish the nation's pride leaves loyal Americans only two choices: succumb to the anti-American ideology and politics of multiculturalism, and thereby engage in a type of national masochism, or fight for their nation's soul in order to preserve its long-held values. . . .

Threats to America's Schools

As all Americans know, the price of liberty is eternal vigilance. One place where they really must be vigilant is in their public schools, on both the elementary and secondary levels. Multiculturalists have infiltrated American schools by pushing their ideology onto teachers and students through their textbooks, which are strongly biased against American culture. Similar to other left-wingers before them, multiculturalists know that they will more likely achieve their goals if they can invade the schools with their ideology. . . .

Americans must become active in restoring the teaching of American history as it used to be taught for generations, when textbooks and teachers taught students about the heroic acts and contributions of men like Patrick Henry, Paul Revere, and others, rather than omit them from texts as is presently true in many instances. Textbooks need to begin giving credit again to Western/Judeo-Christian philosophy and to return to the insights that the Founding Fathers used to found and shape the nation's institutions. Schools must cease pandering to the anointed minorities by teaching unsubstantiated claims as historical facts in order to make them feel good. Ethnic cheerleading has no place in American schools. Teachers are obliged to teach their students about the really significant individuals and events of American history, those that have stood the test of time.

Teachers need to teach students that God gave the United States great presidents when they were most needed—for instance, Washington, Jefferson, Lincoln, Roosevelt, Truman, Eisenhower, and Reagan. These men were not afraid to lead. They filled Americans with pride. They knew that what they were doing was right, and they had no doubts that their decisions would be good for the nation. They did not apologize for acts they never committed, as multiculturalists have persuaded many of our current leaders to do.

The White-Guilt Syndrome

The phenomenon of white guilt has enabled non-Western cultural groups to receive special privileges that no previous groups in America's history have ever received in the past. The time has come for white Americans, who comprise 76 percent of the country's population, to reject the white-guilt syndrome.

White guilt needs to be rejected for several reasons. First, the socioeconomic problems that minority groups experience today are not the fault of the white majority. Second, even if their problems were in part the result of the white majority, blaming others never helps the disadvantaged overcome difficulties. A group that sees itself as victim leads to self-pity, not to character building, self-respect, and self-determination. It leads to looking for special benefits and privileges that only serve to delay progress and development. Third, no white Americans alive today can rightfully be blamed for the enslavement of blacks in the eighteenth and nineteenth centuries, unjust and evil as it was. Nor can the past injustices that American Indians experienced, also more than 100 years ago, be blamed on the present generation of whites. The sins that were committed by some white Americans in the past are not the sins of the present generation. To take ownership of ancestral injustices, which are so readily handed out by multiculturalists, is not only irrelevant but also masochistic. It also does not help the respective minorities in the least.

And so, Americans need to cast off the mantle of white guilt that multiculturalists and radical minority leaders have draped around so many. Minorities today would do well to recall the experience of many minorities of the past, the Germans, the Irish, the Italians, the Poles, the Greeks, most of whom came to America in poverty. Unfortunately, they too were often victims of prejudice and discrimination, and sometimes severely so. But they overcame these obstacles, not by claiming victim status, but by taking advantage of America's unequaled freedoms and economic opportunities. They were content with having equal opportunity which they did not confuse with equal outcome or results, as many leftist politicians tell minority groups today. Ironically, these one-time (old) minorities are now part of the "evil" white majority, which, multiculturalists say, has helped create the "oppressive" Euro-American culture that subjects today's minorities to all sorts of inequalities.

America has long tolerated different views. Its Constitution's First Amendment made toleration a hallmark of freedom. The framers of the Constitution, however, never had the slightest intention of equating tolerance with acceptance. Unfortunately, with the help of multiculturalist propaganda, many Americans now are making this erroneous equation. Hence various behaviors, some of them immoral, which once were only tolerated, are now accepted and socially legitimated.

It is one thing to tolerate something and quite another to accept that which is tolerated. When the latter happens, the distinction between moral and immoral behavior essentially disappears, nullifying the Judeo-Christian standard of morality. Absolute norms and values vanish, everything is morally relative, and facts are irrelevant. When this occurs, the stage is set for a national nightmare, and the rise of coercive power is all but inevitable. Once there is no more absolute truth, or the possibility of it, rational arguments are no longer effective, nor are they tolerated. Coercive power becomes the only means for those who want their ideology—their truth—to prevail.

Ironically, at that juncture cultural relativity comes to an end. Now the relativists become arbitrary absolutists. This is what happened in Nazi Germany and in Communist Russia. To a degree, some of this is already evident with the "politically correct" enforcers on college/university campuses, where many students are being disciplined and expelled for not conforming to the ideology of multiculturalism. America has recently taken long strides toward accepting what it once merely tolerated. And as is often true, when this happens, the next move is toward coercive power. It seems that the nation is beginning to move in the latter direction as many in its midst are forcing a "politically correct" multiculturalist agenda on its people.

> *"Ethnic cheerleading has no place in American schools."*

The United States Needs a Multicultural Identity

by Elizabeth Martinez

About the author: *Elizabeth Martinez, author of* 500 Years of Chicano History, *teaches women's studies at California State University in Hayward.*

For some 15 years, starting in 1940, 85 percent of all U.S. elementary schools used the "Dick and Jane" series to teach children how to read. The series starred Dick, Jane, their white middle-class parents, their dog Spot, and their life together in a home with a white picket fence.

"Look, Jane, look! See Spot run!" chirped the two kids. It was a houseful of glorious family values, where Mom cooked while Daddy went to work in a suit and mowed the lawn on weekends. The Dick and Jane books also taught that you should do your job and help others. All this affirmed an equation of middle-class with whiteness with virtue.

In the mid-1990s museums, libraries, and 80 PBS stations across the country had exhibits and programs commemorating the series. At one museum, an attendant commented, "When you hear someone crying, you know they are looking at the Dick and Jane books." It seems nostalgia runs rampant among many Euroamericans: a nostalgia for the days of unchallenged White Supremacy—both moral and material—when life was "simple."

A National Identity Crisis

We've seen that nostalgia before in the nation's history. But today it signifies a problem reaching new intensity. Today it suggests a national identity crisis which promises to bring in its wake an unprecedented nervous breakdown for the dominant society's psyche.

Nowhere is this more apparent than in California, which has long been on the cutting edge of the nation's present and future reality. California lives up to that questionable distinction again as the stark outline of identity crisis looms in the state once called Golden. Warning sirens have sounded repeatedly in the 1990s, such as the fierce battle over new history textbooks for K–12, Proposition 187's

Reprinted from Elizabeth Martinez, "Reinventing 'America,'" *Z Magazine*, December 1996, by permission of the author.

ugly denial of human rights to immigrants, and the 1996 assault on Affirmative Action which culminated in Proposition 209. When it passed in November 1996 as an amendment to California's constitution, Prop 209 clones were already borning in 35 other states.

The attack on Affirmative Action is not just a politician's ploy. It isn't really about Affirmative Action. Essentially it's another tactic in today's reactionary attack on gains of the 1960s, which plays on Anglo resentment and fear. A major source of that fear: the fact that California will almost surely have a people-of-color majority in 20 or 30 years at most, with the nation as a whole not far behind.

Check out that issue of *Sports Illustrated* with its double-spread ad for *Time* magazine. The ad shows hundreds of newborn babies in their hospital cribs, all of them Black or brown except for a rare white face here and there. The headline says: "Hey, whitey! It's your turn at the back of the bus!" The ad then tells you, read *Time* magazine to keep up with today's hot issues. Alas, that manipulative image with its implications of shifting power appears to be the recurrent nightmare of too many potential Anglo allies.

The ad appeared in the Feb. 3, 1992 issue and the specter of whites becoming a minority casts an even longer shadow for many Anglos today. It could, in fearful imaginations, launch a tidal wave of vengeful retribution by yesterday's disempowered. Right now a profound anxiety centers on the Euroamerican sense of a vanishing national identity. Behind the attacks on immigrants, Affirmative Action, and multiculturalism, behind the demand for "English Only" laws and the rejection of bilingual education, lies the question: with all these new people, languages, and cultures, "what will it mean to be an American?"

If that question once seemed, to many people, to have an obvious, universally applicable answer, today new definitions must be found. But too often Americans, with supposed scholars in the lead, refuse to face that need and

> *"Euroamerican 'civilization' needs the Indian-as-devil to reconfirm its godly mission."*

instead nurse a nostalgia for some bygone clarity. They remain trapped in denial.

An array of such ostriches, heads in the sand, began flapping their feathers noisily with Allan Bloom's 1987 best-selling book *The Closing of the American Mind*. Bloom bemoaned the decline of our "common values" as a society, meaning the decline of Euroamerican cultural centricity (shall we just call it cultural imperialism?). Since then we have seen constant sniping at "diversity" goals across the land. The assault has often focused on how U.S. history is taught, and with reason. For this country's identity rests on a particular narrative about the historical origins of the United States as a nation.

The Great White Origin Myth

Every society has an origin narrative which explains that society to itself and the world with a set of mythologized stories and symbols. The origin myth, as scholar-activist Roxanne Dunbar Ortiz has termed it, defines how a society understands its place in the world and its history. The myth provides the basis for a nation's self-defined identity.

Ours begins with Columbus "discovering" a hemisphere where some 80 million people already lived (but didn't really count since they were just buffalo-chasing "savages" with no grasp of real estate values and therefore doomed to perish). It continues with the brave Pilgrims, a revolution by independence-loving colonists against a decadent English aristocrat, and the birth of an energetic young republic that promised democracy and equality (that is, to white male landowners). In the 1840s the new nation expanded its size by almost one-third, thanks to a victory over that backward land of little brown people called Mexico. Such has been the basic account of how the nation called the United States of America came into being as presently configured.

> *"By now it should be clear that we need a new, more truthful origin myth and a redefined national identity."*

The myth's omissions are grotesque. It ignores three major pillars of our nationhood: genocide, enslavement, and imperialist expansion (such nasty words, who wants to hear them?—but that's the problem). The massive extermination of indigenous peoples provided our land base; the enslavement of African labor made our economic growth possible; and the seizure of half of Mexico by war (or threat of renewed war) extended this nation's boundaries to the Pacific and the Rio Grande. Such are the foundation stones of the U.S. along with an economic system that made this country the first in world history to be born capitalist.

Those three pillars were, of course, supplemented by great numbers of dirt-cheap workers from Mexico, China, the Philippines, Puerto Rico, etc., all kept in their place by varieties of White Supremacy. They stand along with millions of less-than-Supreme white workers and share-croppers.

Downplaying Injustice and Brutality

Any attempt to modify the present origin myth provokes angry efforts to repel such sacrilege. In the case of Native Americans, scholars will insist that they died from disease, or wars among themselves, or "not so many really did die." At worst, it was a "tragedy," but never deliberate genocide, never a pillar of our nationhood. As for slavery, it was an embarrassment, of course, but remember that Africa also had slavery and anyway enlightened white folk finally did end the practice here.

In the case of Mexico, reputable U.S. scholars still insist on blaming that country for the 1846–48 war, although even former U.S. President Ulysses Grant wrote in his memoirs that "We were sent to provoke a fight [by moving troops into a disputed border area] but it was essential that Mexico should commence it [by fighting back]." President James Polk's 1846 diary records his purpose in declaring war as "acquiring California, New Mexico, and perhaps other Mexican lands." To justify what could be called a territorial drive-by, the Mexican people were declared inferior; the U.S. had a Manifest Destiny to bring them progress and democracy.

Even when revisionist voices speak about particular evils of Indian policy, slavery, or the U.S. war on Mexico, those evils remain little more than unpleasant footnotes; the core of the dominant myth stands intact. PBS's eight-part documentary series entitled *The West* is a case in point. It devotes more than the usual attention to the devastation of Native America, but still centers on Anglos. Little attention is given to why their domination evolved as it did and so the West remains the physically gorgeous backdrop for an ugly, unaltered origin myth.

In fact, that myth is strengthened by *The West* series. White Supremacy needs the brave but ultimately doomed Indians to silhouette its own superiority. Euroamerican "civilization" needs the Indian-as-devil to reconfirm its godly mission. Remember Timothy Wight, who served as pastor to Congress in the late 1700s, and wrote that under the Indians, "Satan ruled unchallenged in America" until "our chosen race eternal justice sent." With that moral authority, the "winning of the West" metamorphosed from a brutal conquest into a romance of persistent courage played out in a lonely, dangerous landscape.

Racism as Linchpin of the National Identity

A crucial embellishment of the origin myth and key element of the national identity has been the Myth of the Frontier, brilliantly analyzed in Richard Slotkin's *Gunfighter Nation,* 1992, the last volume of a trilogy. He describes Theodore Roosevelt's belief that the West was won thanks to American arms, "the means by which progress and nationality will be achieved." That success, Roosevelt continued, "depends on the heroism of men who impose on the course of events the latent virtues of their 'race.'" Roosevelt saw racial conflict on the frontier producing a "race" of virile "fighters and breeders" that would eventually generate a new leadership class.

> *"When together we cease equating whiteness with Americanness, a new day can dawn."*

No slouch as an imperialist, Roosevelt soon took the frontier myth abroad, seeing Asians as Apaches and the Philippines as Sam Houston's Texas in the process of being seized from Mexico. For Roosevelt, as Slotkin writes, "racial violence is the principle around which both individual character and social organization develop." Such ideas did not go totally unchallenged by U.S. historians, nor was the Frontier Myth always applied in totally simplistic ways by Hollywood and other media. (The Outlaw, for example, is a complicated figure, both good and bad.) But the

Frontier Myth usually spins together virtue and violence, morality and war, in a convoluted, Calvinist web. That tortured embrace defines an essence of the so-called American Character—in other words, the national identity—to this day.

> *"A more truthful origin myth could help correct the bi-polar model of race relations, which sees only black and white and ignores the other colors all around us."*

The 19th century doctrine of Manifest Destiny served to combine expansionist violence with inevitability based on intrinsic racial superiority, in one neat package. Yankee conquest had to be seen as the "inevitable" result of a confrontation between enterprise v. passivity, progress v. backwardness. Even when that justification or the pretension of virtue failed, race was always there to draw the bottom line.

Linking the national identity with race is not unique to the United States. In the October 1996 issue of *Lingua Franca,* the journal, David Stowe writes that for any society "there is no social identity without a defining 'other'—in terms of class, race, or gender." But the United States has linked its identity with racialism to an extraordinary degree, matched only by two other settler states: South Africa and Israel.

Given its obsession with race and the supremacy attached to whiteness, which demanded absolute racial purity, the U.S. national identity inevitably reserved a special disdain for "half-breed" peoples—above all, Mexicans—even if one-half was European. *The West* documentary series reflects that disdain with its offhand treatment of Manifest Destiny and the U.S. expansionist takeover of Mexico, violations of the 1848 Treaty of Guadelupe Hidalgo, land robbery, colonization backed by violent repression, the role of Mexican people in building vast wealth in the West, and the West as a reflection of Mexican culture. In doing so the series typifies all the other standard historical treatments. Who could care less? is their message.

Mexican Americans are almost always depicted as just another immigrant population, despite the fact that some of us—especially in New Mexico—can trace family back to the 1500s. If anyone in the dominant society remembers Mexicans before this century, it is usually as "bandits" who fought the U.S. occupation, or señoritas on big California ranchos who had the good sense to marry Anglos. Almost never have we formed part of the origin myth. But of course we're not "white."

The racialization of any population is an extended process, as even the history of Mexicans in the U.S. shows; from time to time we have been officially deemed "white." Earlier in this century Irish, Italian, and Polish immigrants were also scapegoated and defined out of the national identity, not being the preferred "Anglo-Saxon." Later, as they embraced Anglo cultural supremacy, and also could be seen as white, inclusion became possible. Immigrants of color, on the other hand, have largely remained outside Americanism.

Chapter 4

Manifest Destiny Dies Hard

Manifest Destiny, with its assertion of racial/cultural superiority sustained by military power, defined U.S. identity for many years. The Vietnam War brought a major challenge to that concept of almightiness. Bitter debate, moral anguish, images of My Lai, and the prospect of military defeat for the first time in U.S. history all suggested that the marriage of virtue and violence might soon be on the rocks. In the final years of the war the words leaped to mind one day: this country is having a national, nervous breakdown.

The Vietnam War continues to arouse passions today. Some who are willing to call the war "a mistake" still shy away from recognizing its immorality or accepting it as a defeat. That resistance reflects the fact that few Americans have the courage to publicly advocate abandoning the idea that our identity rests on being the world's richest and most powerful nation.

By now it should be clear that we need a new, more truthful origin myth and with it a redefined national identity. Instead, we find a massive, stubborn resistance, especially in the world of education. Loudly protesting supposed pressure to be "PC" [politically correct], scholars fiercely reject the idea that "western" values like freedom and democracy could ever have existed in non-western societies (read, among peoples of color). Professor John Patrick Diggins at the Graduate Center of the City University of New York, for example, condemned the new National History Standards for K–12 because they have students "begin the study of history immersed in past cultures whose people perpetuated undemocratic rites and other systems of submission." Diggins claims it was "American exceptionalism" that made it possible "for freedom to flower."

> *"'America' is the name of an entire hemisphere, rich in a stunning variety of histories, cultures, peoples, and not just one country."*

The war over standards for teaching K–12 history continues to rage. Round three in 1996 brought new recommendations to correct the last, supposedly "PC" revisions. On the subject of "How the West Was Won," for example, the previous standards had described the "restless white Americans [who] pushed westward" and how, "animated by land hunger and the ideology of Manifest Destiny" they "engaged in abrasive racial encounters with Native Americans." To make it less "PC," that text would be changed to omit the adjective "white" for those restless Americans. Also, the new version would add another reason for expansion: "the optimism that anything was possible with imagination, hard work, and the maximum freedom of the individual." The Indians just didn't have enough imagination, you see.

Such is the opposition to ideological change. Other societies have also been based on colonialism and slavery but in this country we seem to have an insatiable need to be the Good Guys on the world stage. The need must lie, at least partially, in a Protestant dualism that defines existence in terms of opposites so that if you are not "good" you are bad, if not "white" then black, and so on. Whatever the cause, the need to comply on some level with origin-myth definitions of "virtuous" as opposed to "evil" haunts domestic and foreign policy. Wherever would we be without Saddam Hussein, Omar Khadafi, and that all-time favorite of gringo demonizers, Fidel Castro? I mean, how would we know what an American really is?

Wanted: A New National Identity

Today's origin myth and the resulting definition of national identity make for an intellectual prison where it is dangerous to ask big questions, moral questions, about this society's superiority. Where otherwise decent people are trapped in a desire not to feel guilty, which then necessitates self-deception. To cease our present falsification of collective memory should, and could, open the doors of that prison. When together we cease equating whiteness with Americanness, a new day can dawn. As David Roediger, the social historian, has said, "[whiteness] is the empty and therefore terrifying attempt to build an identity on what one isn't, and on whom one can hold back." In the end, to redefine the U.S. origin myth, and with it this country's national identity, could prove liberating. A new, truly collective psyche might then be born.

Urging a more truthful origin myth, and with it a different national identity, does not mean Euroamericans should wallow individually in guilt. It does mean accepting collective responsibility to deal with the implications of a different narrative.

A more truthful narrative could also shed light on today's struggles. In the Affirmative Action debate, for example, opponents have said that that policy is no longer needed because racism ended with the civil rights movement. But if we look at slavery in this society as a fundamental pillar of the nation going back centuries, it becomes obvious that racism could not have been ended by 30 years of mild reforms. If we see how the Myth of the Frontier idealized the white male adventurer as the central hero of national history, with the woman as sunbonneted helpmate, then we might better understand the ways that women have continued to be regarded as lesser. (We would also better understand why the Angry White Male is so angry today. Poor guy: from Superman to oppressor-on-the-defensive is a big drop.)

> *"The realities of the next century demand a courageous transcendence of old assumptions."*

In addition, a more truthful origin myth could help correct the bi-polar model of race relations, which sees only Black and White and ignores the other colors all around us. That severely limited paradigm further encourages ineffective policies as well as bigger divisions among different peoples of color.

A new origin myth and national identity could help pave the way to a more livable society for us all. A society based on cooperation rather than competition, on the idea that all living creatures are inter-dependent and humanity's goal should be balance. Such were the values of many original Americans, deemed "savages." Similar gifts are waiting from other despised peoples and traditions. We might well start by recognizing that "America" is the name of an entire hemisphere, rich in a stunning variety of histories, cultures, peoples, and not just one country.

The choice seems clear, if not easy. We can go on living in a state of massive denial, affirming this nation's superiority and virtue simply because we need to believe in it. We can choose to reaffirm White Supremacy, with minor concessions. We can choose to think the destiny of the U.S. is still manifest: global domination. We can seek a transformative vision that carries us forward, not backward. We can seek an origin narrative that lays the ideological groundwork for a multi-cultural, multi-national identity centered on the goals of social equity and democracy. It is our choice; after all, myths are not born but made.

There is little time for nostalgia. Dick and Jane never were "America," they were only a part of Anglo life in one part of the Americas. Let's say goodbye to that narrow identity and look ahead. In the end, there is no decent alternative; the realities of the next century demand a courageous transcendence of old assumptions. Will the future be ongoing denial or steps toward that new vision? When on earth shall we abandon the bad habits that imprison so many minds?

At times you can hear the clock ticking.

The White Race Is Endangered

by Kevin Alfred Strom

About the author: *Kevin Alfred Strom is host of the radio program* American Dissident Voices. *This radio program is funded by the National Alliance, an organization that promotes the advancement and protection of the white race.*

Editor's note: The following viewpoint is based on the American Dissident Voices *radio program segment "Worse than Murder," aired on January 13, 1996.*

Let me read you a short article published in *Harper's Magazine*, which is controlled by the super-rich MacArthur family, whose John D. and Katherine T. MacArthur Foundation is almost omnipresent as the opening and closing sponsor of so-called "public television" programs. The article, written by David A. Bush, is headlined "Ozone Anxiety: It's a White Thing":

> A lot has been said recently about the thinning of the ozone layer. Interestingly, it turns out that the whole issue is really of concern only to fair-skinned Caucasians in the Northern Hemisphere, who are threatened with skin cancer and other problems associated with increased ultraviolet radiation. The peoples of the middle latitudes have always been exposed to higher ambient levels of ultraviolet radiation, but their naturally darker skin has acted as protection. It is entirely possible that "lard-white" skin just will not make it in this new world reality! Perhaps the era of the "classic" Caucasian is drawing to a close, and for completely natural reasons. Fair skin might eventually be considered an affliction and impose on those who possess it severe limitations on their enjoyment of the world.

> The far-thinking Caucasian cannot help but realize that the best gift delicate-skinned individuals can give their progeny is a better chance of survival in the coming ultraviolet environment. Fair-skinned individuals should give careful consideration to the selection of a mate who will contribute a darker complexion to the genetic makeup of their offspring.

Reprinted from Kevin Alfred Strom, "Racemixing—Worse Than Murder," *Free Speech*, January 1996, by permission of *Free Speech*, PO Box 330, Hillsboro, WV 24946; www.natvan.com.

I am not suggesting that the government should mandate changes, but it could do a great deal to encourage interracial coupling. First of all, the government could provide some financial incentive to encourage interracial families. Special tax deductions would mitigate some of the problems that these families encounter.

On another level, the government could organize summer camps, or even working camps, where majority children would encounter minority children in a relaxed atmosphere, away from social constraints.

Let me add that when the author says "away from social constraints," what he really means is away from parents and away from peers of the opposite sex and the same race, whose instinctive abhorrence for interracial coupling might "inhibit" the results desired by the author and presumably by *Harper's Magazine* and the MacArthur family. Now back to the *Harper's* article:

> *"When you commit the crime of racial mixing you are participating in genocide."*

Majority girls would participate in camps where they would encounter only minority boys, and vice versa. In such an environment, children would not be subjected to prejudicial pressures or obsolete taboos. Even if relationships did not develop at these camps, the participants would gain a greater appreciation of people who are different from themselves. When they returned home, they might be more disposed to the idea of a different-race partner.

In addition, the public should be educated about the positive aspects of a darker complexion. When mainstream television programming promotes the existence of couples from different races and backgrounds, then cultural and racist barriers will fall and society will move forward. A major benefit will be the fact that the population's general resistance to ultraviolet radiation will be enhanced.

The thinning of the ozone layer is just one more reason for Caucasian parents to bestow the gift of a darker complexion on their offspring. If we continue to lose the ozone, there may not be any options at all for fair-skinned individuals, as they will simply cease to exist. But if Caucasians do the right thing, how comforting it will be for them to look at their children and know they have done their best to ensure them a safe and comfortable future.

Genocide of the White Race

Harper's Magazine published that article in December 1993. It had originally been printed by a glossy magazine called *Interrace*, the primary purpose of which is to promote interracial sex and marriage. We do not know the source of the funding for *Interrace* magazine, but we do know that its reported owner is a person named Candace Mills and the list of its officers consists of only one name repeated for each position, and that name is "Gabe Grosz."

Now David A. Bush may know, and the MacArthur family surely knows that what they are calling for is genocide of the White race. And all of them surely know that their moronic argument about reducing the rate of skin cancer by a minuscule amount is not the real motivation for their call to exterminate our people.

Here we have a major pillar of the liberal establishment calling far more openly for a genocide far more sweeping than that they accuse Adolf Hitler of calling for. And yet we hear of no protests against *Harper's* or its owners, no Million Man Marches of White men and women concerned for the survival and welfare of their kind, no charges of "hate crimes" against the perpetrators of this outrage. No. We hear nothing except a few worried clucks from conservatives that, well, "they probably don't really mean it that way," and approving snickers from Jews and White liberals about how amusing it all is and how wonderful and advanced their thinking is on such matters. Well, I don't think it's funny, and I do think they mean it, and we ought to take this advocacy of genocide through racial mixture very seriously indeed. We must take it seriously because it is happening right now.

Mixed-Race Births Are Increasing

Under the title "Interracial Baby Boom," the following data from the Population Reference Bureau (PRB) was published in the *Futurist:*

> Between 1968 and 1989, children born to parents of different races increased from 1% of total births to 3.4%. U.S. Census Bureau data show that, mirroring changes in laws and attitudes from 1970 to 1991, the number of mixed-race married couples increased from 310,000 to 994,000. PRB researchers observe that this trend is taking place among all racial and ethnic groups, but the patterns for each group are distinctly different.

The article goes on to say that although mixed marriages still represented less than four per cent of the total in 1989, the trend is definitely upward, tripling in less than twenty years. And that trend is probably accelerating. Carry that four per cent forward a few decades—three times four is 12, three times 12 is 36, and three times 36. . . . Couple this ominous trend with the fact that the White birth rate is now below the replacement level, and you see that use of the term genocide is not hyperbole. Also carefully consider this, according to the Population Reference Bureau report "Most mixed births involve one white parent, but by no means all."

> *"Every White man who commits the crime of marrying a non-White will not be fathering any White children."*

Notice the use of the qualifying words, "but by no means all." Why add them? Out of 994,000 mixed-race couples, would anyone expect that every single one of them that had a child would have one White parent? Of course "by no means all." But the extremely significant thing to notice is the report's admission that *most mixed births involve one White parent.* What does this mean? It means that the majority of racial mixing involves the destruction of the White race—Whites mating with Asians, Whites mating with Blacks, Whites mating with Arabs or Jews, Whites mating with *mestizos*, Whites mating with the racially unclassifiable. You have seen it in your shopping centers. You have seen it in the street. You are a witness to genocide. You are seeing it before your very eyes every day. What are you doing about it? If you do not at least speak out against it, you are allowing yourself to be complicit in this horrible crime.

The Crime of Racemixing

The crime is racemixing. It is a worse crime than murder—far worse.

For when you commit murder you kill one man, you end one life, you tragically injure one family and circle of friends. When you commit murder, if your victim has had no children, you do cut off the potential existence of one small branch of the race's future.

But when you commit the crime of racial mixing you are participating in genocide. The probable effect and possible motive for your act is to bring into the world hybrid young, who will not be clearly of one race or the other and which will, by their very existence, increase the probability of future racial mixing and dilute both the gene pool and the sense of identity of the next generation of White children. And don't underestimate the importance of that instinctive sense of identity among our young Whites. Except for efforts like this radio program, which are growing but are still far too small, that sense of identity is about the only thing standing between us and total extinction of the European race. Our young people may be confused, but their innate sense of decency and racial identity has held amazingly firm so far. Even though the Jewish media have been strenuously promoting interracial sex for decades, and even though the so-called "White establishment" has provided no leadership and nothing but treason to our race for the last 30 years and more, about 90 per cent of them are still marrying within their race. This contrasts starkly with the results of a *Washington Post* poll on the subject. According to the poll results, only 47 per cent of White men would not be willing to marry a Black woman; and only 60 per cent of White women would be unwilling to marry a Black man. Quite clearly there is a gap between what White people *say* and what they actually *do*. Why? Even among those intimidated into responding to the question in a Politically Correct manner—even among those who have at some level convinced themselves that they would mate with any arguably human subspecies—the natural instinct to cleave to your own kind is still a powerful determinant of action. Thank God that it is! And to Hell with those who are working in the media and in the schools and in the

> *"The crime of racial mixture . . . is far, far worse than mere murder."*

churches to destroy that healthy natural tendency in our children. They are worse than murderers.

Murderers of Future Generations

And yes, you heard me right, some of these murderers of our future generations have weaseled their way into positions of influence in the churches. That many of these have hidden Communist sympathies or are actually in the pay of our enemies has been documented by many others, and I do not have the time to recapitulate those data today. But their words speak for themselves. Let me give you a few quotations from the March 1994 issue of *Christianity Today*, a mainstream Protestant publication.

> . . . Is it possible God actually calls some Blacks to fall in love with Whites, and vice-versa? If that is true, then we should celebrate.

> Yes, celebrate! Let's rejoice over the beautiful children born to interracial marriages and do everything possible to make them fully accepted. Let's recognize the contributions intermarriage can make toward breaking down prejudice. And though we may not necessarily promote interracial marriages, let's take the lead in defending, protecting, and supporting them in our churches.

> . . . The entertainment industry has attempted to keep pace with the increasing number of intermarrying Americans. Television shows such as *General Hospital* and *L.A. Law* and major Hollywood releases like *Jungle Fever*, *Mississippi Masala*, *The Joy Luck Club*, and *The Bodyguard* have all highlighted interracial romances.

> This is one area where the media may be morally ahead of the church.

> . . . American churches can become havens of safety and support for interracial couples. . . . More creative heterogeneous churches may emerge, becoming places that feel like home to interracial families. . . . We should rejoice over the barrier-shattering potential each Christian interracial marriage brings to our churches.

That is what it says in the March 1994 issue of *Christianity Today*, the chairman of the board and founder of which is the Reverend Billy Graham. No comment should be necessary. I invite you to obtain a copy from your local library if you think I am misrepresenting their position.

Every White man who commits the crime of marrying a non-White will not be fathering any White children. Every White woman who pollutes her body and her spirit by marrying a non-White will not be giving birth to any White children. And by their actions they will be committing the crime of misleading White boys and girls to follow their example. And all those who do not speak out against their racial treason will be complicit in the crime. When your four-year-old sees a Black or an Asian or a *mestizo* with a White mate, and you do not condemn this, that child will believe that what he has seen is normal and that his mommy and daddy approve of it.

Nature—or Nature's God if you prefer to express it that way—created our race through hundreds of thousands of years of incredible hardship and rigorous selection. We have survived the Ice Ages. We have fought against invaders for thousands of generations, from the Moors to the Huns, again and again and again, back beyond the impenetrable mists of history of our race. Our ancestors gave their all so that we might survive, so that we might live. And we *do* live.

> *"I will applaud the growing numbers of members of other races who understand that racial mixing means death for their race and culture as well."*

We *did* survive. Thanks to them. Our race extends back continuously to the mysterious beginning of life itself. It can extend into the infinite future. And its continued existence would undoubtedly be assured by our superior intelligence and unmatched technology, if it were not for those who practice and promote the genocide of our people through racial mixing. By their actions they are killing us. They kill not an individual. They kill the infinite generations of our future. Their crime—the crime of racial mixture—is far, far worse than mere murder.

Seeing the Truth

As long as I live, I will be shouting this truth from the housetops and doing everything I can to encourage more and more of my people to see this truth. And I will applaud the growing numbers of members of other races who understand that racial mixing means death for their race and culture as well. This truth is the one factor that the promoters of the one world government called the New World Order fear. They do not fear the constitutionalist and the legalist "patriots" who avoid the issue of race in order to gain for themselves a measure of "respectability.". . . They don't care how many sacks of gold and silver coins you have salted away. They don't care if the front men for their secret government call themselves conservatives or liberals. They don't care if there is prayer in the schools or not. The one thing they fear more than anything else is racial consciousness, because they know their history, because they know that national and racial loyalty threaten their plan to establish the ultimate multicultural construct, a world government. For this twisted dream of world dominion, they are attempting genocide against our people.

Whites Could Abandon Race Privilege

by Noel Ignatiev, interviewed by ¡The Blast!

About the author: *Noel Ignatiev is coeditor of the quarterly periodical* Race Traitor: A Journal of the New Abolitionism, *PO Box 603, Cambridge, MA 02140-0005.* ¡The Blast! *is an anarchist tabloid published in Minneapolis, Minnesota.*

¡The Blast!: What is a race traitor anyway?

Noel Ignatiev: A traitor to the white race is someone who is nominally classified as white, but who defies the rules of whiteness so flagrantly as to jeopardize his or her ability to draw upon the privileges of the white skin.

"Race" has meant various things in history. We use the term to mean a group that includes all social classes, in a situation where the most degraded member of a dominant group is exalted over any member of a subordinate group. That formation was first successfully established in the 17th century. By then there already existed a trade across the Atlantic in laborers. Traders from both Europe and Africa sold their countrymen and were not held back because they were of the same color as those they sold. Slavery was a matter of economics. At the time it was the most efficient way of guaranteeing a labor force—provided it could be enforced.

As Theodore Allen points out in *Invention of the White Race,* the white race meant not only that no European-Americans were slaves, but also that all European-Americans, even laborers, were by definition enforcers of slavery. In the Chesapeake Bay Colony (Virginia and Maryland), people from Africa and people from Europe worked together in the tobacco fields. They mated with each other, ran away and rebelled together, at first. At the end of the 1600s, people of African descent, even those who were free, lost certain rights they had had before and that even the poorest and most downtrodden person of European descent continued to enjoy. In return for these privileges, European-Americans of all classes came to be part of the apparatus that maintained Afro-Americans in chattel slavery (and themselves in unfreedom). That was the birth of "race," as we use the term.

Reprinted from Noel Ignatiev, "Treason to Whiteness Is Loyalty to Humanity," an interview with Noel Ignatiev by *¡The Blast!* June/July 1994, by permission.

What do you mean when you say that race is a social construction?

We mean that it is the result of social distinctions. Many black people have European ancestors, and plenty of so-called whites have African or American Indian ancestors. No biologist has ever been able to provide a satisfactory definition of race—that is, a definition that includes all the members of a given "race" and excludes all others. At-tempts to do so lead to absurdities: mothers and children of different races, or the phenomenon that a white woman can give birth to a black child, but a black woman can

> *"People are members of different races because they are assigned to them."*

never give birth to a white child. The only possible conclusion is that people are members of different races because they are assigned to them. Of course, differences exist between individuals, and the natives of West Africa in general had darker skin and so forth than the natives of the British Isles, but groups are formed by social distinctions, not nature.

Can you provide an example of a people suddenly becoming "white"?

The Irish are as clear an example as any. In Ireland, under the Protestant Ascendancy, Catholic Irish were the victims of discrimination identical to what we in America call racial, and were even referred to as a "race." Karl Marx, writing from England, reported that the average English worker looked down on the Irish the way poor whites in the American South looked upon Afro-Americans. Yet over here the Irish became "whites," by gaining the right to vote while free Negroes were losing it, by supporting the Democratic Party (the party of the slaveholders), and by preventing free Afro-Americans from competing with them for jobs. The overcoming of anti-Irish prejudice meant that the Irish were admitted to the privileges of whiteness.

Abolishing the White Race

What do you mean by the "new abolitionism"?

We believe that so long as the white race exists, all movements against what is called "racism" will fail. Therefore, our aim is to abolish the white race.

How does your position on race and whiteness differ from the standard political stance of anti-racism?

Racism is a pretty vague term. It has come to mean little more than a tendency to dislike people for the color of their skin. Most anti-racists, even while they oppose discrimination, believe that racial status is fixed and eternal. We hold that without social distinctions, "race" is a fiction. The only race is the human race.

Even if a person declares him/herself a "race traitor," to the vast majority of people in this society, s/he is still white and therefore allowed all the privileges of the "white club." Is it possible to abolish the white race, ironically, only as white people?

The white race does not like to relinquish a single member, so that even those who step out of it in one situation find it virtually impossible not to rejoin it later, if only because of the assumptions of others—unless, like John Brown, they have the good fortune to be hanged before that happens. So-called whites have special responsibilities to abolition that only they can fulfill. Only they can dissolve the white race from within, by rejecting the poisoned bait of white-skin privileges. If that is what you mean by abolishing the white race "as whites," then we have no quarrel.

Race Privilege

What is the relationship between capitalism and racism?

Capital itself is color-blind, and the capitalist system, as such, recognizes nothing but atomized individuals acting independently in the market. There are places in the world where it exists without race. In this country race is central to the system of social control: It leads some workers to settle for being "white" when they could, with some effort, be free.

Is there such a thing as a "white culture"?

No. There is Italian culture, and Polish, Irish, Yiddish, German, and Appalachian culture; there is youth culture and drug culture and queer culture; but there is no "white" culture—unless you mean Wonder bread and television game shows. Whiteness is nothing but an expression of race privilege. It has been said that the typical "white" American male spends his childhood as an Indian, his adolescence as an Afro-American, and only becomes white when he reaches the age of legal responsibility.

In an autobiographical essay, Joel Gilbert says that most of his whiteness has washed away and that he has "plenty of black inside." How is it possible for a white person to have "plenty of black" inside? How is it possible for whites to wash away their whiteness? Should a black person accept a white person's claim to have "a lot of black inside"?

Politically, whiteness is the willingness to seek a comfortable place within the system of race privilege. Blackness means total, implacable, and relentless opposition to that system. To the extent so-called whites oppose the race line, repudiating their own race privileges and jeopardizing their own standing in the white race, they can be said to have washed away their whiteness and taken in some blackness. Probably a black person should not accept a white person's claim to have done that, but should watch how that person acts.

A common theme in Race Traitor *[magazine] is that of whites "crossing over, into black culture," or what you have called "black assimilation."*

> **"Without social distinctions, 'race' is a fiction. The only race is the human race."**

A lot of the examples you cite of people "refusing to be white" involve white people—especially youth—imitating black cultural forms. The line between "crossing over" into black cultures and ripping off black culture is a mighty fine one; where do you draw it? Is there a necessary connection between "crossover" and the abandonment of whiteness? What makes white "cross-over" in the '90s different from white youths and big businesses "crossing over" and ripping off black music in the '40s and '50s?

In culture, the line between rip-off and respect is the willingness to pay the dues, if necessary to forgo the social advantages of being white, in order to achieve genuineness of expression. There is no necessary connection between cultural assimilation and rejection of whiteness: The crowds at professional basketball games prove that; and on the other hand immigrants to this country may speak no English and have no interest in American culture and still refuse to take part in the oppression of black people. But for many, the rejection of whiteness seems to entail some engagement with Afro-American culture, because that is the first cultural expression of resistance they encounter, and it speaks powerfully to them. You are right to point out that whites have been ripping off Afro-American culture for years. Fundamentally, the crossover of the '90s may not be different from that of the past, although it may make a difference that the process of social dissolution is now more advanced. By itself, crossover represents a potential for race treason, not the actuality.

How does wanting to abolish racial classifications avoid doing away with cultural differences, which is what most liberal attempts to "confront racism" do?

> **"Whiteness is nothing but an expression of race privilege."**

For us, black and white are political categories, separate from, although not unrelated to, culture. One of the effects of white supremacy is that it represses the cultures of Afro-Americans and other peoples of color. If that repression were removed, who knows how they would flourish? Moreover, American culture is, as Albert Murray has pointed out, incontestably mulatto. Without race prejudice, Americans might discover that culturally they are all Afro-American, as well as Native American, and so forth.

Race Identity and Race Relations

Abolition also brings up issues of identity. People of color, in struggling against oppression, often turn toward their precolonial cultures and earlier examples of resistance to find an identity that can inspire them today. What can a so-called white person turn to after abandoning whiteness? Does s/he seek inspiration in prewhite cultures such as Judaism, Celtic or Germanic tribes? In ethnic identities such as Irish, Italian-American, etc.? In committing treason against the white race, must we seek these "intermediate" identities, abandon all identities in favor of a universal humanism, or something else?

I don't know. So far as I am concerned, there is nothing wrong with people seeking out the Celtic or Germanic tribes, or ethnicity, or anything else that can provide them with a vital alternative to whiteness, although I have my doubts about how real these are or can be made to be for modern Americans, and the last time somebody built a mass movement around Germanic tribal myths it led to big trouble. We might do better to promote models of amalgamation. The Seminole Indians, as I understand it, were composed of the remnants of several native groups who had earlier been dispersed, plus a number of runaway slaves, plus some deserters from the army. They came together and fought three wars against the U.S. government. They were never really defeated. The Seminole tribe might be a model that could inspire people.

> *"Without race prejudice, Americans might discover that culturally they are all Afro-American, as well as Native American, and so forth."*

Time will tell.

In being a race traitor, to whom do you announce your treason—fellow so-called whites? Is it ever appropriate to tell a person of color that you have abandoned your whiteness?

I would never say that, although I might say I was working on it.

What kinds of relations with people of color are implied when one becomes a race traitor? How does a race traitor act politically with people of color?

Relations must be based on solidarity. People of color have a wealth of experience with white supremacy, from which others can learn, but the fight against white supremacy is not something to engage in as a favor to anyone. All people who wish to be free have an equal stake—yes, an equal stake—in overturning the system of white supremacy. I'm reminded of the old IWW [Industrial Workers of the World, the "Wobblies"] slogan, "An injury to one is an injury to all." Decades of distortion have reduced the message of those words to the idea that you should oppose injustice against others today because if you don't it will come your way tomorrow. We believe in the original intent of the slogan. The Bible offers the same instruction: "Remember them that are in bonds as bound with them."

Race Treason as Revolution

Race Traitor *does an excellent job of providing examples of individuals rejecting their whiteness and joining the human race, but there is little there of collective resistance. Where is the collective political strategy in a politics of abolition? How do we, collectively, abolish the white race?*

For the white race to be effective, it must be unanimous, or nearly so. The reason is that if the cops and the courts and so forth couldn't be sure that every person who looked white was loyal to the system, then what would be the point of extending race privileges to whites? And if they stopped extending race privileges, what would happen to the white race? Our strategy seeks to bring together a determined minority, willing to defy white rules so flagrantly they make it impossible to pretend that all those who look white are loyal to the system of racial oppression.

We wish we could cite more examples of collective resistance. The whites who joined the rebellions in Los Angeles in 1992 and elsewhere were a good example. The Attica prison rebellion was another. The initiative by Love and Rage to launch a campaign culminating in a day of action against immigration controls and anti-immigrant violence was a good project, but unfortunately it never got off the ground. Collective struggle is crucial, but at some point every white person has to choose, like Huck Finn, between being white and striking out for freedom.

In some articles you literally break the world down into a matter of black and white. Have you ever been accused of ignoring the struggles and perspectives of nonblack people of color, and how do you respond to this charge?

Yes, I have been. I think that the line between black and white determines race in this country, and all groups get defined in relation to that line. Don't forget, I am using black and white as political, not cultural, categories. I do not mean to neglect the real and independent histories of people of color who are not of African descent. But in some cases the talk about "people of color" obscures the essence of racial oppression. Chinese are people of color and in the past they suffered fierce oppression in this country, and still suffer the effects of prejudice, but would anyone argue that Chinese in America today constitute an oppressed race? They have been defined as an ethnic group, indeed the "model minority," as shown by the high rate of social mobility among them, the high proportion of marriages with European-Americans, and the presence among them of a substantial number of capitalists who function outside of a segregated market—all in contrast to the situation of Afro-Americans. Of course they might become an oppressed race again. Or they might choose to identify as black in the struggle against white power, as many of the so-called colored of South Africa have done.

> *"All people who wish to be free have an equal stake . . . in overturning the system of white supremacy."*

It seems from your journal and from thinking about your ideas that abolishing the white race would bring about widespread, radical changes in other aspects of social life. Is race treason necessarily revolutionary in that it threatens not only white supremacy but class rule as well?

It would be good if people could forget that they are white and pursue their interests as workers, or women, or whatever else moves them. The problem is that American society does not allow anyone to forget, but injects race into every political controversy. For those in power, the privileges granted whites are a small price to pay for the stability of an unjust social system. While not all forms of injustice can be collapsed into whiteness, undermining white race solidarity opens the door to fundamental social change in other areas. For so-called whites, treason to the white race is the most subversive act I can imagine.

Bibliography

Books

Clint Bolick	*The Affirmative Action Fraud: Can We Restore the American Civil Rights Vision?* Washington, DC: Cato Institute, 1996.
Peter Brimelow	*Alien Nation: Common Sense About America's Immigration Disaster.* New York: Random House, 1995.
George E. Curry, ed.	*The Affirmative Action Debate.* Reading, MA: Addison-Wesley, 1996.
Harlon L. Dalton	*Racial Healing: Confronting the Fear Between Blacks and Whites.* New York: Doubleday, 1995.
Dinesh D'Souza	*The End of Racism: Principles for a Multicultural Society.* New York: Free Press, 1995.
Chester Hartman, ed.	*Double Exposure: Poverty and Race in America.* Armonk, NY: M.E. Sharpe, 1996.
bell hooks	*Killing Rage: Racism.* New York: Henry Holt, 1995.
Robert Emmet Long, ed.	*Immigration.* New York: H.W. Wilson, 1996.
Wendy L. Ng et al., eds.	*ReViewing Asian America: Locating Diversity.* Pullman: Washington State University Press, 1995.
Harry Pachon and Louis DeSipio	*New Americans by Choice: Political Perspectives of Latino Immigrants.* Boulder, CO: Westview Press, 1994.
Jack Salzman and Cornel West, eds.	*Struggles in the Promised Land: Toward a History of Black-Jewish Relations in the United States.* New York: Oxford University Press, 1997.
Stephen Steinberg	*Turning Back: The Retreat from Racial Justice in American Thought and Policy.* Boston: Beacon Press, 1995.
Barbara Tizard	*Black, White, or Mixed Race? Race and Racism in the Lives of Young People of Mixed Parentage.* New York: Routledge, 1993.
Tom Wicker	*Tragic Failure: Racial Integration in America.* New York: William Morrow, 1996.
Patricia Williams	*The Rooster's Egg.* Cambridge, MA: Harvard University Press, 1995.

Bibliography

Periodicals

Regina Austin and Michael Schill	"Black, Brown, Red, and Poisoned," *Humanist,* July/August 1994.
Michael Barone	"Racial Preferences Just Died: What Comes Next?" *American Enterprise,* January/February 1997.
Black Scholar	Reader's forum on Ebonics, Spring 1997.
Christopher Boerner and Thomas Lambert	"Environmental Injustice: Industrial and Waste Facilities Must Consider the Human Factor," *USA Today,* March 1995.
Ellis Cose	"Color Blind," *Newsweek,* November 25, 1996.
Terry Eastland	"Formula 209," *American Spectator,* January 1997.
Jerelyn Eddings	"Counting a 'New' Type of American: The Dicey Politics of Creating a 'Multiracial' Category in the Census," *U.S. News & World Report,* July 14, 1997.
William H. Frey and Jonathan Tilove	"Immigrants in, Native Whites Out," *New York Times Magazine,* August 20, 1995.
John Kennedy and Louis Farrakhan	"One in a Million," *George,* October 1996. Available from Headquarters, 1633 Broadway, 41st Fl., New York, NY 10019.
Randall Kennedy	"My Race Problem—and Ours," *Atlantic Monthly,* May 1997.
Joel Kotkin	"The Emerging Latino Middle Class," *Wall Street Journal,* October 9, 1996.
Norman Matloff	"How Immigration Harms Minorities," *Public Interest,* Summer 1996.
Joshua Muravchik	"Facing Up to Black Anti-Semitism," *Commentary,* December 1995.
Debbie Nathan	"Dangerous Crossings," *In These Times,* September 16, 1996.
Orlando Patterson	"The Paradox of Integration," *New Republic,* November 6, 1995.
Eric Pooley	"Fairness or Folly?" *Time,* June 3, 1997.
Alejandro Portes and Min Zhou	"Should Immigrants Assimilate?" *Public Interest,* Summer 1994.
Jamin B. Raskin	"Affirmative Action and Racial Reaction," *Z Magazine,* May 1995.
Mayer Schiller and Dinesh D'Souza	"Racial Integration or Racial Separation?" *American Enterprise,* January/February 1996.
Peter Schrag	"So You Want to Be Color-Blind: Alternative Principles for Affirmative Action," *American Prospect,* Summer 1995.
Thomas Sowell	"Ebonics: Follow the Money," *Forbes,* January 27, 1997.
Jack E. White	"I'm Just Who I Am," *Time,* May 5, 1997.

Organizations to Contact

The editors have compiled the following list of organizations concerned with the issues debated in this book. The descriptions are derived from materials provided by the organizations. All have publications or information available for interested readers. The list was compiled on the date of publication of the present volume; names, addresses, phone and fax numbers, and e-mail and Internet addresses may change. Be aware that many organizations take several weeks or longer to respond to inquiries, so allow as much time as possible.

American Immigration Control Foundation (AICF)
PO Box 525
Monterey, VA 24465
(703) 468-2022
fax: (703) 468-2024

The AICF is a research and educational organization whose primary goal is to promote a reasonable immigration policy based on national interests and needs. The foundation educates the public on what its members believe are the disastrous effects of uncontrolled immigration. It publishes the monthly newsletter *Border Watch* as well as several monographs and books on the historical, legal, and demographic aspects of immigration.

Anti-Defamation League (ADL)
823 United Nations Plaza
New York, NY 10017
(212) 490-2525

The ADL works to stop the defamation of Jews and to ensure fair treatment for all U.S. citizens. Its publications include the periodic *Dimensions* and the quarterly *Facts* magazines.

Association for Multicultural Counseling and Development
c/o American Counseling Association
5999 Stevenson Ave.
Alexandria, VA 22304
(703) 823-9800

This association of professional counselors works to develop programs to improve ethnic and racial empathy and understanding. It publishes the quarterly *Journal of Multicultural Counseling and Development*.

Cato Institute
1000 Massachusetts Ave. NW
Washington, DC 20001
(202) 842-0200
fax: (202) 842-3490
Internet: http://www.cato.org

The Cato Institute is a libertarian public policy research foundation dedicated to limiting the role of government and protecting individual liberties. It researches claims of discrimination and opposes affirmative action. The institute publishes the quarterly magazine *Regulation,* the bimonthly *Cato Policy Report,* and numerous books.

The Heritage Foundation
214 Massachusetts Ave. NE
Washington, DC 20002
(202) 546-4400
fax: (202) 546-0904

The foundation is a conservative public policy research institute dedicated to free-market principles, individual liberty, and limited government. It opposes affirmative action and believes that the private sector, not government, should be allowed to ease social problems and to improve the status of minorities. The foundation publishes the quarterly journal *Policy Review* and the bimonthly newsletter *Heritage Today* as well as numerous books and papers.

Hispanic Policy Development Project (HPDP)
1001 Connecticut Ave. NW
Washington, DC 20036
(202) 822-8414
fax: (202) 822-9120

The HPDP is a nonprofit organization that encourages analysis of public policies affecting Hispanics in the United States, particularly the education, training, and employment of Hispanic youth. It publishes a number of books and pamphlets, including *The Future of the Spanish Language in the United States* and *Make Something Happen: Hispanics and Urban High School Reform.*

Human Rights and Race Relations Centre
141 Adelaide St. West, Suite 1506
Toronto, ON M5H 3L5
CANADA
(416) 481-7793

The center is a charitable organization that opposes all types of discrimination. It strives to develop a society free of racism where each ethnic group respects the rights of other groups. It recognizes and awards individuals and institutions that excel in the promotion of race relations or that work for the elimination of discrimination. The center publishes the weekly newspaper *New Canada.*

National Association for the Advancement of Colored People (NAACP)
4805 Mt. Hope Dr.
Baltimore, MD 21215-3297
(410) 358-8900
fax: (410) 486-9257

The NAACP is the oldest and largest civil rights organization in the United States. Its principal objective is to ensure the political, educational, social, and economic equality of minorities. It publishes the magazine *Crisis* ten times a year as well as a variety of newsletters, books, and pamphlets.

National Network for Immigrant and Refugee Rights (NNIRR)
310 Eighth St., Suite 307
Oakland, CA 94607
(510) 465-1984
fax: (510) 465-1885
e-mail: nnirr@igc.apc.org
Internet: http://www.nnirr.org

The network includes community, church, labor, and legal groups committed to the cause of equal rights for all immigrants. These groups work to end discrimination and unfair treatment of illegal immigrants and refugees. The network aims to strengthen and coordinate educational efforts among immigration advocates nationwide. It publishes a monthly newsletter, *Network News.*

The Poverty and Race Research Action Council (PRRAC)
1711 Connecticut Ave. NW, Suite 207
Washington, DC 20009
(202) 387-9887
fax: (202) 387-0764
e-mail: prrac@aol.com

The PRRAC is a nonpartisan, not-for-profit organization convened by civil rights, civil liberties, and antipoverty groups. Its purpose is to use social science research and advocacy work in order to address problems that affect poor minorities. The council publishes the bimonthly *Poverty & Race* as well as several booklets and symposia.

Project RACE (Reclassify All Children Equally)
1425 Market Blvd., Suite 1320-E6
Roswell, GA 30076
(770) 433-6076
fax: (770) 640-7101
e-mail: Projrace@aol.com
Internet: http://www.projectrace.mindspring.com

Project RACE advocates for multiracial children and adults by hosting educational and community awareness programs as well as by influencing legislation. The project supports a multiracial classification on all school, employment, state, federal, local, medical, and census forms. Its website provides information on state and federal legislation, news articles, and links to other sources and sites concerning the multiracial and interracial communities.

Resisting Defamation
2530 Berryessa Rd., #616
San Jose, CA 95132
(408) 995-6545
e-mail: ResistDef@aol.com

This organization fights stereotypes and discrimination against European Americans. It provides free seminars and publishes a syllabus entitled *Sensitivity Toward European Americans.*

Index

Index

and decline in income, 169
and high birth rates, 141, 143
negative attitudes about, 53
as scapegoat community, 145
school dropout rates of, 170
stereotypes about, 42
success of, 53-57
  and importance of families, 55-56
  and tension with African Americans, 156
  see also environmental racism
Holmes, Steven A., 141
hooks, bell, 86

Ignatiev, Noel, 194
immigration, 111, 113, 184, 197, 199
  and changing demographics, 141-47, 181
  and denial of benefits, 105, 181
  and divided population, 149-53
  and job competition, 145, 152
  motivation for, 158-59
  need for control of, 81, 162-63
    popular support for, 149
  and requirements for citizenship, 112
  as threat to community, 157
  and white flight, 155, 156, 159
  see also affirmative action; English as official
    language
Interrace magazine, 189
Israel, 73, 162, 184
  see also Jews
Izumi, Lance T., 80

Jackson, Jesse L., 42, 68, 73, 93, 100
  and ebonics, 119, 125, 129
Jefferson, Thomas, 82, 162, 175, 178
Jewish Community Relations Advisory Council, 67
Jews, 66, 162, 191
  and unity with African Americans, 67-68, 88, 91
  as myth, 69-73
  strategies for, 87, 89-90
  see also anti-Semitism; Israel
Jim Crow laws, 67, 106, 107
Joint Center for Political and Economic Studies, 176

Kelly, Michael, 94, 95, 96
Kennedy, Randall, 82
Kerner Commission, 172
King, Martin Luther, Jr., 78, 84, 86, 167
  legacy of, 88, 89
King, Rodney, 34, 107
Koprowski, Gene, 46
Koreans. *See under* Asians
Kristol, William, 19
Krouch, Stanley, 43
Ku Klux Klan (KKK), 75, 76, 77, 79, 124
  and history of targeting churches, 78

Leach, Jim, 46, 47, 49
Lee, Charles, 29
Legal Defense Fund, 67
Lerner, Michael, 85
liberals. *See* political left/liberals
Lincoln, Abraham, 82, 162, 178
Los Angeles, California, 35, 57, 126
  City Council Personnel Department, 34
  and ebonics, 126

immigrants in, 116, 145, 150, 151, 152
Police Department, 34
riots in 1992, 80, 81, 144, 199
Los Angeles Times, 107, 129

MacArthur family, John and Katherine T., 188, 189,
  190
Macey, Jonathan R., 47, 49
Malcolm X, 78, 82, 86
Marshall, Thurgood, 67, 84
Martinez, Elizabeth, 180
Marzulla, Nancie G., 50
Mayfield, Kenya, 135
McCall, Nathan, 63
Mexican American Legal Defense and Educational
  Fund (MALDEF), 37
Mexico, 144, 182, 184
Mfume, Kweisi, 119
Million Man March, 32, 190
Modern Language Association, 130
Mortgage Disclosure Act (HMDA), 22, 23, 24, 27
Muhammad, Elijah, 78
Mullings, Leith, 17
multiculturalism, 147, 196
  American symbols attacked by, 174
  American values endangered by, 80, 160-62, 163,
    173, 177-78
  and national identity crisis, 180, 184
  challenge of, 164-66, 170
  and hope for racial harmony, 83-84
  and hyphenated names, 176-77
  and hypocrisy, 157-58
  need for, 186-87
  promise of, 167-68, 171-72
  and reality of cultural divisions, 81
  and responsibility, 169-70
  unrealistic idealism of, 82, 148-49, 160
  and white guilt, 178-79
  see also affirmative action; Census Bureau; white
    race
Murray, Charles, 43
Muwakkil, Salim, 28

NAACP (National Association for the Advancement
  of Colored People), 29, 42-43, 67, 119, 123
Narasaki, Karen K., 115
National African-American Leadership Summit, 30
National Association of Latino Elected Officials
  (NALEO), 34
National Council of Churches (NCC), 94, 95, 96
National Council of La Raza, 53, 143
National Endowment for the Arts, 145
National Environmental Justice Advisory Council, 30
National Fire Protection Association (NFPA), 76, 77
National Urban Coalition, 176
National Urban League, 44, 67
Nation of Islam, 78
Native Americans, 52, 100, 172, 178
  early injustices to, 165, 179, 182, 183
  loan default rates for, 47
  at margins of society, 155-56
  Seminoles, 198
New York, 33, 67, 73, 96, 144
  antiblack prejudice in, 62
  criminal police officers in, 109
  and immigration, 150